Institutional Research in the University

A Handbook

Paul L. Dressel
and
Associates

Foreword by
Frederick deW. Bolman

Institutional Research in the University

Jossey-Bass Inc., Publishers
San Francisco · Washington · London · 1971

INSTITUTIONAL RESEARCH IN THE UNIVERSITY: A HANDBOOK
by Paul L. Dressel and Associates

Published in Great Britain by
Jossey-Bass, Inc., Publishers
St. George's House
44 Hatton Garden, London E.C.1

Library of Congress Catalogue Card Number LC 75-159264

International Standard Book Number ISBN 0-87589-099-7

Manufactured in the United States of America

JACKET DESIGN BY WILLI BAUM, SAN FRANCISCO

FIRST EDITION

Code 7125

The Jossey-Bass Series
in Higher Education

Editors

JOSEPH AXELROD
*San Francisco State College
and University of California, Berkeley*

MERVIN B. FREEDMAN
*San Francisco State College
and Wright Institute, Berkeley*

Foreword

Amerian higher education is scrutinizing itself as never before in a history going back several hundred years. The academic community has developed for society some of the most effective research tools ever known, but now it is taking a close look at its own modes of operation—from input to output—with full realization and determination that many necessary reforms must be made. Some say that in this regard colleges and universities are only one step ahead of the sheriff since the reforms have been so long in coming.

The fact of the matter is that many of the best tools for self-analysis and decision have been devised only recently. The whole technology of institutional research has taken giant steps in a relatively few years as methods which originated in the university proved their worth outside and it became apparent that some methods developed outside could be successfully applied within the university. Thus, from institutions of higher education, from government, and from industry, insight and skill for the analytic manipulation of data have evolved. These techniques can be of great and lasting benefit to our colleges and universities.

That is the purpose of *Institutional Research in the University*—to help in a rebirth of American higher education. For that reason, it is addressed not just to those engaged in institutional research but more especially to presidents and chancellors, to members of governing bodies, to statewide educational planners, and to those in the federal government concerned with education. This broad audience should be concerned with institutional research because it is essential that they understand that a new tool is now available which can be a prime asset to every college, university, and statewide system—and a national asset as well.

On a modest and fragmented scale, what is termed institutional research came into being before World War II. In the first few years after the war, as enrollments burgeoned, some further progress was made in the field. Since 1960, however, with the advent of new analytic technologies, institutional research has grown in sophistication and has begun to emerge as a quite new field. Although sometimes narrowly interpreted, the activities associated with institutional research can extend to so broad a subject as the systems analysis of the entire educational enterprise in one or many institutions of higher learning.

Gathered in this handbook are discussions of institutional research by many of the leading practitioners. There have been earlier monographs on the subject, but this is the first volume to deal with the promise offered by new techniques for the seventies and beyond. It is a volume not only to stimulate the imagination but to show pathways to vitally needed reform. Institutional research, when properly used, can act as an early warning of impending crises, can help to redefine the role of the university, and can be of great value in aligning modes of operation to avoid disaster and to achieve the true goals of higher education.

New York   FREDERICK DEW. BOLMAN
September 1971   *Executive Director*
                                              Esso Education Foundation

Preface

Institutional research, in the broadest sense, is certainly nothing new in higher education, but in recent years the attention given to it and the tendency to consolidate many formerly unrelated data collection and study activities into a single office have placed institutional research in a new light. Institutions of higher education have a special obligation to carry a program of institutional research beyond the obvious concerns for efficiency and effectiveness. Higher education must be dedicated to the production of individuals who are capable of making wise judgments. This commitment bears out the conviction that choices and decisions based upon extensive knowledge and evidence are better than those made without knowledge or evidence. In support of this broad educational objective, the deliberations and the decision-making patterns of a college should constitute models for students to readily recognize as at least attempts to reach ideals which they are supposed to emulate. Unfortunately, the deliberations of faculties and the decisions of administrators are too often quite inconsistent with the behavior which universities attempt to produce. Emphasis on institutional research is at least one approach to the improvement of this situation.

The nature of institutional research, its functions, its placement in the university structure, and its relationship to other research are not yet resolved. Development of information systems and emphases on program budgeting and planning may ultimately lead institutional research to take a different form than that which it originally had. In various chapters of *Institutional Research in the University*, especially in the last chapter, the authors discuss some of the possibilities, and I hope that the volume as a whole contributes constructively to development of ideas and, eventually, to consensus. Chapters overlap somewhat, but differences in focus and in points of view justify this. Institutional research simply cannot be divided into a completely independent set of discrete topics.

Institutional research is not confined to large universities, although the problems are obvious there simply because of size. Smaller universities and colleges have the same problems, especially in improvement of resource utilization. *Institutional Research in the University*, though written by persons associated with large universities, is equally applicable to the small colleges.

As general editor and major contributor, I have profited greatly from the discussions and interchanges with my cocontributors. Each has added significant dimensions to this volume. Lou Anna Kimsey's accumulation of the resource materials in Appendix A was an almost accidental, certainly unplanned development, but a useful one. Sally B. Pratt deserves particular commendation on her review of literature, which was helpful in this volume and also resulted in a separate publication, *The World of Higher Education: An Annotated Guide to the Major Literature* (San Francisco: Jossey-Bass, 1971).

Others contributed greatly though less directly to *Institutional Research in the University*. To both Ruth A. Frye and Marion M. Jennette are due many thanks for their assistance in taking care of correspondence, typing, and proofreading and generally in keeping the task progressing in an orderly fashion. To Phyllis Applegate, who assisted F. Craig Johnson in the search of literature, and to Clara and Daniel R. Coleman, who assisted him in preparing the typescript, thanks are also due. Frederick deW. Bolman, executive director for the Esso Education Foundation, who has had for some years a deep personal interest in institutional research, provided very helpful ideas.

East Lansing, Michigan   PAUL L. DRESSEL
September 1971

Contents

⊰⊱⊰⊱⊰⊱⊰⊱⊰⊱⊰⊱⊰⊱

Authors

FREDERICK deW. BOLMAN, *executive director, Esso Education Foundation, New York*

ELWIN F. CAMMACK, *assistant vice president for planning and analysis, The University of Wisconsin*

PAUL L. DRESSEL, *assistant provost and director, Office of Institutional Research, Michigan State University*

F. CRAIG JOHNSON, *professor and research associate, Division of Instructional Research and Service, The Florida State University*

LOU ANNA KIMSEY, *graduate assistant, Office of Institutional Research, Michigan State University*

DONALD C. LELONG, *director, Office of Institutional Research, The University of Michigan*

THOMAS MASON, *director, Office of Institutional Research, University of Colorado*

SALLY B. PRATT, *assistant professor, Office of Institutional Research, Michigan State University*

JOE L. SAUPE, *university director of institutional research, University of Missouri*

Institutional Research in the University

A Handbook

CHAPTER 1

Major Problems in Higher Education

Paul L. Dressel

⚭⚭⚭⚭⚭⚭⚭⚭

Higher education in the United States includes a very mixed collection of institutions. The range is suggested by the distinct categories into which we commonly group them: private and public; graduate schools, four-year undergraduate schools, and two-year junior colleges; professional schools, technical institutes, and liberal-arts colleges; and coeducational and single-sex (men or women) institutions.

Distinguishable trends have been recognized for particular kinds of institutions. Data from *A Fact Book on Higher Education* show that from 1955 to 1968 the total number of institutions increased by 651 (from 1,886 to 2,537), but public institutions increased by 376 while private institutions increased by only 225 (American Council on Education, 1969a, p. 9117). During the same period, enrollments in private institutions decreased from 44 to 29 per cent and may further decrease to 20 per cent by 1975 (American Council on Education, 1970a, p. 40.9). Meanwhile the number of high school graduates attending college increased from 50 to 60 per cent, and this figure is expected to reach 66 per cent by 1976 (American Council on Education, 1970a, p. 70.7).

During the same period of time both junior colleges and institutions granting graduate degrees increased in numbers. Those granting graduate degrees increased by over 40 per cent (from 191 to 278), and two-year institutions increased by 65 per cent (from 525 to 867) (American Council on Education, 1969a, p. 9118). The increase in doctoral-level institutions resulted largely from the addition of programs to institutions already offering baccalaureate and master's degrees.

The tripartite category of professional, technical, and liberal arts colleges does not lend itself to statistics; professional, technical, and liberal education may be offered in the same institution. Many liberal arts colleges offer some professional or technical programs, although costs and competition are forcing many to take a second and perhaps final look at programs such as nursing, medical technology, and home economics. The status of many technical institutes —post secondary but not on the level of liberal arts or professional schools—further complicates the scene. New schools of medicine, law, and social work are being developed in state universities to meet the professional needs in our society, but some private universities are reviewing the increasing costs of their professional programs with concern.

Separate colleges for men and women, long an accepted and prestigious segment of American higher education, may become curiosities. Cost, especially for offerings differentially attractive to the sexes, is one factor. A physics major attracts few women yet its absence in a women's college can be perceived by critics to denote a lack of balance. Psychological and social considerations of students are other factors. Coeducation is attractive to most young persons, and the weakening if not elimination of the surrogate parent tradition, which assumed responsibility for student morality,

makes segregation of the sexes less meaningful. The women's liberation movement seriously questions the use of sex as an admissions
consideration. Demands for equal rights may ultimately eliminate
even the traditional male sanctuaries found in the service academies.

The changes or trends within institutional categories suggest many of the problems in higher education. Contributing to all
the problems is the vast increase in enrollment: 2,660,000 in 1955;
6,928,000 in 1968; and a projected 10,318,000 by 1975 (American Council on Education, 1970a, p. 70.5). Accompanying the
increase in enrollment is a rise in expenditures—from 3.5 billion in
1955–1956 to a projected 28.3 billion by 1975–1976 (American
Council on Education, 1970b, p. 70.106). Earned degrees increased
from about 380,000 in 1955–1956 to about 870,000 in 1967–1968
(American Council on Education, 1969b, p. 9188). Demand for
higher education has been increasing so dramatically that, even
with the larger number of institutions, many individual campus
enrollments have increased. The percentage of institutions with enrollments over five thousand increased from 5 per cent in 1950 to
15 per cent in 1968 (American Council on Education, 1969a, p.
9123). Size tends to complicate the life of the student and to produce the facelessness that is at the root of much student dissatisfaction.

Some part of the growth and of the attendant problems in
higher education result from the varied expectations of those who
approach institutions. Differing expectations are fostered by lack
of clarity in institutional goals and in the goals of higher education
generally. Prospective students expect the college or university to
provide courses or programs for every interest and every ability—
and to give degrees for these courses of study. Individuals, businesses, and communities expect institutions to provide them with
consultation and services on a free or marginal cost basis. The federal government and its agencies view universities as a market in
which to purchase research at cut-rate prices. On and off the campus, others would have the university enter into and resolve problems of racial discrimination, pollution, poverty, and overpopulation.

Education, regarded as the magic solution to all the problems of our society, has become the butt of criticism and suspicion
because of the known failures in its application to those problems.

Institutions of higher education collectively and individually are unclear as to their social purposes. Internal priorities and operations render them almost incapable of solving their own immediate problems, much less the collective problems. Higher education is in trouble.

Narrow and Broad Views

The recognized purposes of higher education are transmission of the cultural heritage, organization of and addition to the cultural heritage, and extension of knowledge and research to the solution of social and economic problems. These purposes give rise to certain institutional functions: instruction to transmit the cultural heritage; research and integrative scholarship to expand the cultural heritage; and continuing education, extension, and applied research for fulfillment of the public service obligation. The extent to which these three purposes and associated functions constitute obligations for all institutions of higher education is not a matter of complete accord; all universities and most colleges recognize research as desirable, and public service activity is often encouraged as resources are available.

Although the educational purposes have traditional acceptance, their interpretation is subject to debate and to gradual change. In part, this interpretation may be seen by examining specific educational objectives stated for students. These are concerned with specification of knowledge in the disciplines and associated cognitive abilities; with affective considerations of attitudes, values, and character development; and with preparation for a vocation. In part, the changing manifestation of purposes may be seen in the new institutions developed. So successful were the land-grant colleges, which extended education to numerous vocational fields and emphasized applied research and service through experiment stations and extension programs, that all state universities, many private ones, and even the smaller private liberal arts colleges have adopted the model. The growth of community colleges and technical schools is a further expansion of vocational education and of community service activity.

Higher education, which originally served as a source of educated and specialized manpower, has come to be viewed broadly as a natural resource. World War II focused attention on specialized training and caused faculties and facilities to be viewed as resources essential to national security and development. Today higher education is seen by many as the major prop of a decadent society. Thus a narrowly academic interpretation of higher education objectives is gradually being replaced by a broader social definition of those objectives. The contrast (and conflict) is suggested by the following list:

Objective	Narrow Academic View	Broad Social View
Transmission of culture	Western heritage only	All cultures
Development of values	Middle class career-oriented values	Career and social values
Vocational education	Professions	All occupations
Research	Pure research (disciplines and professions)	Applied research (social problems) as well
Service	Extension instruction	Public services plus social action
National resource	Specialized manpower	Manpower plus pressure for social change and individual opportunity

In the face of these shifting interpretations of purposes and the demands based on them, institutions find their resources inadequate. The traditional autonomy of individual institutions has made them vulnerable to self-serving opportunism, competition, and expediency. In trying to satisfy administrative and faculty aspirations as well as student and public demands, institutions have often confused their needs and aspirations with social needs, resulting in uneconomical use of resources and a tendency toward mediocrity.

A responsible institution should limit itself to meeting needs for which it has unique capabilities and for which adequate resources can be found. It should leave to other institutions responsibility for meeting other needs more suited to their capabilities and resources. Unfortunately, institutions appear to be incapable of exercising this restraint, and they strongly resist state and regional role definitions. Even the private liberal arts college has difficulty in eliminating courses and programs for which demand is limited— especially when another college regarded as competitive is providing them. Continuing operational deficits are often the ultimate cause for program cutbacks which might have been made earlier because of sound educational considerations. Planning has not been effective in this regard, for planning is most attractive and accepted when it involves expansion in program and facilities. The most significant and most difficult problem faced by any college or university is that of reexamining and clarifying purposes and subsequently interpreting these to its publics. If this process is carried out successfully, understanding can be achieved and programs can be defended or rejected on grounds implicit or explicit in the recognized purposes.

Fiscal Problems

The vast increases in financial support required for higher education have led to detailed study of fund sources and of ways in which funds may be most effectively allocated. State legislators in despair of ever satisfying the demands have become increasingly suspicious that inefficiencies in operation and unreasonably low faculty teaching loads generate much of the demand. Thus, in 1970, the Michigan higher education appropriation contained a section indicating that the legislature expected a minimum of ten, twelve, or fifteen classroom contact hours for each faculty member, depending on the institution. Endowments of private institutions have failed to keep pace with the needs, and alumni and donors have evidenced reluctance to increase or even to continue their contributions in the face of doubts raised by student unrest and by student and faculty radical activism.

Increases in private college tuitions and fees have reached the point of diminishing returns. Greater costs of college attendance have generated demands for student aid, especially where effort has been made to enroll those from the lower economic groups. Borrowing money to attend college has been advocated by those who see higher education as contributing the primary benefits to the individual. But, to others who emphasize the social benefits and doubt the wisdom of saddling socially and economically deprived students with major indebtedness, this proposal is entirely unsatisfactory. A study made in California by Hansen and Weisbrod (1969, Chapters 4 and 6) purported to show that, in respect to higher education alone, lower-income groups are already making tax contributions disproportionate to the benefits received. This would seem to support increased tuition for those able to pay. Peckham (1970, pp. 361–370), director of economic studies for the Brookings Institution, seems to have repudiated this study on methodological grounds, and he argues that free or almost free access to public higher education for all qualified students is the simplest and most efficient method of ensuring enrollment of qualified poor students. Whether values or research dictate conclusions is sometimes uncertain.

The federal government is widely regarded as the prime source of additional support. This view recognizes that higher education is a national resource and also that only the government can find the resources required to run it. Here a debate is joined as to whether the support should be in the form of direct grants to students; income tax deductions; support of research, graduate, or other special programs; funding of facilities; or general institutional grants based on enrollment or degrees granted. Adequate loans at reasonable interest rates depend upon federal guarantees and funding of associated costs. Private and public education lobbies do not support the same causes, and current attitudes toward education in Washington do not inspire confidence that federal policies to relieve the financial dilemmas of higher education will soon be formulated and activated. The problems of equity (removing financial barriers to higher education) and of efficiency (maximizing the return on investments) are complex and possibly conflicting.

The salary costs of tenured faculty, the costs of essential administrative services, and the maintenance costs of the existing physical plant, which are fixed costs arising from long-term commitments, account for a high proportion of income. Harris (1969, p. 487) reports that receipts earmarked for plant funds were 11 per cent of the educational and general income in 1939–1940, 29 per cent in 1949–1950, and 35 per cent in 1964–1965. Donors tend to favor buildings rather than faculty salaries. Classroom and lecture facilities compete for funds with specialized technological equipment, laboratory facilities with expensive instruments, seminar and conference rooms, and private offices for faculty. Many of the costly facilities are not fully utilized. Student station utilization rates are commonly under 50 per cent on the basis of a forty-four hour week (Harris, 1969, p. 504). When all facilities—classroom, laboratory, library, student union, auditorium, gymnasium, residence, and recreational space—are tallied, most institutions have five or more spaces per student. Classroom and teaching laboratories generally account for less than 25 per cent of the assignable square feet available in colleges and universities (Dahnke and Mertins, 1970, p. 22).

By more efficient use of instructional space, most colleges could accommodate two or three times their present student body. However, faculty and students alike resist elimination of small classes and avoid late afternoon and evening classes. For much of the year, facilities stand idle. In spring 1970 Michigan State University had a campus enrollment of over 40,000 students. Yet 25 per cent of the undergraduate classes had enrollments of twenty or fewer. Observatories, planetaria, museums, exhibition halls, and sports areas which have limited use are additional luxuries contributing to high maintenance costs.

New administrators are frequently accorded the privilege of expensive remodeling of old facilities. Seldom is a new facility in use for more than a year before some remodeling is required to adjust to personal whims. While facilities do require renovation and updating, costs are high and must often come from current income. New facilities which earn no income require deferment of operating expenses to debt payment. Faculty and student involvement in the planning of facilities may be wasteful in time as well as in financial costs. Utilization of new facilities may force changes in courses and instructional methodology. Because faculty and student stays at an institution are often relatively brief, those who participate in planning may not be those who use a facility. State planning and architectural requirements cause further irritation in some states. They slow down planning and construction and force standardization which can destroy the plans originally conceived by those who use a building.

Budgetary procedures are largely ineffective in reallocation of funds. Departmental autonomy makes it virtually impossible to recapture funds from the established base of the previous year. Yet central administration seldom knows in any detail how departmental resources are utilized. Management data systems are inadequate, and data that are accumulated are manipulated if not actually falsified to gain departmental ends. In publicly supported institutions, gains in enrollment yield additional funds. These are employed largely in staff expansion, but they also provide some flexibility whereby new programs can be introduced and administrative prerogatives and goals can be asserted. Only as enrollment stabilizes or income is restricted or both of these things happen does the opportunity arise for serious application of program budgeting or other procedures involving appraisal of effectiveness and redistribution of resources.

Administrative Roles

The role of administration in higher education has changed from one of enunciating policies and making decisions to a mediating and coordinating role involving extensive consultation and communication with students, faculty, board members, and even the general public. Consulting and communicating, which require large investments of time by all concerned, make it difficult for an administrator to act quickly in response to urgent needs or to unreasonable demands or threats. To the administrator, it seems that no segment of the university or its public has confidence in any other and that each one's price for acceptance of a policy is his personal involvement in its formulation. The reactionary elements can be counted upon to reject any policy inconsistent with any of their demands. The once-justifiable revolt against unreasonable and irrelevant rigidities imposed by administrators, faculty, and social mores has led institutions into other and equally crippling rigidities. Through endless procedural due process, with its attendant committee meetings, the grist of each cause is ground ever finer by other competitive causes. Unfortunately, too, those who remain involved after the vast majority of students and faculty have returned to their primary concerns are not necessarily representative or well informed.

As the bargaining patterns developed by labor and industrial unions become common in higher education, university groups find themselves competing for scarce resources. Clerical employees, administrative and professional staff, custodial and operative personnel, graduate assistants, and tenured and nontenured faculty present their demands. At the bargaining table, salary increments, fringe benefits, and work specifications become fixed, and administrators find much of their power is subsequently curtailed or dissipated. Their responsibilities still remain.

Improved communication, extensive consultation, and collection and dissemination of data have been urged as correctives. Yet, even assuming some alleviation of the present tensions, the long-time trends indicate a fragmentation of decision making. The traditional pattern of authority delegation—from governing board to president, to dean, and then to departmental faculty—and of influence in the reverse direction now has several competitors. Senates and committees comprised of faculty, administration, and students deliberate on policies regarding budget, salaries, records, curriculum, grades, appointments, tenure, and promotion. Bargaining decides other issues. Meanwhile legislatures and boards of both private and public institutions, exasperated at rising costs, student and faculty recalcitrance, and other signs of ineffective management, attempt to reassert their authority. "Who decides who decides?" is not simply an amusing question.

Academic Programs

The academic program, the original and still primary justification for the existence of higher education (although curricular irrelevancies and excesses are at the root of many problems), is sometimes forgotten in the struggle for power. Demands for open admission, having some basis in the inadequacy of admissions criteria but apparently assuming that all individuals regardless of prior experience and education have adequate potential for college success, are put forward without regard to institutional roles or resources. New courses and programs are urged despite the course proliferation and overspecialization already existing within and among departments, colleges, and institutions, and the lack of adequate support for many existing programs.

Concern about the flight of faculty from the classroom and for the inept and indifferent performance of many instructors when they do appear before students leads to futile and temporary programs of faculty evaluation and to special recognition or awards for good teaching which all too often miss the devoted, self-effacing teacher, especially if he lacks a list of publications. Occasionally, the acknowledged deficiencies of undergraduate programs result in a residential, inner, or cluster college development which leads a hazardous existence because of the constraints imposed upon it by the traditional and prestigious departments. These new units, too, tend all too soon to assume a rigid structure; and their faculties, recognizing their tenuous existence, avoid the critical evaluation which may enhance their experimental character and justify, by evidence of quality, continued existence (Gaff and associates, 1970, pp. 216–239).

This discouraging picture is a result of the established value system of higher education. Faculty members and administrators tend to evaluate a department or an institution by the number of courses and programs it offers rather than by the character of the graduate. Prospective students and their parents also are impressed by the range (richness?) of the offerings. When attention is turned to the product, assessment is based on the number of degrees awarded and the number and percentage of graduates who receive fellowships or continue to an advanced degree. Departmental and disciplinary organization tends to focus on mastering of subject matter rather than on individual development. With instruction reduced to a part-time assignment by demands for research, service, and participation in governance, time and funds for improvement of courses and curriculum and for enrichment of learning experiences through use of technology are not readily available. And there is no assurance of acceptance or reward for efforts toward academic excellence by faculty associates or administrators. Even students sometimes appear more impressed by an entertaining egoistic and provocative oddball than by a professor who consciously places restraints on his own performance to gain maximum student involvement and self-direction in learning.

Further evidence of the higher education value system is seen in the apparent absence of consistent, sequential effort to improve curriculum or instruction (Dressel and DeLisle, 1969). Promising starts fizzle because of changes in faculty or administrative personnel or because some new development attracts attention and support. Innovation claims more attention and support than do existing programs. Hence institutions periodically wrestle with improvement of curriculum and instruction but only occasionally persevere until a new level of performance is attained and institutionalized. Too frequently the results of only a particular effort are institutionalized, and dedication to continuing innovation and improvement is forgotten. The effects of sporadic curriculum review are temporary if not illusory. Left to the departments, instruction and curriculum review at the undergraduate level result in mere updating of content because of narrow disciplinary interests, departmental priorities, and ignorance about alternatives to traditional practices. Only if one or more individuals can be assigned responsibilities and funds for instructional and curricular development and can be relieved of other responsibilities will long-term results occur.

Student Demands

The studies of sociologists and social psychologists have destroyed some myths but have also reinforced some of the conventional wisdom about higher education. An example of the latter is the demonstration by Clark and Trow (1966) of the existence on the campus of academic, vocational, nonconformist, and collegiate subcultures. Keniston (1965) has written about alienated youth, and the Berkeley, San Francisco, and Columbia episodes have created a flow of studies and rationalizations about students, especially those involved in protest. Still, academic, vocational, and collegiate subcultures of students ignore, curiously watch, or participate for kicks in campus unrest, thereby confusing the situation in regard to numbers involved, intensity of student feeling, and actions that should be taken to resolve difficulties or control destructive activity. Gross (1970, pp. 41–53), reviewing the situation, has described three groups of students: (1) the alienated—a highly visible group, but probably less than 1 per cent of the students on most campuses; (2) the apathetic—the dominant group, approximating the collegiate and vocational groups described by Clark and Trow and accounting for 60 per cent of most student bodies; and

(3) the activist—a vocal minority estimated to constitute 5 to 10 per cent of most student populations.

Gross sees two subclasses of alienated students. One is composed of radical revolutionists—rebellious, militant, and out to destroy the university and the society it represents. The other is made up of hippies or yippies who find society intolerable and seek to withdraw from it. The apathetic student tends to be vocationally and materialistically oriented. He lacks concern and involvement in society and seeks its benefits without attending to its problems. The activist generally accepts the goals of higher education but dislikes the means and controls used. He seeks reform and is vociferous in his demands. Frustration can lead him to attempt coalition with the alienated rebels, although he generally disowns their destructive and irrational activities.

The above categories and population estimates should not be taken too literally. The percentages Gross has suggested account for only about 70 per cent of the student body. The balance may be accounted for by the academic group of the Clark-Trow categories, but such speculation is highly dubious and altogether useless. The significance of the subcultures among students (and faculty as well) is that policies acceptable to one group can be objectionable to those in other groups. Many students are no longer satisfied with student government which is peripheral to the main thrust of the institution, dominated (perhaps tactfully) by student personnel officers, and largely disregarded by the faculties as irrelevant. Enough students want a piece of the action to ensure that they will attain it in varying degrees. Admission of more students from minority groups can only increase tensions.

Coordination and Cooperation

Morton (1970, p. 297) reports that there are presently seventeen state governing boards and twenty-seven state coordinating boards. These agencies, in varying degrees, require and process data from institutions, review and approve budgets, review and approve new programs, assign institutional roles, and plan for new institutions. At one extreme are statewide boards of control which take over the powers of, if they do not entirely replace, institutional boards. Other boards exercise authority over matters such as programs, facilities, and student numbers. And some can make recommendations but have no authority to enforce them. To be successful, a board must maintain the respect of both the institution and the legislature. Advocating the needs of institutions and trimming budgetary requests to meet the demands of the legislature are competing roles combined effectively in relatively few instances. The demands for comparable data grow, along with the quest for valid formulas to simplify decisions and to provide a semblance of equity. As studies of needs, admissions, and space utilization—once done by individual institutions, if at all—become state enterprises, institutional research moves in part from the institutional to the state level.

Another response to the increasing complications in higher education is the pooling of resources to ease the strain on finance, faculties, facilities, and curricula through interstate compacts and consortia. Three interstate compacts have been established. The Western Interstate Commission for Higher Education (WICHE) covers the western area mainly, although the Management Information Systems developed by WICHE has been opened nationally to all interested institutions. The Southern Regional Education Board (SREB) and the New England Board of Higher Education (NEBHE), like WICHE, attempt to strengthen the quality of education and to avoid duplication of effort through extensive planning and through research projects. On a still broader scale, consortia and other systems attempt to establish priorities and activities for a group of campuses. Moore (1967, in an explanatory note) has reported over a thousand consortia, with the larger proportion of these functioning at the graduate level. Most of these have a limited purpose and informal exchange. Only a small number (about thirty) have a structural organization and a wide range of activities. Some of the consortia cover a limited number of institutions in a restricted area. Examples include the Associated Colleges of the Midwest, which involves ten private liberal arts colleges in four states, and the Great Lakes College Association, involving nine liberal arts colleges and three universities, all private, in three states.

Purposes of consortia include the following: (1) expanding opportunities in areas such as cooperative courses, joint study abroad, and summer institutes, which typically have low enrollments and are expensive or for which teaching personnel are difficult to obtain; (2) increasing the availability of courses, resources, and facilities to a wider group of students, especially through facilitating intercampus exchange of students and faculty members; (3) promoting economy and efficiency through cooperation in admissions, financial aid, purchasing, data collection and processing; (4) developing programs involving experimentation and innovation not easily supported by single institutions; (5) collaborating in attacking major social, environmental, and economic problems; and (6) augmenting research and library facilities.

Need for Institutional Research

Higher education has become a very large enterprise, much too complicated to be run on improvisation guided by expediency, opportunism, and competition. While the operation of institutions has become complex and difficult to understand, growing demand for resources has increased concern about efficient operation in utilizing those resources. Administrators suddenly aware of these complications find themselves confronted with inadequate management information systems and procedures for institutional study, highly charged demands for immediate action, and insistence on the part of faculty and students that these groups be given a voice in all deliberations and decisions.

Institutional research is certainly not new. In trying to trace its origin to a particular date, W. H. Cowley suggested the founding of Yale in 1701 and referred to various study committees set up in later years. However we can assume that over earlier centuries study committees and accumulations of data were in one way or another used in reaching decisions involving the changing forms of higher education. The current scene in American education, with increasing numbers of students, rising costs, and insistence from students and the supporting clientele that their voices be heard in establishing priorities for higher education, has given institutional research larger, more formal dimensions. Institutions need data about costs, educational programs, the impact of various educational policies, the relationship of student characteristics to academic success, the utilization of space, the effects of administrative decisions, and especially the relationship of expenditures to results. The latter can be used to establish that institutional priorities rather than departmental aspirations guide the allocation of resources.

The various forces shaping higher education in the present era have a number of identifiable consequences which can be understood and dealt with through institutional research. These interrelated forces include (1) public resistance to higher education budgets; (2) a shift to large-scale, low-cost education away from small college (high cost and presumed quality) systems; (3) continuing pressure for federal support; (4) increasing use of educational technology; (5) increasing student dissatisfaction with the way colleges are run and with the kind of education provided; (6) demands for cost benefit or cost effectiveness studies; (7) need for broad institutional review and reform of curriculum and of instructional practices; (8) improvement of the governance process increasing participation while yet maintaining some reasonable flexibility and clarity in dealing with problems; and (9) increasing coordination among institutions and acceptance of role assignments by individual institutions.

This cacophony of demands makes it necessary for institutions to know what they are doing, to have rational bases for their decisions, and to be honest and open in dealing with all their various publics. They need to stop promoting liberal arts degrees as necessities for everyone, to stop regarding vocational education—particularly programs of less than four years—as second class education, and to recognize that significant education can be provided outside of formal, structured institutional arrangements.

Institutional research and management information systems cannot bring about utopia in higher education; but higher education cannot be rational and open until it has the factual basis in data collection and study to permit sound evaluation of resource allocation and of the consequent quality of education provided. No institution can know how to improve itself without knowing in some detail how it has been and is operating. When those responsible for the development and improvement of an institution become aware of this, institutional research becomes essential.

Bibliography

American Council on Education. *A Fact Book on Higher Education,* issue 3. Washington, D.C., 1969a.

American Council on Education. *A Fact Book on Higher Education,* issue 4. Washington, D.C., 1969b.

American Council on Education. *A Fact Book on Higher Education,* issue 1. Washington, D.C., 1970a.

American Council on Education. *A Fact Book on Higher Education,* issue 2. Washington, D.C., 1970b.

CLARK, B. R., AND TROW, M. "Determinants of College Students Subculture." In T. M. NEWCOMB AND E. K. WILSEN (Eds.), *The Study of College Peer Groups.* Chicago: Aldine, 1966.

DAHNKE, H., AND MERTINS, P. F. *Distribution of Physical Facilities Among Institutions of Higher Education Grouped by Level, Control and Environment Size.* Washington, D.C.: Government Printing Office, 1970.

DRESSEL, P. L., AND DE LISLE, F. H. *Undergraduate Curriculum Trends.* Washington, D.C.: American Council on Education, 1969.

GAFF, J. G., AND ASSOCIATES. *The Cluster College.* San Francisco: Jossey-Bass, 1970.

GROSS, R. F. "The College and University Student Today." In *The Trustee.* Washington, D.C.: Council for the Advancement of Small Colleges, 1970.

HANSEN, W. L., AND WEISBROD, B. *Benefits, Costs and Finance of Public Higher Education.* Chicago: Markham, 1969.

HARRIS, S. *The Economics and Financing of Higher Education in the United States,* a compendium of pages submitted to the Joint Economic Committee, Congress of the United States. Washington, D.C.: Government Printing Office, 1969.

KENISTON, K. *The Uncommitted.* New York: Harcourt Brace Jovanovich, 1965.

MINTER, W. J., AND SNYDER, P. O. *Value Change and Power Conflict in Higher Education.* Boulder: Western Interstate Commission for Higher Education, 1969.

MOORE, R. S. *A Guide to Higher Education Consortiums: 1965-66.* Washington, D.C.: Office of Education, 1967.

MORTON, B. L. "Perspective from a State Coordinator of Higher Education." *Educational Record,* 1970, *51,* 296-300.

PECKHAM, J. "The Distributional Effects of Public Higher Education in California." *Journal of Human Resources,* 1970, *5,* 361–370.

ROURKE, F. E., AND BROOKS, G. E. *The Managerial Revolution in Higher Education.* Baltimore: John Hopkins University Press, 1966.

CHAPTER 2

Nature of Institutional Research in Self-Study

Paul L. Dressel

❦❦❦❦❦❦❦❦

I nstitutions of higher education are heavily committed to research. Although research is usually thought of as a function of universities, there is probably no college in the country in which administrators do not take pride in the research activities and publications of their faculty. Even in small budgets many find some way in which to provide support or reward for the publishing researcher. The total expenditures for research in universities are difficult to determine accurately. In 1969, the total federal obligations for research at ten universities (six public, four private) exceeded fifty million dollars (American Council on Education, p. 4). Support from the funds of an institution is more

19

difficult to determine because reduction in load without specific assignment of salary dollars for research is the common pattern. Estimates made in a study of research activities in Michigan public institutions (Dressel and Come, 1969, p. 39) suggest that from 15 to 20 per cent of the general fund (legislative appropriation plus student fees) may support research. Most of this activity pertains to graduate instruction, but also included is a general commitment to scholarship and search for truth—a commitment which supports the concept of academic freedom. This assures the right to study or research on any topic appropriate to one's competencies and the right to publish or speak as that research may dictate.

Despite broad commitment to research, most colleges and universities spend limited sums on studying their own operations. Effort is aided in small ways by many people in a university, such as professors studying their courses, registrars studying their problems of record keeping, and admissions officers making studies of the effects of various admissions policies. But the total cost of these efforts is probably not a very significant item in most budgets. A great deal of research activity, while it must in some sense be called institutional research, is done in such a limited way and is tied so closely to the existing pattern of operations that one may question its significance. In reference to the total university budget, the dollar commitment for salaries and operations in institutional research is minimal. At Michigan State University, with one of the larger offices of institutional research, the total annual budget of the office in 1971 was roughly one-fourth of 1 per cent of the institutional budget. Even this small percentage has been questioned. Are the benefits greater than the expenditures? This question reveals not only why institutional research is essential but also why it is often ignored.

The human failings of administrators and faculty members constitute another problem. Though institutional research may be justified by increased efficiency in use of resources—space utilization, elimination of small classes, and other possible savings—some persons regard these efforts with suspicion and alarm. They prefer to run their own show without anyone looking over their shoulders. Administrators preferring to operate by the seat of their pants and committees concerned with compromising the emotionally stated convictions of members are not receptive to studies that may provide a firm basis for their deliberations. Within a milieu committed to research and to considered judgment are made many decisions for which no data were collected and for which no clear statement of assumptions, purposes, or objectives was ever developed. A good many decisions in colleges and universities are made on the basis of individual and institutional values and aspirations rather than on the basis of carefully considered study of consequences. Colleges accept money for a new program or a new building simply because the money is there. Institutions shift and temporize or plunge ahead as pressures and expediency dictate. Always alert to the activities of sister institutions, they engage in competition. Despite demand by institutions as well as the units within them for economy, studies which cast doubts on the plans of entrepreneuring institutions and individuals are not greeted with pleasure.

Studies of higher education generally or of systems of higher education in a particular state or region are regarded by those who guide institutions as inapplicable to them, unless the results suggest, encourage, or provide for expansion into new areas of interest to the faculty and administration. When expansion is uppermost, the range of factors applied to study data is usually limited. Further discouragement of critical analysis results from diffusion in the responsibility of the various groups involved. Decisions made on the basis of opportunism, expediency, or competition are always subject to time pressure, and data used must be immediately available.

Curiously, too, the very assumption that they are committed and highly intellectual professionals causes many institutional planners to demand autonomy, blithely ignoring the conflicts of interest involved. Assignment to faculty of responsibility for the curriculum unhappily results in curriculum decisions based more on the self-interest of faculty than on the needs of the individual student or of society. Decision-making in higher education is simply not a good model of the process as stated in the decision-making objectives formulated for its students.

Discrepancies between ideals and practices are part of the heritage of humankind, but the extent of the discrepancies in the case of higher education is both disillusioning and dangerous. Institutional research alone cannot repair the damages. But well-conceived and properly executed research can, if widely disseminated, serve as a precondition for improvement in institutional functioning. Facts and data based on examination of the implications of various courses of action will eventually confound those who propose solutions based on atypical instances, contrived data, and personal interest or prejudice.

Effective and adequate institutional research cannot be provided by the efforts of one person alone. No one individual, and probably no office group, can have the range of knowledge and competencies necessary to carry out studies in all aspects of higher education operations or even to deal with all problems which arise in any single operation. To staff an office of institutional research with all the special competencies required at various times is uneconomical and strategically unwise. Backgrounds required include educational research, statistics, economics, accounting, systems analysis, computer science, sociology, and psychology. Such a complete staff would be unreasonably costly. It would deny extensive involvement of personnel from other departments, especially in the case of faculty members. Involvement of faculty expertise is economical as special problems arise; it is also likely to gain widespread respect for and acceptance of institutional research.

An office of institutional research embedded in a single institution is not in a good position to carry out studies involving other campuses, especially if the several institutions are competing for students, faculty, and resources. Hence institutional research activity is also essential in coordinating or control boards and in regional agencies of cooperation or consortiums. A distinction between institutional research and the broader study of higher education exists but is not definitive. Some studies conducted by institutes and centers for study of higher education and by federal or state commissions qualify as institutional research; they focus on problems of widespread concern and provide data analyses and recommendations which lead to policies or guidelines for individual institutions. Thus some of the studies of the Kerr Commission, supported by the Carnegie Corporation, may reasonably be regarded as institutional research in an extended sense. Extended studies can significantly affect governmental policies in the long run, and they have immediate value in helping to form views affecting decisions made regionally, and individually. However, at this point, we turn to discussion of the nature and purpose of institutional research and self-study as it operates on a single campus.

Basic Purpose

The basic purpose of institutional research is to probe deeply into the workings of an institution for evidence of weaknesses or flaws which interfere with the attainment of its purposes or which utilize an undue amount of resources in so doing. In the search for flaws, no function, individual, or unit should be regarded as off limits. In the process of searching, evidence of effective and perhaps excellent functioning can and should be produced, but perfection is unlikely to be found and improvement is always possible. Studies which overemphasize the positive are not conducive to improvement and may encourage such pervasive satisfaction and complacency that deterioration results from the suspension of self-criticism. Some years ago an eastern college sought a self-study grant from the Ford Foundation. The final report stated that the study was initiated after some hesitation and largely because of the virtual certainty of getting the money; the institution saw no real need for self-study. At the conclusion of the report, satisfaction is voiced because the study convinced them that they were really better than they originally thought. Self-study which contributes to such a state of mind is not only wasted effort but is deleterious to continuing critical examination and improvement without which any institution becomes moribund.

Types and Sources of Projects

Need for standardized definitions of basic data and data categories is responsible for an undue proportion of time spent in the definition, collection, organization, and dissemination of data. Local administrative and faculty demands cause idiosyncratic definitions affecting the process of counting groups such as students, majors, and faculty. Some departments regularly grant many master's degrees but list all their graduate students as candidates for the doctorate. Other problems of terminology affect phenomena such as faculty load. On some halcyon day we may have information systems based on uniform definitions which will provide print-outs of data organized in almost any fashion we desire. At present much data still must be almost literally dug out of records and then tabulated and organized by hand.

Studies requiring crossovers among various data systems (commonplace to institutional researchers but not to offices operating their own systems) run into inconsistencies in definition and discrepancies in numbers. Details (such as waiver by a dean of a curriculum requirement) are frequently not recorded thereby foiling study of the extent to which graduates have fulfilled all specified requirements. Few institutions can readily produce full data over a span of years on departmental faculty, enrollments, budgets, majors, and load.

Demands for data on federal, state, accrediting agency, and other questionnaires as well as on those sent by others whose primary goal is research require many hours of time, especially because there is no standardization in the form of the requests. Outside requests and even occasional requests by individuals and offices internal to the institution are sometimes based on definitions irrelevant to the major problems which should be confronted in an office of institutional research. Yet the office usually tries to respond at the cost of many hours of effort which probably could be put to better use.

Studies undertaken by an office of institutional research often originate from requests, usually by administration or faculty. An office of research welcomes such requests but frequently finds that the urgency of a demand requires extra work and temporary discontinuance of other projects. At times these requests display more curiosity than consideration for a decision to be made. Naivete about the nature of data available or collectible sometimes necessitates extensive consultation for clarification. An inquiry about the percentages of students who work full time or part time, for example, requires at least a sample survey and may be complicated because students working full time are for several reasons less likely to respond than those working part time. Students in either group are less likely to respond than those who do not work. A research office must set priorities based on established principles lest it become ineffective simply because it attempts too much. Factors that should not be considered in reviewing requests are the prestige or the administrative title of the person making the request. Institutional research can all too easily serve only administrative desires, ignoring important faculty and student requests.

Another major source of studies is the office itself. Studies that originate internally should arise from identification of problems, inconsistencies or seeming inequities, or possible ineffective uses of resources. Such studies aim to curb or disturb; they may be unwanted and they may stimulate irritation and rebuttal. So be it. If laboratory requirements in a department appear excessive relative to usual standards, fairness to students and concern for costs justify a study designed to exhibit the facts and their implications. If the hypothesis is found to be correct, expectation of modification is fully justified. An office of research which has not the time, the acceptance, or the sensitivity to identify and carry through unrequested studies which may be construed as impertinent is not performing its true function. This problem again raises the issue of priorities.

Priorities and Cooperation

An office of institutional research must continuously examine its priorities. It can readily become an agency reacting only to requests from others rather than developing its own program. Thus the first concern must be with balance between servicing requests for data and studies and conducting studies which the institutional research staff believes to be desirable. It is not always easy to take a firm position on such matters. However, the requests of administrators can sometimes be discussed with them; during discussion the costs involved and the other projects that would have to be shoved aside can be pointed out. A detailed salary study requested by one office was withdrawn when questions were raised about its use and when it was indicated that, while it could be done, a number of other projects of concern to others would have to be postponed. Priority applies, too, to those projects which are accepted. Dates for board meetings and committee meetings as well as due dates for external reports establish priorities in at least a limited sense.

More significant considerations of priority involve meaning, utilization, and ultimate effect of a given study or collection of data. At one extreme are individuals interested in having a historical picture of institutional development to identify. Purely historical data by themselves decide nothing, win few friends, and influence no people. Unless they can be related to planning or to budget allocation, their collection and organization are wasted effort. There are always demands for the current picture of the university—for the number of students, the number of staff, or the size of the budget. Such data should be provided routinely with minimal staff involvement. A study designed to ascertain in some depth how faculty resources are utilized in a current quarter can be a major task requiring the full time of a number of people in institutional research and many hours of time of faculty members and administrators. Interesting as current data are, it is important to raise two questions concerned with the future: Where are we going insofar as present trends are identifiable? Where should we be going? Priorities should be given to studies which will be interpreted and used to examine where the university is going and to raise questions about how these developments correspond with the avowed purposes of the university and the current needs of the society which it serves. Institutional research which does not bring about reevaluation and change is not necessarily wasted, but it never has the impact on the university that occurs when implications for future development are highlighted.

There is an area of danger for priorities in the planning and executing of institutional research projects. If an office of institutional research has time for its own projects, it may still operate on the basis of present or past orientation which renders its studies useless. For example, the office may consider examining what alumni are doing and what they think about the institution. However, most of the programs through which alumni have gone have changed and some programs may no longer exist. Therefore it is difficult if not impossible to interpret to a faculty the suggestions of alumni. If, because of curriculum revision, there is widespread concern about the impact of educational experience after several years of work experience, the alumni survey may be useful. Other reasons for a survey of alumni include the cultivation of interest prior to a fund-raising campaign. But, in view of limited time for developing studies, priority should be given to existing major problems and to major problems which may develop in the next two or three years.

Many months can be involved in collecting data and completing a study. If a research office is successful in guessing a trend, a study may appear at the time when the importance of the problem strikes the faculty and administration. Too much research falls on fallow ground because no one is interested in the problem at the time it is revealed, because circumstances surrounding some power bloc or personality make it impossible to move, or because the data in the report do not deal with an issue in a manner which is relevant to faculty concerns. The future-oriented project may be planned to generate awareness and concern or to become shrewdly available about the time the seriousness of the problem is realized.

Special considerations of priority emerge in considering projects which probe new problem areas and involve new interrelationships and cooperation within and among institutions. It is unwise to undertake the same kinds of studies year after year; even though they may be of significance and receive special attention, the burden of updating or redoing them may usurp all the resources of an office. Effort should be made either to routinize the procedure on studies which must be done every year or every few years or to turn such projects over to some other person or office that may have become interested and found them particularly useful. An office of research cannot afford to get bogged down in a repetitious routine activity. It should be committed to encouraging everyone in the university to think in broad, analytical terms about the operation of the university. A problem which comes from a group not previously involved or which requires the cooperation of several groups should be given priority over a problem of equal importance that is rather traditional or a problem which comes from a group already calling upon the office of institutional research.

Many problems of higher education are concerned with limited resources. They cannot be stated in terms of absolutes though some would take that point of view. (Some faculty members, and administrators too, argue that every institution of higher education should offer Latin and Greek even though enrollment is small and costs are high.) Most money matters studied in institutional research—salaries, costs, specifications for tenure, faculty load, and the like—involve comparison with what is being done in other institutions. Budgets are usually based on some insight into what similar institutions are doing. But regard for higher education as a national resource should provide even greater incentive for co-operation among institutions in order to achieve good and widely available education at minimal cost. Cooperation among institutions on institutional research projects, then, has two implications: it provides comparable data which help to give meaning to each institution's own data, and it may become the basis for further co-operation involving more important aspects of education.

Though institutions prize individuality and autonomy, they are very conscious of their sister institutions. Since there are no absolutes determining faculty loads, salary, or utilization of space, many institutional research studies have limited meaning until data from similar institutions are obtained. The definition of *similar* varies with purpose. If the intent is to make the institution look good, the word involves a different group of institutions than it does if the intent is to justify funds for salary increases. A state university does not hesitate to make comparisons with regional colleges and universities when defining library deficiencies, salaries, or computer needs. Informal networks existing among administrative officers and research directors for regular exchange of certain data such as salaries and for ready accommodation on other data as requested serve the purpose of survival more than that of cooperation.

Fundamental cooperation among institutions is increased when studies are jointly sponsored and carried out and when such studies are encouraged or sponsored by outside agencies. These include state and regional cooperative or coordinating agencies; centers or institutes for study of higher education such as those at Berkeley, Temple, and Georgia; federal agencies such as the U.S. Office of Education and the National Science Foundation; and national associations such as the American Council on Education, the National Education Association, the American Association of University Professors, and the American Association of Collegiate Registrars and Admissions Officers. Studies or reports from these groups are described in Dressel and Pratt, 1971. Other groups with a national impact include the Brookings Institution and the major foundations—Ford, Carnegie, and others. The Kerr Commission in its extensive studies, supported by the Carnegie Corporation, has involved many researchers studying all facets of higher education and has made recommendations for future support and directions of development. The Management Information Systems project, sponsored by the Western Interstate Commission on Higher Education, will undoubtedly affect institutional research on every campus.

Institutional research, interinstitutional research, and suprainstitutional study of higher education are interwoven and interdependent for various reasons: norms are needed to interpret local studies; problems of quality and costs are complex, and cooperation among institutions in the study of them is essential if the results are to be useful; all institutions, whether operating independently or as part of a state or regional system, are part of a total national system and thereby require more than localized knowledge to understand problems of future development and to plan for it; increasing demand for higher education and resistance to increasing support require institutions to have complete data for their internal decisions as well as to provide detailed justification for resource requirements; and in their research and demands for data, coordinating and control agencies, state and federal agencies, foundations, and scholars develop procedures and instruments useful in individual institutions. Both methodology and instruments have resulted from these joint efforts. Instruments developed include (1) the much-used Omnibus Personality Inventory, which was developed by the Center for Research and Development in Higher Education at Berkeley in some of its early studies of institutional and student diversity; (2) the Institutional Functioning Inventory, which originated in a study by Earl McGrath, then at the Institute of Higher Education at Columbia; and (3) the College and University Environment Scales, which have gone through several modifications and were originally constructed as part of a research project at Syracuse University investigating differences in students and in their perceptions of college environments. The last two instruments are now available from the Educational Testing Service as part of their Institutional Research Service.

Various state coordinating and control agencies have contributed to the improvement of studies of space utilization (Bayless and associates, 1970). AACRAO (American Association of Collegiate Registrars and Admissions Officers) helped to standardize definitions related to records and to admissions (AACRAO, 1962). The U.S. Office of Education, through its data collection and report system based on HEGIS (Higher Education General Information Survey), has also been a strong force for standardization of definition and reporting (Osso and associates, 1968). The AAUP (American Association of University Professors), in its collection and reporting of data on salaries, has contributed methodology to both and collection utilization of comparative data ("The Annual Report on the Economic Status of the Profession, 1969–70").

Institutional research studies arise from different sources: from administrators, faculty, students, and boards for campus control; and from many agencies and individuals off the campus. Because of the need for comparability in resource allocation and planning, data definitions are gradually being standardized. Methodology and instruments, too, emerge from numerous cooperating sources. Yet institutional research is far from standardized. Management information systems adequate to the complexities of large universities have yet to be agreed upon. Cost studies or cost effectiveness analyses call for information not obtainable without faculty involvement, yet faculty members are not always amenable to definitions, instruments, and procedures developed elsewhere. Because of closer contiguity with and necessary involvement of faculty, institutional research on a campus takes a somewhat different turn than does research planned at a distance from the campus. Unless the trend toward democratic participation of students and faculty in decision-making is reversed (and this is unlikely), institutional research on the campus will not become totally standardized. Demands for uniformity and standardization from off the campus will result at best in local systems of data collection and analysis which are compatible with (translatable into) the externally improved systems. At worst, data will be amassed (or manufactured) to meet external demands, while internal operations continue unaltered.

High priorities of institutional research on the campus include responsiveness of effort to local stresses and full disclosure of the data used, explaining how it is analyzed and interpreted. If institutional research is to contribute answers for the basic question

—where the university should be going—then its activities must not be determined by externally imposed priorities.

Subjects

The subjects of institutional research can be divided into three major topics: the institutional environment, the processes and operations carried on in that environment, and the ultimate outcomes achieved. These topics can be applied to an input-output model of higher education in which the environmental elements represent inputs; the processes and operations, acting upon these, produce the outputs or ultimate outcomes. Since immediate results are more available, in practice they are used more than are ultimate outcomes and are regarded as indices of those outcomes. Input-output analysis involves relation of dollar resource input to the economic benefits of education. This is an analysis of interest, but it is fraught with problems because of the difficulty of assigning dollar values to the personal and social benefits.

Environment. The environment in a university is a composite of philosophical commitments, physical facilities, and the interactions and values of the individuals and groups using these facilities. The philosophical commitments include the purposes of higher education and the more specific purposes, assumptions, and goals of the institution. If these were specified as clearly as some philosophers of education believe they should be, facilities would be planned around them, only faculty and administrators who affirmed these commitments would be hired, and students would be selected because they desire to achieve the goals specified. In this case, students could be regarded as a controlled part of the environmental input; they would be receptive to experiences designed to produce change in the directions specified by the goals. In some limited sense this reality exists in a few small colleges, but most universities have multiple and often conflicting commitments. Administrators, faculty members, and students differ in personal values and goals as well as in perception of institutional purposes, goals, and priorities.

The prime goal of most public universities and some private ones appears to be growth and expansion—more students, more faculty, more undergraduate programs, more research, more facility, and more money. The "mores" of higher education make it difficult to plan facilities in reference to educational goals and to develop an environment conducive to learning. Institutional research can study the environment to point up some of the inconsistencies and contradictions imposed by expansion, but studies of the environment will probably not evoke more than passing interest on most campuses. Faculties show more concern for their research than for the classroom; business officers are preoccupied with residence hall income; and the aspirations and plans of administrators are increasingly circumscribed by accommodation to student and faculty demands.

However, studies revealing the disparate views and concerns of the subcultures of the university may at least result in a consensus of concern for certain phases of the operations through which needed changes and directions of change can be reached. While the residential or inner college in the university represents an admission of the inadequacy of the dominant environment for some students, this innovation also demonstrates inability to modify that environment except by introducing a special unit based on recognition of the problem.

Processes and Operations. All activities carried on in a university can be classified as processes or operations. The list can be extended almost indefinitely depending on the detail desired. Because relationships of processes and operations vary according to administrative organization, a list should be viewed only as categories of activity in which, at one time or another, a research office should be conducting studies.

Student personnel services offer many opportunities for study, although institutional research perhaps does less in these areas than in others. Included are admissions, records, financial aids, placement, testing and counseling, health services, student activities, athletics, and residence hall operation. Inactivity in these areas results from at least two basic causes. First, some of these services include staff who regularly make studies. This is often the case for counseling, admissions, and residence halls. A second problem is compatibility of student records. Confidentiality complicates accessibility and standardization of records. Retention, transfers, completion of requirements, and other phenomena can be routinely studied only if records are maintained to facilitate this. Relationship of admissions data to later success should be a major effort merging with studies of instruction and the curriculum.

Curriculum and instruction are highly important yet rather sensitive areas of study. Faculty members regard them as their domain and are inclined to resent incursions. Nevertheless, the heart of the academic program is where many of the greatest problems arise. Grading, poor instruction, course proliferation, unduly small classes, and teaching load are among the sources of student irritations, of inefficiencies, and of high costs.

Although space planning and allocation are not usually (and should not be) a function of institutional research, study of space utilization certainly should be. Inefficiencies in the use of space are often related to problems of curriculum and the organization of instruction. Unless class size, numbers of sections, repetitions of courses from one term to another, and hourly usage are monitored regularly, the preferences of faculty and of students yield poor utilization. Institutional research, by pointing up the reasons for this inefficient use, provides deans with the information required to demand improvement.

Plant and business operations certainly require study, but institutional research personnel can seldom deal effectively with them unless they have impinged rather directly on the academic program and have become a source of concern or complaint from academic units. Close collaboration between the business office and institutional research can be aided by development of a management information system which makes budget information readily available. Such a system should relate expenditures for each unit from various fund sources to the function, object, and program for which expended. Payroll records should at least be compatible and accessible, though they need not be fully integrated with other files. Cost studies and other studies involving expenditures may well be cooperative endeavors between institutional research and the business office.

The communication and decision-making systems of the university are seldom satisfactory to everyone and hence are deserving of institutional research study. However, the sensitivity of these areas makes it difficult for the office of institutional research to initiate and complete studies without a request from or close collaboration with faculty and students. Furthermore, the closer a study gets to the administrative lines of authority in which institutional research is itself involved, the less objective institutional research can be and the more suspect the study becomes. In such sensitive areas, institutional research can perhaps be most effective by aiding an outside group to design the study, define data, develop instruments, and summarize results. Interpretation, reports, and recommendations are always more likely to be accepted and heeded if they come from participants in the operations studied rather than from the office of institutional research. Indeed, in studies involving outside participants, the study procedure may itself be more beneficial in provoking self-examination and consequent improvement than is the ultimate report. Institutional research can often be most effective when its efforts are unobtrusive and solely facilitative in nature.

In study of processes and operations, descriptive summary data are necessary. Some processes, such as admissions, yield relatively immediate data on results. The success of students in their first term is an immediate (though partial) indication of the effectiveness of admissions criteria. Withdrawals (enforced or voluntary) also constitute an index of effectiveness in processing students suited to the programs of the institution. The number of credit hours produced for a term, an immediate result of the instructional program, has no meaning until related in some manner to the resources used. Student credit hours per full-time-equivalent faculty member, descriptive of instructional organization and faculty load, constitutes a criterion of performance useful (within limits) for comparison among departments or for year-to-year comparison within departments. Some variables may be regarded differently for various purposes. At times they are merely descriptive. For other purposes, they may serve as criteria of effectiveness or efficiency in performance. Or they may be perceived as immediate results of a particular process. Among these are class size by department and course level; course offerings by department and course level; grade distributions by department and course; total service load of faculty by department and rank; number of majors by department; and enrollments by course, department, and student level. Since each of the above provides information about departments and persons therein, statistics widely deviant from the averages usually provoke great interest.

Other variables affecting study of processes and operations represent a further step toward output measurement but are still very immediate results of the process and provide no measure of quality or efficiency. Faculty publications and degrees granted, like variables noted earlier, can be related to costs, to number of faculty, or (in the case of degrees granted) to the original group of students beginning a program in order to obtain indices possessing some comparability and therefore useful as performance criteria.

Studies of student achievement, of curriculum planning and development, and of departmental operation are examples of complicated and typical institutional research. Studies such as these do not lend themselves to simplistic summarization in a few statistics or indices. When statistics or indices are applied, differences in the disciplines and consequent variations in instructional patterns require that adjustments be made. Without adjustment, injustices can be done or staff members, fearing injustices, can be pushed toward falsification of data. Economy, efficiency, and effectiveness are not attainable by imposition of formulas any more than they are by leniency, which permits and thereby encourages waste.

Ultimate Outcomes. If immediate outcomes such as degrees produced and papers or books published are regarded as inadequate measures of the impact of education, long-term or ultimate outcomes must be sought. Questions such as the following might be considered as bases for study. What are the contributions and accomplishments of the graduates? In what ways do the graduates live richer, more satisfying lives as a result of their education? What has been the impact on higher education and on society of the research done by faculty? What are the social, economic, and political benefits to the nation, state, and community which result from higher education? However these questions are not likely to be answered in any objective or convincing fashion by an office of institutional research or by any other agency. Merely to raise such questions with some faculty and administrators is to risk condemnation as a skeptic incapable of understanding educational values and prone to sacrificing them to the almighty dollar or at least to the science of measurement.

In place of such investigations, data on salaries, positions held, postgraduate degrees awarded, publications, awards, and listings in *Who's Who* are submitted. These indirect evaluations beg the question of the real benefits of education, ignoring effects on individuals and on society. Another way to sidestep the question is to produce evidence of an enhanced reputation for the institution— evidence of reputation achieved by the faculty, growth of the institution, and rating of the university as a graduate school. Many faculty and administrators apparently believe that whatever is good for them and for Old Siwash is good for the quality of the education provided and, consequently, is good for society. For accreditation studies and annual reports institutional research must at times play this game, but it serves best when it casts doubts on such evidence, insisting that it is largely self-glorification irrelevant to the real issue.

Widespread interest in cost effectiveness or cost-benefit analysis also becomes involved in assessment of outcomes. Opinions among economists active in institutional analysis differ strongly as to the relative weight of personal and social benefits. Some argue that the benefits are primarily personal and that each individual should therefore pay the full cost of his education. Educators generally believe in and espouse the social benefits. Since many benefits of education are intangible, not interpretable in dollars or even in observable social effects, it is not likely that research will resolve the argument. Though institutional researchers find cost analysis of interest, it probably must remain a peripheral activity because of its difficulty and because any effort devoted to it is unlikely to have much immediate impact within the institution. Fortunately economists, legislators, and donors have been raising questions about cost effectiveness in a manner which commands attention. But ultimate outcomes still evade quantitative investigation.

Bibliography

AACRAO, Committee on Data and Definitions in Higher Education. *Handbook on Data and Definitions in Higher Education.* Washington, D.C. 1962.

American Council on Education. "Total Federal Obligations to 100 Universities and Colleges Receiving the Largest Amounts, Fiscal 1969." *Higher Education and National Affairs,* 1970, *19*(30).

"The Annual Report on the Economic Status of the Profession, 1969– 70." *AAUP Bulletin,* 1970, *56*(2), 174–239.

BAYLESS, P. C., AND ASSOCIATES. *Higher Education in Indiana: The Future Space Requirements. Long Range Needs and Resources.* Indianapolis: Indiana Advisory Commission on Academic Facilities, 1970.

BRUMBAUGH, A. J. *Research Designed to Improve Institutions of Higher Learning.* Washington, D.C.: American Council on Education, 1960.

DRESSEL, P. L., AND COME, D. C. *Impact of Federal Support of Science on the Publicly Supported Universities and Four-Year Colleges in Michigan.* Washington, D.C.: National Science Foundation, 1969.

DRESSEL, P. L., AND PRATT, S. B. *The World of Higher Education: An Annotated Guide to the Major Literature.* San Francisco: Jossey-Bass, 1971.

DREWRY, G. N. (Ed.) *The Administrative Team and Long-Range Planning.* Athens, Ga.: Institute of Higher Education, University of Georgia, 1967.

FINCHER, C. *Planning in Higher Education.* Athens, Ga.: Institute of Higher Education, University of Georgia, 1966.

KNORR, O. A. (Ed.) *Long-Range Planning in Higher Education.* Boulder: Western Interstate Commission on Higher Education, 1965.

OSSO, N. A., AND ASSOCIATES. *Higher Education Facilities Classification and Inventory Procedures Manual.* Washington, D.C.: U.S. Office of Education, 1968.

RUSSELL, J. D. "The Purpose and Organization of Institutional Research." In R. G. AXT and H. T. SPRAGUE (Eds.), *College Self Study: Lectures on Institutional Research.* Boulder: Western Interstate Commission on Higher Education, 1959.

STECKLEIN, J. E. "Institutional Research: Current Status and Future Requirement." In *Current Issues in Higher Education.* Washington, D.C.: Association for Higher Education, National Education Association, 1962.

STICKLER, W. H. "The Expanding Role of Institutional Research in American Junior Colleges." *Junior College Journal,* 1961, *31* (9).

TYRRELL, P. H. "Programming the Unknown: Guideline for the Conduct of Institutional Research." *Journal of Experimental Education,* Winter 1962, *31,* 92–94.

CHAPTER 3

Planning and
Executing Studies

Paul L. Dressel

❦❦❦❦❦❦❦❦

Institutional research is different from the research of faculty members in a number of ways. It does not share the mantle of academic freedom; it is primarily utilitarian and therefore has a distinctive set of values; and its ultimate success depends less on the research findings than on the promotion of action to alleviate functional weakness and to increase the effectiveness of the institution. In this chapter I attempt to demonstrate the validity of these statements.

Academic freedom extends to the faculty member the right to study any problem within his competency and to publish or present the conclusions and views arrived at, no matter how unpopular they may be. The institutional researcher does not share this freedom. His role gives him access to confidential information, and in his analysis of it he may find evidence of malfeasance, misfeasance, and sheer ineptitude which publicly reported would be highly destructive to the institution and to individuals. Although most studies should be widely disseminated within an institution, some studies must be restricted to a few individuals or to the specific unit requesting them. The existence of an office of institutional research and of requests for studies indicates a desire for detection of weakness and for improvement. Confidentiality in reporting is frequently essential to permit opportunity for improvement and certainly is essential to build confidence and generate further requests. Unquestionably this confidentiality is overdone. The weaknesses in the records of an admissions office, for example, are usually widely suspected if not documented. Undue administrative restrictions on reporting and sharing of data raise doubts rather than allay them. Open admission of error, providing it is accompanied by indications of corrections, would be wise when error does occur.

The ethics of institutional research have not been clarified in detail, but the ethical issue does arise. When a department or other unit requests a study, the question inevitably raised is whether the results will be given to the dean or president. Institutional research may operate under a charter which requires that all reports go to the president, but such a policy is undesirable. If this necessity exists, the department should be so informed. The desirable situation is one in which the results of a requested study are released to others only with the consent of the unit concerned. A study of a unit requested by an administrator over that unit poses a very different problem since an effective study usually requires the cooperation of those studied. Full discussion of the situation and consideration of the implications of noncooperation usually solve the problem. On occasion, however, highly confidential studies of individuals or departments using data already available may be requested by administrators as a basis for possible direct action on their part. Unusually high failure rates, high cost ratios, low morale and feuding, or strong student criticism generate such situations. The institutional researcher must not become a spy or an intelligence agent; a limited private investigation and report usually resolve such difficulties without generating a major confrontation.

Institutional research must be conducted with integrity and impartiality. Data presented should be accurate, or the possible sources and amount of error should be indicated. Otherwise erroneous conclusions may be drawn. Moreover an irritated individual can use an error, however minor, to discredit an entire report. Courtesy and tact in the conduct of studies and in the collection of data are essential both as a matter of appropriate conduct and as a practical recognition that impolitic behavior at this stage can arouse antagonism inimical to the reception of the report. Many reports indicate clearly that confidential data on salary, age, and other personal factors have been used. Sensitive individuals need assurance that institutional research employees do regard such data as confidential and that adequate security measures are in effect when such data are collected and analyzed. Reports which note extremes, such as the lowest salary, certainly should not include names, and they should be edited so that curious readers cannot readily identify individuals. Persons who have responsibilities which require such knowledge can always obtain it.

Academic freedom applied to research includes the privilege of stating personal views or tentative conclusions as well as documented ones. The institutional researcher must be chary of such expressions. As a person, he has a right to his own opinion, and, if he is unusually experienced, his opinion may be very significant and influential. An institutional research report, however, should be an objective analysis of a problem and a presentation of relevant evidence. The researcher who presents his own solution jeopardizes the effect of the report by focusing attention on his solution and arousing antagonism at his presumption in making it. He may reasonably suggest several solutions and attempt to indicate the assumptions and values involved and how available evidence relates to these. Thus he forwards deliberation and decision-making without attempting to force it.

The major use of institutional research should be in the facilitation of decision-making and policy formation. Strictly informational roles are not insignificant. Even in an institution with an extensive computerized management information system, institutional researchers frequently find the need for data that are not routinely collected. There is little alternative but to collect the data on the spot. In addition, selection, organization, and updating of certain kinds of data provide a fund of general information for administrators and faculty and may be provocative for discussions and identification of issues which would not otherwise come to light. Data may be also used and even specifically collected for publicity purposes, for fund-raising, or for the speeches of administrators. In moderation, such uses of institutional research are justifiable.

The institutional researcher must be mindful that the policies and decisions formed from his data are always made in reference to some set of values. Thus, he should identify a number of values and consciously keep them in mind as he organizes and presents data. The following exemplify some of the relevant values. Many studies grow out of a concern about the representativeness of the institutional population on such factors as race, sex, geographical sources of students, and institutional sources of degrees held by faculty. This is one of the major concerns currently with respect to minority groups and women.

A second value is that of equitability, which is in some sense involved in representativeness but becomes more explicit when attention is turned to the salaries of men and women, the grading patterns of various instructors, the size of departmental budgets relative to the load carried, and the faculty loads within and among departments. As with many values, it is easier to make a commitment to the value than it is to be sure that the value has been adequately met. The range of considerations (including period of service, quality of research and teaching, and market competition) involved in the determination of salaries makes it very difficult to determine equitability. And the distinctive elements in the work of such departments as music and mathematics make it difficult to ascertain the equitability of the staff load across departments.

A third value is feasibility. Such a pragmatic concern may not be readily accepted as a value. Yet in starting a new program it is necessary to know whether resources will be available. Research of any kind involves the development of new conceptions, distinctions, and definitions. But the feasibility of a definition or the attempt to use a distinction may eliminate it from consideration. Thus, in collecting data on the use of faculty time, someone might suggest that distinctions be made for time spent on scholarship, on creativity, and on research, and someone who attempted to use these categories might conclude that this is not a feasible distinction.

Another value may be described as suitability, appropriateness, or relevance. It becomes apparent in examining the relationship of grades to the abilities of students or the relation of admission standards to program requirements and success in programs. The educational program of a college must have an appropriate relationship to the kind of students with which it deals; and when it becomes apparent either that unusual numbers of students fail or that the standards of particular fields are too high for the students, some adjustments must be made.

Another highly pragmatic value is necessity, which involves a judgment of the importance and the reality of the social needs to be met by an institution. Studies oriented to this value attempt to document the deficiencies which need to be corrected or ameliorated by development of an educational program. Necessity plays a major role in almost all proposals in higher education. Faculty members presenting a new program are sure that it is necessary; students are convinced of the necessity of anything that they demand; and the public—despite its complaints about the expenditures of higher education—also makes demands upon it. Necessity is not an absolute. It merges into the determination of priorities.

The determination of priorities is a major and continuing task in higher education, as it is in most enterprises. Resources are never adequate for the many "necessary" demands which are presented. Improvement in salaries and fringe benefits may be given high priority, but if resources are at the bare operational level, nothing much can happen. Pragmatically the first priority is always the continuing operation of the institution, even though for some institutions outsiders may doubt that this is the wisest course. On most campuses the library holdings and staff are considered somewhat inadequate, but other program requirements frequently are given higher priority. Buildings and equipment are a continuing problem which involves so many factors that priorities are seldom fixed.

Efficiency is a central concern in many of the efforts of the office of institutional research. It is a focus in studies involving degree or credit hour costs, section size, space utilization, operation of the library, registration, and the enforcement of policies and requirements. The ultimate concern of efficiency is maximizing the rate of return for the investment in higher education.

Quality is a major value, especially in reference to publications, fund-raising, and other uses of data emanating from the institution. Number of staff in *Who's Who*, number and place of publications, faculty graduate record examination scores, test scores of students, fellowships awarded to graduates, graduate school applications and acceptances—all are examples of data collected in an attempt to determine the quality of an institution. Unfortunately, many of these turn out not to be statements of quality but to be statements which are presumed to document quality.

In planning a study, an institutional researcher should consider the various uses that may be made of it and the various values that are involved in connection with those uses. Data collection and interpretation may then be designed to give particular consideration to the values. Values are also relevant in considering alternative courses of action.

Once it becomes clear that values provide the basis for the development and use of institutional research studies, it becomes evident that institutional research is more than data collection. However its reports and conclusions cannot be based simply upon values or interpretations of values by those conducting the study. How does one decide whether an operation is efficient? How does one discern the quality of an institution? What are the criteria for judging the feasibility of a project? There are at least five rather distinctive bases for judgment. The first of these is comparison with other relevant data or with similar institutions. Comparisons may be internal or external, depending on the nature of the concern. The staff of one department may feel that their salaries are not comparable with those in another, or they may feel that there are inequities in load. Cases for improvement of salaries are almost always based upon comparisons with other groups of institutions usually carefully chosen to suggest that the institutional salary level is inadequate. Tuition and fee charges also tend to be adjusted with an eye to the charges in other institutions. Some comparisons are more or less informative, and some involve relationship of data to established norms. Studies of grade distributions made within the institution or in comparison with like departments in other institutions may be regarded primarily as informative, although highly deviant distributions may result in pressures for modification toward an average. But, for library holdings, standards suggested by various authorities have become the basis for a normative judgment as to adequacy or inadequacy.

The second basis for judgment is the existence or the development of theoretical or empirical models. After a study of grades, recommendations have been made on some campuses that grade distributions approximate a certain pattern (A's 5 to 10 per cent, B's 20 to 25 per cent). Curriculum requirements are often based on a model which implies that a student has a certain breadth and depth in his studies as well as certain specific experiences in areas such as writing and a foreign language. Some institutions have developed formulas for determining the staffing of a department or the total institution on the basis of specified loads, average salaries, and the like. Generalized campus models suggest how classrooms, library, housing, and maintenance facilities may be arranged in order to facilitate movement, create a strong educational environment, and encourage a community spirit. Through the use of the computer, it has become possible to develop fairly elaborate models of the operation of an institution. These models can become the basis either for planning or for appraising operations to determine in what respects either they are inefficient or the model is inappropriate.

A third basis for judgment is the application of absolute standards. Tenure regulations tend to be highly specific and are adhered to vigorously. Student records provide another example of the need for absolute accuracy; even occasional errors are a matter of great concern. Statements of due process prescribe standards and steps to be utilized in particular circumstances, with any variation becoming the basis for complaint.

A fourth basis for judgment is cost-benefit or cost effectiveness analysis. In this program budgeting approach the benefits of a number of different alternatives are examined in relationship to costs and a decision is made on this basis. Implicit in this approach is the element of comparison, but the comparisons may become very elaborate as various aspects of benefits are taken into account. Though much discussed and strongly recommended, this approach has been little utilized because of the difficulties in assessing benefits or effectiveness.

The fifth basis, consensus, is concerned with participation in judgment. Consensus moves beyond the judgments of individuals to the collective judgment of those concerned with a decision. In practice, consensus may result from presentation of a report along with other information to a group which ultimately through discussing, politicking, or exerting pressure attains unanimity as to action to be taken or an acceptable compromise. When students and faculty become involved in policy determination, problems are likely to be resolved on a consensus basis. By disseminating pertinent data, the office of institutional research can contribute to making this a somewhat more rational process than it would otherwise be.

Given these bases for judgment, what approaches to problems can institutional research take? I previously discussed the three major subjects of institutional research—the environment, processes and operations, and the immediate and ultimate outcomes. In the consideration of processes and operations I focused on certain broad areas, such as student personnel and plant and business operations. These areas, in some limited sense, correspond to entities in the organizational or administrative structure of the institution. But in the study of any one of these areas one or more distinctive approaches may be chosen. The emphasis may be placed on the functions performed, that is, one may examine instruction, research activities, or the service rendered by a specific unit—functions which constitute its contributions to the major purposes of the university as a whole. Alternatively, one may look at a function such as counseling and find it carried out in a number of different areas— health service, counseling center, deans' offices, and departments. At points it becomes inseparable from the advising function. Instructional services, library, admissions, scholarship, financial aid, student records, curriculum planning and administration, and faculty work load—all involve alternative approaches. Selection of approach depends on the emphasis of a study. With studies involving many units, the selection of approach can be critical.

Another approach, less useful than the concept of function but sometimes helpful, is the object-expenditure classification used by the business office. An investigation of the inadequacy of the supplies budget in a department could be based on this classification. Travel expenditures could also be studied with this focus. Studies involving the use of equipment or aimed at determining the computer needs of a campus are also object-expenditure oriented. Expenditures for repair, maintenance, and communication services are probably seldom studied by institutional research, but phone costs, rented equipment, and maintenance and service contracts do constitute a significant expenditure. If the subunits of an institution have considerable autonomy in these arrangements, occasional study is perhaps desirable to determine whether more control or alternative patterns are desirable in the interests of economy.

Another approach to institutional research is investigation of human aspirations, experiences, and interactions. Here one becomes concerned with satisfactions and gripes and with the nature of interactions. Investigation of the communications system—the clarity of assignments or requests to students or faculty—is appropriate to many problems. When low morale, the decision-making process, or some other aspect of governance is of concern, a study may approach the matter through examination of the influence patterns relating individuals, offices, and administrators, and the extent of confidence or distrust exhibited. Occasional studies of aspects of committee membership, such as changing membership, time involved, and percentage of faculty serving over a period of time, may be a useful way to determine the extent of faculty resource utilization and involvement in governance. A study of the interaction patterns among students, faculty, administrators, board, donors, legislatures, and public is very complicated indeed but may be deemed essential to reveal why misunderstandings and antagonisms arise and how they influence the development and support of the institution.

A study may be designed in relation to the organization and facilitating structures in the institution. Here, one may start with the organization chart depicting the maze of line and staff relationships, examining the clarity of assignments and relationships among various units and individuals and exploring how the various elements in this structure operate and interrelate in policy-making, interpretation of policy, and policy enforcement. Institutional research may have difficulties in carrying on an objective study because of its involvement in this organization. It is evident to anyone who has examined existing structures and suggested reorganizations, however, that structures which appear quite clear and seem satisfactory to individuals at the top of the pyramid are very frequently malfunctioning for and disconcerting to those lower in the hierarchy. Extensive overlapping in responsibilities, which clouds the appropriate point of contact on a particular problem and impedes prompt response, is a frequent difficulty.

A study may be launched in reference to institutional purposes and objectives. In this case one becomes concerned with the clarity of these statements and with the consistency of such statements emerging in various contexts and from various individuals. Knowledge of and acceptance by faculty and students of the institutional purposes and the educational objectives are other concerns. A particular program may be examined in relationship to its fulfilment of or contribution to purposes and objectives; and ultimately any program and indeed the institution itself are to be evaluated in terms of their effectiveness with regard to stated purposes and objectives.

Still another approach to institutional research is through examination of the environmental characteristics. Here environment is interpreted in a very broad sense. It may include the attractiveness of the facilities and grounds as a significant demonstration of the concern of the institution for esthetic values. Environmental studies examine the various emphases (perceived and actual) in regard to the academic program, cultural activities, sports, social activities, and political concerns. The study of environmental characteristics is likely to move beyond these concerns to determine the extent of involvement of individuals in various groups. It certainly becomes concerned with the existence of subcultures in colleges, residence halls, and various groupings of students and faculty such as in the resident or the commuting population, minority groups, professional programs, technical programs, and liberal arts programs. Finally, a study of environmental characteristics is probably concerned with the extent to which the environment presently satisfies or meets the needs of various groups and is in accord with the purposes and objectives to which the institution is committed. To the extent that it is unsatisfactory in some respects, a study may examine how the characteristics of the environment may be changed. This planning usually proceeds reasonably well as long as the primary concern is in changing the physical environment and funds can be found to do so. To the extent, however, that the environment is made up of vested interests, strong subcultures, and long-established faculty priorities, planned environmental changes may be difficult or impossible to accomplish.

A final approach to institutional research is through the utilization of comprehensive management programs, which are implied by such phrases as input-output analysis, systems analysis, operations research, cost-benefit or cost effectiveness analysis, program budgeting, and long-term planning. Each of these comprehensive management approaches has many complications and is so far-reaching that institutional research can at most promote such activity or utilize it when it already exists. If institutional research attempts to impose upon an institution any one of these elaborate systems, it moves from institutional research into management. Yet each of these systems does suggest a pattern of analysis and demand an extensive data system, which tremendously influence and expedite certain types of institutional research. However, these management approaches may develop flaws or have inherent weaknesses which endanger the essential character of the institution. Institutional research needs to guard against being constrained by them. Program budgeting may have been developed with an inappropriate or an inadequate definition of programs. Long-term planning may have developed with too much attention to the financial aspects and insufficient attention to the academic program. Institutional research must be aware of these possibilities and develop its studies in some broad sense, which will permit examining the effectiveness of any program.

Any particular institutional research project may cut across these various approaches. Nevertheless, in designing a project a researcher should consciously think through which one or combination of the several approaches is going to be emphasized and how this approach relates to the various bases for judgment and values which will ultimately be involved in reaching decisions. Thus, in the planning of a project attention must be given to the decision-making process and the politics involved, for action may be promoted or discouraged by the approach and the emphasis of the study.

If studies are to be selected, planned, and carried through in a manner which is likely to produce alteration and improvement, very serious thought should be given at the first consideration of a project to each of the following questions. What is the use or the purpose of the study? What difference will the study make? What specifically is the problem or decision with which the institution is confronted? What are some of the possible courses of action? If these questions cannot be answered in rather specific terms, it is doubtful that a study should be undertaken at all unless it can be initially directed to providing answers to these questions. The attempt to answer these questions forces some redefinition of the nature of the study and helps in deciding on the data to be collected and the procedures to be used.

A second set of questions revolves around identification of the values which will be utilized in reaching a decision. Are we concerned with values such as representativeness, equitability, and feasibility, or are we primarily concerned with the importance and the necessity of particular operations and the priorities among them? Is the problem one of appropriate adjustment between functions, or is it one of efficiency in operations? If the focus is on quality, are we primarily concerned with self-glorification or with improvement?

We also need to give consideration to the bases upon which judgments are made about the values which are served and the extent to which various possible solutions are consonant with the values. These questions lead us into consideration of possible courses of action and the effects of each. While one is unlikely to identify all of these at the beginning of study, to the extent that alternatives are visualized, it may be possible to plan the study so that the data accumulated and the analyses made permit comparison of the significance of various courses of action and the benefits involved.

All too frequently a study causes questions to be raised about some highly relevant missing factor. The researcher can only reply lamely that he never thought of it. Thus, a degree of imagination, originality, and creativity is desirable in planning any study. Undoubtedly in many institutions, right at this moment, the problem of improving instruction is being investigated, but the thinking is limited entirely to traditional classroom patterns with instructors face-to-face with students. When this limitation is imposed, the data considered are very narrow in scope, and the range of solutions is so severely limited that it cannot readily take into account much that is current in educational technology, methods for independent study, off-campus educational expeciences, and the like.

Although institutional researchers to be effective must be continual irritants, they should also be sufficiently politically minded to give cautious attention to the matter of strategy and tactics in getting action on the problems which give rise to their studies. One factor is the timing of studies. If institutional research responds only to requests, it is usually in a rush to meet demands for quick action on the part of administrators or committees who have deadlines for the completion of their deliberations. To the extent that institutional research can identify problems in advance of their formal identification for study, studies can be launched and completed so as either to provide the basis for encouraging attention to the problem or to be placed in the hands of an administrator or committee at the strategic moment when deliberations begin. Repetition is the time-honored way of getting action. As the dripping water wears away a stone, so repetitive studies of certain points gradually develop awareness of these problems and bring about action. Particularly is this true when the increasing awareness of certain problems comes to the fore in connection with demands. For example, a department which schedules all its courses in the morning and resists any modification may at some later point demand more classrooms and can then be made aware of the problem. A department with many small sections can be brought to examine the matter when the overall load increases and more staff is requested.

Although, as we have indicated, institutional research reports are not to be widely distributed without attention to the rights and concerns of those who are studied, widespread dissemination of studies is, on the whole, more conducive to developing awareness of a problem and bringing about change than is limited distribution. Costs are a factor, particularly if one attempts to prepare reports in a way which encourages reading and filing for reference. A major budgetary item for publication is required if attractive reports with tables and illustrations are to be prepared in large numbers. Hence the distribution of reports may be delimited as much by the budget as by any other factor.

However, an office of institutional research which loads the desks of administrators and faculty with large numbers of reports containing extensive data is likely to find that the reports are largely unread and that the office develops the reputation of being very busy but not very effective. The natural tendency of the researcher is to include all the data and details of discussion in a report, at most yielding to an insistence that there be one or two summary pages at the beginning which mention the major points and list the recommendations. Though the omission of data may provoke some readers, it is perhaps far better on the whole to make reports brief and to indicate that certain substantiating data are available in supplementary appendices or by visiting the office of institutional research. By this approach, costs can be reduced and reading induced.

A typical ploy of researchers is to end with inconclusive statements and an indication of the need for further research. This course is unwise, for it provides an opening for those who are satisfied with the status quo to indicate that the report is so inconclusive it should be ignored. An institutional research report should be as definite as possible at the various points where it interprets data. It should not hesitate to point out alternative interpretations, and it should avoid specific recommendations other than when they are presented as alternatives with some indication of how they are related to the evidence presented. If the institutional researcher has the stature or feels compelled to make a specific recommendation on his own or both, this recommendation is best included in a covering letter and commentary attached to the report when distributed.

Institutional research reports should be written in specific terms addressed to the audience on the campus rather than to higher education at large. A report written for an administrator or group of administrators may be quite specific on a number of points, naming departments and even individuals. But a report more widely distributed should not do so. Therefore the researcher should visualize the widest possible distribution of a report on campus and prepare it accordingly. Supplementary comments may be prepared providing the details for a more limited audience. If a researcher feels that what he has done merits publication for a wider higher education audience, considerable rewriting and editing will probably be necessary. Rarely does an institutional research report, in its original form, communicate effectively to a national audience. The company of institutional researchers themselves is something of an exception to this statement since involvement in similar studies often means that locally prepared reports are of more significance to them than are rewrites of these reports directed to the wider audience.

Those who conduct institutional research and hope to promote action must always be aware of the possibility of conflict of interest. Reports may run into trouble because administrators or faculty members have made judgments influenced by an unrecognized conflict of interest and vigorously defend their judgments on professional grounds. Reports may also run into trouble because the implications appear to others to be to the advantage of the office of institutional research. Others are then convinced that this motivation was a dominant factor in preparing the report. Institutional research, perhaps more than other research, strikes at traditional practices and cuts across vested interests. But the facts and objective interpretations often play less of a role than does discussion in bringing about a recognition of basic values and in developing an awareness of the role that bias and personal interest have played in past practices.

If institutional research is to be acceptable, it must be presented in a form that will attain a degree of receptivity. Irritating in some ways it must be or it is unlikely to attract attention or get action; however some measure of restraint must be exercised else the whole endeavor will be rejected. I am reminded of the story of the individual who was unable to get his stubborn mule to move. He appealed to a stranger who immediately picked up a 2 × 4 and hit the mule on the nose, remarking that it was necessary to get the mule's attention before giving him any orders. That is almost precisely the problem of the institutional researcher: he must get attention.

CHAPTER 4

Collecting and Utilizing Basic Data

Joe L. Saupe

❧❧❧❧❧❧❧❧

A basic institutional data system contains the detailed information routinely kept in the files of the college or university, including the simple counts and tabulations made from that information. The basic data on students maintained in folders, punch cards, or computer files provide for basic enrollment tabulations. There are also basic data and basic tabulations on programs, staff, facilities, and finance.

The familiarity of most types of basic data suggests an absence of great issues in dealing with it. Indeed, a college president may wonder why it is apparently so difficult to find out the total number of faculty, or he may not even recognize that there is a

53

difficulty because someone has provided him with a count. Difficulties involve fundamental issues in defining, collecting, and using basic data. Careful planning of the data to be collected and equally careful planning for processing and utilization are essential to institutional operations and to institutional research aimed at understanding and improving those operations. Failure at any of these three points can mean that the data maintenance operation is inefficient, a source of continuing irritation, and an expense which is not justified by the benefits provided.

Applications

Meaningful and consistent basic institutional data are essential to the college or university for understanding the problems and operations of the institution and for day-to-day decisions. In probing into operations and examining the effects of actual or prospective decisions, institutional research uses basic data to analyze the effectiveness of past operations and to predict the varying impacts of alternative future decisions. Five general applications of basic data can be identified.

First, counts and tabulations of basic data provide a description of the institution that is essential to an understanding of it. The description provided by quantitative information is never complete, for it does not reveal purposes and aspirations, but it is certainly fundamental. A college or university is typically described by statements of number—how many students it enrolls (and how many are in undergraduate, professional, and graduate programs); how many faculty members there are (and at what academic ranks); the size of the campus, the number of buildings on it, and the number of square feet in them; the amount of income available (by source) and the total expenditures (by purpose); and combinations of such counts, as in the student-to-faculty ratio. The numbers and types of degree programs offered along with counts of students pursuing each reveal something of the purposes and academic emphases of the institution, which may or may not correspond to statements of purposes and plans.

Counts and tabulations of basic data over time contribute to understanding of the growth and development of the institution and of trends in this growth. They can show rates of growth for the institution as a whole and differential rates for components.

Basic quantitative descriptions of the institution and of its history provide a context for a broad range of considerations in planning and decision-making. A specific issue may be identification of the implications of decreasing numbers of physics majors for a plan to add three new physics courses to the upper division of the department.

Second, basic data, compiled historically, are used in making projections. Some procedures for projecting enrollments, staff, physical facilities, and fiscal resource needs involve the extension of past trends. Even when new principles for controlling growth are deemed more appropriate than continuation of the trends of the past, projections need to be made in the context of historical data to ensure the feasibility of the growth planned and the validity of the control procedures to be employed.

Third, basic data are used in analytical and special purpose institutional research. Quantitative analyses resulting in information on class sizes, teaching loads, unit costs, and instructional space utilization involve statistical manipulations of basic data. The products and implications of such analyses can be no more sound than the basic data used in them. The use of analytical models for planning and for resource allocation requires sound basic data to operate the models. The nature of analytical models was suggested in Chapter Two, and applications are discussed in Chapters Eight, Nine, and Ten.

Special studies also depend upon basic data in one way or another. For a survey of dropouts, one must be able to identify who is and who is not a dropout and to associate other basic data such as prior grade average, sex, major, and geographic source with each individual. If sampling is to be used for a survey of enrolled students, basic data on sex, major, and class level are needed to define the sampling procedure.

Basic data are required for specific issues, such as the rate of attrition of students or of employees. When it becomes necessary to study the status and prospects of an entire academic department, much basic data, current and historical, are required. Chapters

Five and Six suggest items of basic data which may be essential in such studies.

Fourth, extensive files of basic data are required for responding to external requests for information. The office of institutional research often bears responsibility for these requests, which can be viewed as a troublesome burden. However, the accountability of the institution to its publics frequently requires accurate responses to their questions. In some cases, justification for the effort applied to questionnaires can be found in political expediency. It is interesting, at least, that many efforts at refining the collection of basic institutional data can be traced to external requests for information. To the extent that the external agency, federal, state, or other, asks for the type of basic information the college or university should have available for its own purposes, this development cannot be considered altogether undesirable.

This category of uses of basic data includes data used in budget request and development procedures, that involved in accreditation self-study reports, and that required in requests and proposals for project or grant funding by federal agencies or others. There are also legitimate requests for information to be used in research conducted by graduate students and faculty members. The university, by its own commitment to research, is obligated to cooperate whenever the requests are reasonable and confidential information is not involved.

Finally, basic data can be integrated in the development of a management information system. A comprehensive information system ensures that basic data inform through organization into a usable system. The final section of this chapter suggests guidelines for establishing an information system, and Chapter Eight deals specifically with system development and use.

Basic institutional data are, or should be, collected in the normal processes of operating the institution. Fortunately, there is a considerable parallel between the information required in operations and that required for management, planning, and many types of institutional research. Even where specific items of data needed for management are not inherent in operating procedures, it is usually more advantageous to make provisions for collecting them there than to develop ad hoc information collection systems. Thus, even though in the initial appointment process it may not be essential to collect complete biographical information on each faculty member, the biographical information form should be incorporated in the appointment process. Uniformity of procedure and controlled collection are potent advantages.

Information on expenditures is collected in the normal process of carrying out expenditure transactions. In view of check records and cumulative totals of expenditures, it would be absurd for the accounting office to ask a department for a report of expenditures. But department chairmen are asked, no less absurdly, to report the numbers of students taught in their department, the number of research grants held by the departmental faculty, and even the number of individuals on their faculty. These types of basic data should be collected in the processes of registering students in courses, accepting research grants, developing the annual budget, and appointing faculty. Efficiency and accuracy are as important in collecting data concerned with numbers, qualities, and activities of people as in collecting expenditure data, and an audit trail of records on human data is just as desirable as one on financial data.

Requirements

The first requisite for any type of basic data is that of definition. Elements of basic data must be clearly defined, and the definitions must be accepted and understood by all those who deal with the data. It is not at all uncommon for two individuals to count the faculty of a college or university and arrive at quite different totals. This discrepancy may be disconcerting to the consumer of the counts, but both may be correct in reference to the definition used or the purposes for which collected. It should not be expected that the faculty count of the budget analyst be the same as that of the faculty senate. Ideally, however, the two should come from the same data source and should be reconcilable. This requirement suggests the need for carefully developed definitional systems and consistently used terminology. The budget analyst may count full-time-equivalent academic staff appointed to departmental and instruction research accounts. This count may be quite different from a head count of academic staff appointed under tenure regulations. In this illustration, the term *faculty* has been purposely abandoned to avoid confusion.

The need for systems of definitions exists with almost any type of basic institutional data. The definition that should be used in a specific case depends upon the use to which the data will be put. The use of an inappropriate count of faculty in a student-to-faculty ratio calculation can be either disastrous or dishonest. In neither case is it likely to benefit the college or university in the long run.

Basic data derive from data elements, which are discrete items of information that cannot be subdivided (Lawrence, 1969). Data elements for faculty include academic rank, salary, salary account number, percentage of full-time appointment, and many others. Faculty counts and other aggregations of faculty data are derived from data elements and are meaningful only in terms of the precise uses of component data elements in the derivation.

Derived data must be based on verified elemental data. A common dilemma in institutional research is to find that a total count has been modified or corrected without adjustment of the items of detail. Subsequent calculations from the original detail cannot reconcile with the corrected total. Corrections should be made to elemental data as of a specific date and all further counts or calculations are then verifiable providing they refer to that date.

Basic data involve definition of categories as well as of elements and derived data. For example, the element *academic rank* is delimited in terms of the category of employees to which it applies and is described in terms of its meaning. The categories for academic rank include professor, associate professor, assistant professor, instructor, lecturer, and perhaps others including one or more for graduate students with academic appointments. A category may need careful definition, although in some cases this is trivial. In our example, it may be necessary to specify the circumstances under which a graduate student may be appointed with each available title. Unrecorded changes in definitions cause difficulties in comparisons over time. Definition of derived data reveals further complication in our example. The term *academic staff* may include all individuals appointed with a given set of titles (academic rank). But if the president is also a professor of history, is he a member of the academic staff? If so, the fact that he is also counted in the administrative staff must be recognized.

Definitions of elements, categories, and derived data can be idiosyncratic to a particular institution for sound reasons. But basic data are collected, tabulated, reported, and used on an interinstitutional basis. For uniformity, data need to be maintained in such a fashion that they can be translated into the interinstitutional format (Lawrence, 1969). The need for translatability may lead to maintaining more detailed data than are required for purely local purposes, but this result is probably unavoidable.

Internal consistency is a second requirement for basic data. A system of definitions which provides for reconciliation of differing aggregations of similar data illustrates one type of internal consistency. Another kind of consistency has to do with the comparability and consistency with which data on different subjects are collected and reported. Many types of data are collected and reported in categories representing the academic organization of the institution, that is, by department and school or college. Because data reflecting various categories are compared, whether by design or not, close attention needs to be paid to this type of comparability. If the number of faculty members in a teaching load analysis is different from that in a salary tabulation or a directory listing (and, of course, it is very likely to be), someone is almost certain to note this discrepancy and demand an explanation or simply reject all such reports as being inaccurate.

One difficulty with the category of departmental organization is that the key data elements used by people in different offices reflect different institutional functions. Consider the key elements used by the following people: admissions officer (major of student), registrar (course number), accountant (account number), dean of faculty (subject field or academic rank), and payroll officer (office address). This list may be extended, but it makes the point that differing institutional functions lead to differing concepts of institutional organization. The result can be misleading basic data. If the term *department* is defined as an organizational unit with a designated administrative head and a budget, then it is likely that none of those named above could provide basic data by the departmental organization.

Internal consistency is further complicated when, in complex institutions, there is not a one-to-one relationship between majors offered and departments as defined. Particularly troublesome are interdisciplinary majors. Some departments, for example foreign languages, are responsible for more than one series of course numbers yet some courses may be the responsibility of no single department. Account numbers may come close to revealing the departmental organization, but there can be exceptions. Professors of psychology are sometimes appointed to medical schools, and if there is no department by the name, it is not obvious to which department the professor of genetics belongs. The office address to which the payroll check is mailed may have little to do with anything else. The problem is compounded as elements are collected and updated from time to time in varying ways differing in reliability.

If basic data are to be collected, displayed, and analyzed on a departmental basis in an internally consistent fashion, compatibility between data elements and data files is essential. Unless those responsible for the separate institutional functions attain an institutional perspective on the total data problem, this compatibility may be difficult to accomplish.

A third requirement is that of consistency over time. Basic data are often most revealing and useful when tabulated over a period of years. Consistency is essential if trends are to be accurately revealed. Two sources of difficulty may be noted. First, as colleges and universities move in refining their collections of basic data, the refinements can interrupt established trends. New and refined definitions constitute a specific illustration. Another problem is consistent cutoff dates for data reporting. In early years enrollments may have been reported as the number of students processed through registration before the first day of classes. Later, a rudimentary procedure for adjusting student full-time-equivalents by some special treatment of part-time students may have been developed and applied. Finally, a refined full-time-equivalent counting procedure may have been developed and the counts taken at a standard time two to four weeks after classes had begun, with late registration accomplished. In this case, the three types of enrollment counts should not be used uncritically as a basis for establishing enrollment trends.

Second, changes in institutional organization also disrupt consistency over time. Organizational changes are not uncommon, and the impact of them on compilations of historical basic data should be considered. The creation of a new department from a reorganization of two or more existing departments is one illustration. The division of a single department, for example speech and theater, into two separate units is another. The combination of two existing departments into a single new one, while a less common occurrence, is relatively easy to reflect. Changes or refinements in budgeting procedures or the chart of accounts can produce inconsistencies in trends in financial data, even without changes in organizational arrangements. The assignment of faculty fringe benefits to departmental accounts immediately destroys direct compatibility of departmental expenditures with those of previous years.

When a revised definition or procedure for collecting basic data is established or a change in the structure of the college or university occurs, consideration can be given to reconstituting data for prior years. Often such a procedure is unfeasible, if not downright impossible. In some cases it may be possible to overlap two procedures for a year or two so the impact of the new procedure on basic data is revealed. If discontinuities in trend tabulations of basic data are unavoidable for one or more of the reasons mentioned, at least the fact of discontinuity can be highlighted in the tabulations.

A fourth requirement of basic data is availability. The first priority of the admissions office is to admit students, and the registrar's office must act efficiently to enroll students, to register them in classes, and to collect and post grades. But the production of basic data from these operations cannot be left to chance or to available time. The production of basic data from operational procedures must be carefully planned, not only in regard to content, but also in regard to an established schedule. Enrollment information, often in considerable detail, is needed early each fall semester for public information purposes, for internal and external reporting, and for budget planning for the next academic or fiscal year. Data on courses taught and on the enrollments of students in sections are basic to instructional program analyses and must be available early enough for results to be used in program and budget planning for the next year. Class rolls established at the end of registration can be supplemented by summary tabulations of teaching loads for each department to assist administrators in last-minute decisions on staffing caused by unexpected developments in student enrollment.

The timeliness of other types of basic data is no less important. Adherence to a schedule for the production of all types of basic data and associated tabulations and reports allows users to know what to expect and when to expect it, thus contributing to an orderly and systematic use of it. Failure to maintain the schedule encourages the user to collect his own data or to utilize some alternative procedure.

An additional requirement of basic data is that it be authoritative and understood. To be authoritative it must be accurate and come from a responsible source. When the same types of data are produced in two or more places, they are very likely to differ even though all reports may be correct in respect to definitions and time of collection. A dean's count of his faculty is almost certain to differ from the official count of the staff budget officer or a count made by the office of institutional research. All may be correct, but the use of different counting procedures undermines the authenticity of each. The president needs to be able to rely on the information he receives; he has no need for conflicting sets of basic data. Legislators and the general public simply do not understand such discrepancies and tend to suspect either the intelligence or the integrity (or both) of those who present conflicting reports.

If basic data are produced by a single source on the basis of agreed-upon definitions and procedures, the probability of their being authoritative and understood is enhanced though by no means made perfect. The key to understanding basic data is the definitions used in producing it. Specific definitions must be used, and the consumers of the data need to understand the definitions and agree that they are appropriate. If the dean and the staff budget officer use the same definitions, procedures, and dates in counting faculty, their counts will agree, and, under this circumstance, there will be no need for the dean to make his own counts. But if the dean is jealous of faculty size and insists on counting five persons appointed but not due on campus until the next quarter, inconsistencies arise.

Types of Basic Data

The following sections devoted to discussion of specific types of basic data deal with definition, implications, and use. The coverage of basic institutional data is not complete, but many salient types are considered, and there should be implications in these discussions for items not specifically mentioned. Discussions are developed and presented on the basis of data being collected for programs, students, staff, finance, and facilities. Focus is on application of basic data to the generally agreed upon university functions—instruction, research, public service, and supporting service. Input-output models are sometimes used in demonstrating data/function relationships, and these enter discussions in terms of the construction elements commonly used—resources (representing input), activities (representing processes), and products (representing output).

Basic data of different types measure different variables. In only a limited sense does a count of students, of faculty, or of total expenditures have meaning apart from what it is expected to indicate concerning the institution. The count used depends upon the variable that needs to be measured. For example, if a measure of the faculty resources (an input) available for offering instruction (a dependent function) were required, one type of count of institutional staff (basic data) would be made. This count would measure one variable; a count relevant to faculty resources for research would measure another; and other counts of faculty made for other purposes would be concerned with still other variables.

Programs. Basic data on programs include the inventory of programs offered by the college or university and descriptions of these programs. Program categories include instruction, research, public service, and supporting services. Each kind of program is a distinct type of resource for the institution. Programs change, so the inventory needs to be kept up to date. Much of the information on programs is more descriptive than quantitative, but it is certainly basic.

Every college and university collects and reports extensive amounts of basic data on fiscal affairs, but there are few, if any, comparable sets of basic data on central program variables. Requirements of fiscal accountability and the fiscal basis of institutional operation and planning explain the attention given to fiscal transactions and to the basic data resulting from them. But program variables determine the fiscal ones and are at least as important. Academic transactions should be recorded as systematically and carefully as fiscal ones.

For the function of instruction, program data include information on the curriculum, the degrees and majors offered, the course requirements of individual programs and groups of programs. They include information on the courses that have been authorized to be taught.

That curriculum data are not always systematically maintained is illustrated by the experience of one multi-campus university in developing a simple inventory of the several degrees approved for offering at each campus and the majors available for each degree. General catalogs did not contain the information in any systematic, consistent, and complete manner. The apparently simple project took a year to complete, and even then there were indications that the published inventory needed to be called tentative, pending further study. The responsibility for maintaining basic data on instructional programs and courses offered should be centrally vested, perhaps in the curriculum committee, a group vitally concerned with acting upon programs and courses. Help should be made available from the office of the registrar and the office of institutional research.

There is a parallel between fiscal transactions and curriculum actions. Auditable records of basic data should result from each. In the preparation of the college catalog, it is a common practice for each department to submit copy for the programs and courses it offers. The result is the familiar discontinuities in style and content of the resulting catalogs. This problem can be avoided by centralized curricular information.

Having consistent basic data on instructional programs and courses allows a number of important questions to be answered and serves additional purposes as well. The inventory of majors and degrees reveals something about the program balance and emphasis of the institution. Are the balance and emphasis consistent with the college or university mission or purpose? In combination with other basic data, for example the number of students enrolled in each major, what programs are candidates for discontinuance? Having consistent data on the course requirements of individual majors permits investigation of the relationship of the requirements to program objectives and may raise questions about the consistency among programs in terms of requirements. Is the balance among general and specialized courses appropriate? How are prerequisites used? Is there an appropriate balance between lower- and upper-level undergraduate courses? Furthermore, the consistent inventory of course requirements is a first step in the utilization of computer procedures for certifying that students have completed or are completing on schedule the requirements for the degrees they are seeking.

The official inventory of courses and sections approved for offering permits the numbers of classes listed and the growth in the list to be compared on a trend basis, by department and by course level. There is general agreement that colleges and universities offer more classes than are desirable, but few have been successful in reducing the number. Data from the inventory can at least call attention to the problem. If the inventory of courses is in computer records and contains sufficient data for each course, it can be used in the initial stage, at least, of the preparation of the schedule of classes to be offered each academic term or semester.

The idea of an inventory of research programs may also be considered. What departmental research projects are underway? What are the organized or separately budgeted research activities, centers, and institutes of the university? What are the sponsored research projects in the various stages between proposal submission and project completion? How many are pending and active, and what departments are most active in sponsored research? As revealed by such an inventory, are the level, balance, and thrust of research activities consistent with institutional purposes?

A number of colleges and universities operate data banks on sponsored research projects and find them useful for a variety of purposes. These data banks contain records initiated at the time a proposal is forwarded to the sponsoring agency, updated when the sponsoring agency acts on the proposal, and maintained for the duration of the project (or indefinitely). The data thus maintained can be used to reveal the rates of success of the faculty and subgroups of it in securing funding. Data on sponsored research in progress can be classified by sponsoring agency, by department and school or college, or by the subject matter of the research. A data bank can also be used by individual members of the faculty to identify ongoing research in areas and on topics in which they are interested. Several universities have utilized data banks in preparing reports of research in progress in response to requests from state governments or from coordinating boards.

The public service programs of an institution may also be enumerated and described in a basic fashion. The term *public service* has come into use for want of a better and more widely understood designation for those activities through which the knowledge and expertise of the college or university are made available to the community served. Public service is a traditional function of land-grant institutions and is increasingly performed by all types of colleges and universities. As with programs for instruction and research, basic data for budget and accounting are generally available, but basic data on programs may need to be developed through special efforts. There are comprehensive extension divisions, continuing education centers paralleled by cooperative extension services, adult education centers, and other similarly designated organizational units. In addition, special departmental services may be rendered separately from the activities sponsored by the specially designated units. An up-to-date inventory of public service programs being conducted can be revealing in itself and is also basic to analyses of the activities and products of the public service function.

Finally, there are the institutional support programs, which provide student services, general administration, plant operation and maintenance, and other services. For administrative and accounting purposes at least, there must be and usually is some type of listing of these programs and of the purposes of each. The activities of these programs are essential to the effective performance of the three primary functions, and meaningful basic data on them are important to an understanding of the total functioning of the institution.

Students. There are many varieties of student data (National Center for Educational Statistics, 1968). Although some students, for example graduate assistants, are also staff, student data are relevant primarily to the function of instruction. Special considerations pertain to students in public service programs, and these are discussed at the end of this section.

Numbers and characteristics of students, on the one hand, can be used as measures of input or of the raw resources for instruction. At the same time, numbers of students and associated data are measures of work load, which are central measures of instructional process. Furthermore, when instruction is viewed as an institutional objective, the number of students taught is a measure of output. Thus, the meaning of a count of students is specific to the institutional attribute it is intended to measure.

The first question usually raised about a college or university is the number of students enrolled. There may be as many answers to this question for any given college or university as there are people who ask it. Clearly, there are a variety of reasons for asking the question. Some reasons border on idle curiosity; others are more germane. The reason needs to be considered before the answer is provided.

The most common enrollment count is the number of different students enrolled for a given academic period—for example, the fall semester or quarter. This apparently straightforward measure is not without its difficulties and limitations. It needs to be taken at an agreed-upon and consistent point in time each academic period. Part-time students and students enrolled in special courses and workshops which do not coincide with the regular calendar also must be considered. More fundamentally, the student head count is an inflated measure of the instructional work load of and the educational service provided by an institution. Many institutions have been reluctant to count and report enrollments in any other context.

A head count of full-time students is one way of avoiding

the difficulty presented by part-time students. The rationale for this count is that it represents individuals who are fully committed to seeking education and not elsewhere involved in the economy. The resultant counts may be appropriate for manpower and economic analyses but should not be expected to reveal the sizes of individual colleges and universities with accuracy.

Separate counts for full-time and part-time students along with the total head count are often reported. Such counts are more revealing than either of the preceding types of counts, but they do raise the question of defining a full-time student. There is some agreement that an undergraduate student who is registered for twelve or more credit hours is full-time, but there is less agreement on what constitutes a full-time graduate student. A graduate student would probably need to register for twelve or more credits each semester or quarter to complete a graduate program in the customary time period. On the other hand, is not the graduate student carrying six or nine credits and holding a graduate assistantship also devoting full time to his graduate education? If he is a research assistant, he almost certainly is, for his research activity will probably contribute to accelerated completion of his dissertation. It is awkward to have one definition of a full-time student for one purpose and another definition for a second purpose.

If the enrollment figure is to be used to reflect the instructional load of or the educational service provided by the institution, a count of full-time-equivalent (FTE) students should be used. Two principal procedures for determining FTE student counts are used. In one, the number of full-time students is supplemented by some fraction of the number of part-time students. The fraction may be one-third of all part-time students, or it may be determined on the basis of the total number of academic credits for which part-time students are enrolled. In either case, two facts are ignored: full-time students also enroll for varying numbers of credits, and there are institutional and departmental differences in the average load generated by full-time students. In engineering colleges most students carry sixteen to eighteen credits; in other types of colleges twelve to fifteen credits is the average load.

This difficulty is overcome when FTE student counts are based entirely on a credits-for-which-enrolled measure. In this procedure, the total number of academic credits for which students are registered (student credit hours or, more simply, student credits) is divided by some constant representing a normal student load. For undergraduate students, the constant may be fifteen on the basis that this is a semester or quarter segment of a degree program of 120 semester credits or 180 quarter credits.

The significance of the two procedures becomes clear from an example. Assume that nine students are enrolled for the following numbers of course credits: twenty-six, twenty, eighteen, sixteen, fifteen, thirteen, eight, three, one. Six students are enrolled for twelve or more credits and the remaining three for a total of twelve credits. By the first procedure, this enrollment yields an FTE student count of seven. The sum of all the credits is 120, which, when divided by fifteen according to the second procedure, yields an FTE student count of eight. Which figure better represents the work load of or educational service provided by the institution? On a large scale there can be large differences in the results of applying the two procedures. If state appropriations are based on, for instance, a thousand dollars per FTE student, the possible financial implications are obvious. In these implications can be found many of the difficulties of agreement on data reporting common in a group of institutions competing for resources.

To continue with the second procedure, a smaller constant than fifteen is frequently used for graduate students and a distinction is made between master's and doctoral students, the rationale being that course loads are typically lighter at the graduate level and that graduate education, more than undergraduate study, involves student-faculty contact in experiences for which academic credit is not granted. Another argument that has been advanced for differential weighting of graduate credits is that graduate education is inherently more expensive and that the FTE counts should reflect this fact. The premise of this argument may be valid, but the conclusion does not necessarily follow. There also are inherent variations in the costs of undergraduate programs, but there is little merit in confounding measures of enrollment with the factor of cost. If a budget allocation system is based upon aggregate student credit or FTE student counts, there may be no alternative to differential weighting of them. Budget allocations are more meaningful, however, if based on individual programs and the work loads they generate at each level. The topic of resource allocation is considered in Chapter Nine.

Perhaps the most straightforward enrollment count intended to reflect work load and output is provided by the numbers of student credits generated by each department or program and tabulated by student level. The difficulty is that the figures are large and unfamiliar, and for this reason the raw student credit count is reduced by division by one or more constants to get an FTE student count as substitute for the more familiar head count measure. An advantage of student credits and FTE student counts derived from them is that they permit classifications by student major or groups of majors and by departments providing instruction. The student credit is a useful and relatively simple unit for these types of institutional analysis and also provides a meaningful link to other analyses, for example those of class sizes and teaching loads.

Basic data on students for enrollment counting purposes involve more than head counts and full-time-equivalents. Data elements to be defined and recorded include age, sex, class level, program level, major, location, admissions status, source, and geographic origin. Each of these provides a set of categories for enrollment counts, and combinations can be used to produce meaningful cross-tabulations. Race is also a data element of concern in admissions, in studies of retention, and in enrollment reporting. But the legal status of this datum and the sensitivity surrounding it result in obtaining the required data indirectly, perhaps surreptitiously, and consequently with a minimum of knowledge or confidence of accuracy. Age and sex are basic attributes which reveal salient characteristics of the raw resources of the college or university. They may also be used as variables in enrollment projection calculations.

Enrollments are typically counted and enrollment analyses are made by class level: freshman, sophomore, junior, senior, master's, and doctoral. These categories and their definitions can be subjects of concern. Is there a need for a fifth-year undergraduate category? Should master's and doctoral level students be separately counted and should postdoctoral students be counted and how? In universities, particularly, the distinction between master's and doctoral students is not always clear cut. Is the beginning graduate student who proposes to bypass the master's degree a doctoral-level student? Students in professional programs such as dentistry, law, medicine, and veterinary medicine are usually counted separately by year level within the program.

The degree level of the student indicates the level of the degree for which he is working or at which he is enrolled. Associate, bachelor's, professional, master's, and doctoral are the usual categories. Students who are not seeking a degree may be designated as special or unclassified at the level of the highest degree they hold or at the level of the course work they are taking.

The major of the student is another item that needs to be recorded as a basis for both individual planning and program planning. The uses of data on student majors are sufficiently critical that enrollment in and changes of majors should be official actions producing the required basic data. Where such data are generated less systematically, it is not uncommon for the registrar's count of majors in a field to be at variance with the count produced by the department chairman. The responsibility and credit for majors in interdisciplinary programs and for candidates for secondary-school teaching certificates are often problems. Students pursuing two or more majors present a similar problem which must be resolved in terms of how the basic data are kept.

The number of majors in a department does provide a measure of the size of the program sponsored by the department and of its work load of student advising. However, it is not a measure of instructional work load. The majors in a given department generate teaching loads in many different departments, with a variable proportion in the home department. Fortunately most college budget officers now recognize that the dean's claim on a portion of the institutional budget cannot be based upon the number of majors for which he is responsible.

The location variable is pertinent in multi-campus institutions and in those which offer credit courses or degree programs at locations other than the main campus. Residence centers may need to be distinguished from off-campus centers offering credit courses and students classified accordingly. Often, off-campus course offerings are budgeted separately, and enrollments need to be counted separately for this reason. In some instances all students, on and off campus, have been counted and reported in support of a request for legislative appropriations for instruction and the off-campus students counted again in support of the extension or continuing education request. Such a practice should not be condoned, even as an oversight. Basic data on students should contain the distinctions needed to align enrollment counts with budget categories.

Admissions status categories include first-time college student (Is the one who begins in the summer still first-time in the fall?), transfer, returning (from prior semester or quarter), and readmitted. A distinction between a student's original and current admissions status can be made. Data on admissions status are important in describing the student body and as variables in enrollment projection studies. Colleges and universities have been surprised to discover that the impact of expanding numbers of junior colleges is felt in transfers to the sophomore and freshman classes as much or more than to the junior class. Similarly, mobility of college students (as reflected by transfers) and irregular attendance (as reflected by readmissions) may have implications for the undergraduate curriculum, which is typically but erroneously based on the notion of four years of continuous attendance at the college.

Source, another data element, is used to identify the specific institution—high school for first-time students, or college for transfer and new graduate students—from which the student came. The geographic origin of a student is his home state or county. For private institutions which seek to maintain cosmopolitan student bodies, basic data on these items are important to reviews of the performance of the admissions office. They are important to state supported colleges and universities for other reasons; they bring additional funds from nonresident charges (until the student from another state can establish he has become a resident), but they also bring expressions of concern from the legislature.

Basic data on enrollment are revealing and useful in simple tabulations as suggested above. They are also used in analyses of enrollment trends, in preparing enrollment projections, and in analyses of instructional activities.

A longitudinal analysis of student flow through the institution is made possible by consistent and cumulative student enrollment data and can produce findings with implications for the college or university. Many colleges still base their programs on the traditional model of uninterrupted attendance at a single institution. It is also assumed that the student who is in attendance one semester but not the next is a dropout and should be considered a loss. A systematic student-flow analysis can reveal what proportion of entering freshmen continues uninterrupted to graduation, what proportion drops out at one point and returns later, and what proportion of the student body consists of transfers from other institutions. As new freshmen discontinue before earning a degree and transfers continue to be added to the student body, it should not be surprising to discover that the graduating class in any given year includes appreciable numbers of students who came to the institution as transfers and others who had earned academic credit at other institutions along the way. What are the implications of such findings for the integrity of tightly planned four-year programs of undergraduate study and for tightly planned and scheduled sequences of interdependent courses?

Student flow analyses can lead to mathematical models of student attendance behavior which are useful in enrollment projections and in estimating the consequences of policy changes. Such a model may permit, for example, the estimation of the long-range impact on enrollment resulting from a restriction prohibiting transfers from junior colleges without program completion. If residence were a variable in a model concerned with attendance patterns in respect to in-state and out-of-state students, the impact on attendance of a change in the out-of-state quota could be similarly estimated.

Mathematical models applying attendance behavior to systematic enrollment projection procedures are based upon basic data on the sources of different types of students and on the flow of different groups through the college or university. Enrollment projections are essential to program, financial, and facilities planning, and enrollment projection models facilitate estimates of the effects of proposed changes in enrollment policies. If the basic data are adequate, an enrollment projection model can include projections of enrollments in specific academic majors or groups of majors and, on the basis of the course selections of students in different majors, can be extended to include projections of enrollments in courses or groups of them. Because it is the departmental teaching loads that generate specific needs for faculty, space, and operating funds, these types of projections are crucial for planning. The decision to increase the size of the freshman class in engineering is usually accompanied by a request from the engineering dean for more staff positions. In this case, immediate needs for additional staff are probably greatest in the mathematics department and in other departments which teach freshman engineers. Projecting the basic data may even reveal that, in a year or two, when the increment in students does reach engineering courses, it will fill up existing course sections rather than create a demand for new ones.

Another revealing analysis of basic data is that of changes in declared majors. How many times does a typical student change majors during his four undergraduate years, and what are salient patterns of major changes? How many of the new freshman engineering majors of the preceding paragraph can be expected to remain in engineering as they become sophomores and juniors? Coupled with evidence on student flow, evidence of major changes can cause important questions to be asked.

Enrollment and student registration data also lead to analyses of the instructional program. Data on the curriculum in action provide measures of work load and activities of instruction. Instruction is the central function of all colleges and universities, and it is important that basic data on the manners in which it is provided be available. Educational as well as fiscal considerations require such data (McGrath, 1961; Ruml and Marsison, 1959). Instructional program data include semester-by-semester or quarter-by-quarter information on each section of each course taught. They include the enrollment in the section; the credit value of the section; the designation of the section as a lecture, laboratory, or other teaching arrangement; and the instructor or instructors assigned responsibility for the section. They also include the times and places the section meets. These data can be obtained from the normal course scheduling and registration processes.

The analyses suggested here illustrate that institutional research often utilizes basic data from different sources. The requirements for consistency among the different types of data and for collection of data in forms applicable to various interrelated analyses are clearly evident to the institutional researcher. Basic data on sections taught are produced in the process of scheduling courses. The student registration procedure produces the counts of students enrolled in each section, and some other procedure may need to be used to identify the instructor for the course or section. If the data are used for unit cost analyses, faculty salary data from financial records are required. These same data, when supplemented by student station and square footage data from the inventory of physical facilities, lead to studies of the utilization of instructional space.

Derived data on the instructional program include measures of the volume of instruction provided by different departments and for different groups of students. The numbers of different courses and of different sections taught, the numbers of course or section credits or class hours taught, the numbers of students enrolled in different courses, and the number of student class hours and of student credits taught are measures used. Average class or section sizes and frequency distributions of class sizes are produced. Average faculty teaching loads and distributions of teaching load values are also prepared. The index of student credit hours taught per full-time-equivalent faculty member is more useful than the familiar student-to-faculty ratio.

If the basic data on each course or section taught include not only the total number of students registered but also their distribution by class level and major, the data can be used to generate tabulations showing the sources of students for individual courses and for groups of courses. The cross-over matrix is useful in revealing which departments provide appreciable service-load instruction to students from other departments. By showing where given types of students generate teaching loads, data on courses are fundamental to many types of analytical approaches to projections and planning and also facilitate examination of the correspondence between student class levels and intended levels of courses.

These instructional program data, when retained on a cumulative basis, also provide a basis for answering other questions about instructional program processes. How frequently are listed courses taught? What courses have not been taught for a period of years? Which courses are offered repeatedly for small numbers of students?

Are course prerequisites observed? To what extent are the programs of students, as revealed by their cumulative records, consistent with the catalog descriptions of program requirements? Experience in preparing analyses of these types and in sharing them with faculty and administrative groups has revealed that they can contribute to actions designed to increase both the effectiveness and the efficiency of the educational program.

Certain types of basic student data collected more or less routinely depending upon the policies and procedures of the college or university are used as measures of the raw material for instruction. Data on freshman student aptitude, as represented by records of high school academic performance, and college entrance test scores obtained in the admissions process should be retained in an accessible place for research on the institution. Placement testing programs also produce test scores which should be considered as basic institutional data.

Summaries of freshmen student aptitude data over a period of time are useful in evaluating admissions policies and practices and are fundamental in considerations of purposes and objectives. Student aptitude data may also be drawn upon in special institutional studies and analyses. They can serve as control variables in research on teaching effectiveness and as classificatory data in dropout studies. It is provocative to examine the ways in which grade point averages vary or do not vary as the overall level of freshman aptitude changes over time.

The student application form can be a source of other data that reveal central characteristics of the student body and changes in it. Interests, motivation, experiences, nonacademic achievements, socioeconomic status, and other background factors may be among the information included. The specific uses made of such data vary from one institution to another. The key point is that these items are basic data and may have value after the admissions decision has been made. Unlike those items of basic student data that are repeatedly used, these types may not need to be stored mechanically. It may be more efficient to recall them from the forms on a selective basis as needed for special studies.

Applications for financial aid contain appreciable amounts of basic student data and should be viewed as a resource for institutional study. Financial aid actions also generate basic data descriptive of the aid program, which can take on added utility if systematically associated with the basic data generated in the admissions and registration processes. If the financial aid officer records type, source, and amount of aid by a student identification number, these data can be added to other student files for comprehensive analyses of the aid program.

Personality tests, attitude inventories, and related types of questionnaires may be more or less regularly administered to students as part of the institutional self-study and evaluation program. Uses of basic data of this type are discussed in other chapters of the volume.

The grades awarded students in individual courses are basic institutional data which provide measures on one aspect of the product of instruction. Grade averages are traditional criterion variables for studies of admissions standards. Studies of the grading practices for different courses and departments can suggest varying practices which deserve to be called to the attention of the faculty (Petersen, 1967).

The numbers of degrees awarded by a college or university provide concrete evidence of the product of its instructional program. Degrees awarded are tallied by type of degree, major, educational level, and date granted. These tallies yield information on the flow of trained manpower into the economy from individual institutions and from groups of them.

Some analyses of degree production for individual institutions have been made by comparing the number of degrees awarded in one period with an enrollment count for an earlier period. Comparisons of this type may reveal general trends but are likely to be misleading because of irregular attendance and transfer phenomena. If "degree awarded" is added as a data element on individual enrollment records, refined analyses of degree production are made possible. Even with provisions for credit by examination and efforts to encourage year-round operations, few students earn undergraduate degrees in fewer than four years of continuous attendance. Some students require more than four years. This fact presents implications for the efficiency of curricular requirements.

Extension organizations are often responsible for administering courses for academic credit at diverse locations. This is a public service function as well as an instructional one. Basic data on these courses are or should be similar to those on regular on-campus courses. Major portions of public service activities are in fact instructional in purpose, and the public service student is as real as a student in a regular academic program. Thus basic data on the work load and the product of public service activities can be developed on the basis of numbers and types of public service students served. As illustration, consider the following forms of public service instruction: group instruction, which includes formally organized conferences, short courses, workshops, seminars, and similar activities involving identifiable groups of participants or students and amounts of instruction that are quantifiable at least on the basis of the durations of the activities; independent study, which takes place when self-instructional material is provided individual students; individual instruction, which involves a one-to-one relationship between the instructor and the student in forms such as face-to-face contact, telephone contact, and correspondence contact; and mass media instruction of a public service nature, which can be provided by radio or television, or by newspapers and other publications.

The numbers of students served in these activities (with the exception of mass media instruction) may be counted, often from registration records. But the raw head counts are not at all comparable from one activity to another and are thus of limited utility as basic data. By developing conventions similar to those used for regular students, one can develop public service FTE student counts. For group instruction situations, the convention may be that a hundred student hours of organized activity designates an FTE student. A two-day conference of fifty registrants with six hours of conference sessions per day would then generate six ($12 \times 50 \div 100$) public-service FTE students.

By assigning a unit of academic value, perhaps on the academic credit scale, to independent study packages, FTE counts can be based upon the number of such units provided. Similar conventions, based upon actual or estimated student effort, can be developed for each form of individual instruction. The work of a national task force on the Continuing Education Unit (CEU) has promise for guiding the development of basic data on public service students (Williams, 1966). The basic recommendation of this task force is that the CEU be defined in order that attainments of individuals in continuing education experiences may be recorded and accumulated in much the same fashion as is done with academic credits for degree-seeking students. The CEU is defined as ten hours of instruction and may be recorded in tenths. Each experience offered for CEU credit is certified in much the same manner as credit courses are authorized. This proposal has been the subject of pilot projects at twenty colleges and universities. It is likely that the practice will be widely adopted. As with the academic credit, the CEU can serve not only as a certification of an educational experience but also as a measure of work load and of educational product. In the latter sense, CEU equivalencies could be associated with many or all public service teaching activities and could thus provide a basis for measures of work load and of product.

Staff. The staff, both academic and other, is a principal resource of the college or university. Basic data on staff yield measures of this resource for the functions of instruction, research, public service, and supporting services. Basic data on staff activities contribute to measures of work load and of the processes by which each of the functions is carried out. The activities and accomplishments of the faculty result in basic data which are indicative of product or outcome, particularly with respect to the function of research.

The academic staff of a college or university may be defined to include those individuals who, on the basis of training or experience, are employed to carry out instruction, research, and public service. It includes the faculty, but this term has so many different meanings that it is used sparingly here. This definition of academic staff includes teachers in the classroom, researchers in the laboratory, and professional staff carrying the expertise of the college or university to the public. It may also include professional staff in the library, in an instruction and research computer center, and in services which provide direct support to academic activities. The academic staff, but perhaps not the faculty, includes graduate students who also have responsibilities in instruction, research, and public service.

Basic data on academic and other staff, particularly counts, should be collected in the appointment and budgeting processes. The information required for categorizing and counting staff should be available in these processes. Verifiable counting and good management both require it. If a professor is appointed to the psychology department and paid from the psychology budget but works full time in the counseling center, it is awkward to subtract him from the count of psychology staff when calculating the teaching load of that department, and inconsistent reports may result. The budget should reflect the intended deployment of resources and should be updated as necessary.

Counts and other basic data on academic staff are less useful in the aggregate than when given in terms of categories. One set of categories is that provided by ranks or titles. Senior or top-four-rank academic staff include those in the instructor to professor ranks. Junior academic staff include the several types of graduate assistants; and a category of other academic staff may be needed to account for lecturers, research associates, postdoctorals, and others.

Another set of categories based upon function or institutional organization defines the major distinctions for academic staff as instruction, research, service, support (appointed to educational, research, or service units), and administration. These categories are only illustrative. They do, however, indicate staff resources for the several academic functions. The calculation of student-to-faculty ratios should be based upon some count of the academic staff for instruction. Unfortunate comparisons among colleges and universities have too frequently been made on the basis of ratios computed from counts of all academic staff or of some undefined, inconsistent, or inappropriate count of faculty. Even within an individual institution such inappropriate calculations are less than meaningful because departments may, by accident or plan, vary greatly in the proportions of staff assigned to various functions. Judgments about the sizes of other components of the academic staff should be made on other bases.

The person attempting to develop a system of definitions for academic staff meets numerous difficult problems and needs to deal with each. The multiple appointment problem created by individuals who are assigned to more than one administrative unit is particularly troublesome and is considered in the following paragraphs.

As with students, both head counts and full-time-equivalent counts can be made for academic staff. In concept, the counting of the number of different individuals on the academic staff is straight-forward, but in practice it is not unusual for such counts to be equivocal. Some individuals may hold academic rank but work in positions not normally in the academic organization. The president is an example. The coach of an intercollegiate sport who may teach physical education courses in the off season is another. The business manager who at one time was a professor of business administration and has retained the title is a third.

If the head counts are by some set of categories, additional difficulties arise from multiple appointments. A professor may teach in and be paid from the budgets of two or more departments. Another has part of his salary paid from a research grant. The coach may be paid from the physical education and the inter-collegiate athletics budgets. Such individuals, in effect, have two or more part-time positions. They may be counted in each if the resultant double counting is explicitly recognized. For head count purposes they may be counted in that organizational unit with which the largest proportion of their salary is associated. If the split is 50–50, the choice should be made by some rational and agreed-upon procedure, not merely by the flip of a coin.

Many of the difficulties of counting can be resolved by the designation, in the appointment and budget process, of a principal or primary appointment for each individual. Head counts of prin-cipal appointments can be made and supplemented by counts of individuals with secondary appointments in each category. The primary appointment should also designate the unit in which the individual votes on all-institutional matters.

Full-time-equivalent counting circumvents several of the difficulties of head counts and results in data that more precisely reveal overall amounts of academic staff and show how this resource is distributed among organizational units and functional categories. The full-time equivalencies of full-time individuals with multiple appointments may be apportioned among counting units in pro-portion to the amounts of their salaries that are paid by each, and part-time staff may be similarly reflected. Full-time-equivalent counting of part-time staff requires that the equivalency of each appointment be systematically recorded as part of the appointment and budgeting process. This proportion of a full-time-equivalent should reflect the relationship between the salary of the individual and the salary he would be paid if his appointment were on a full-time basis. Ratios of 0.25 or 0.33 for individuals with half-time teaching assignments reflect the abominably low rate of pay for part-time staff.

Some faculty and administrators, too, argue that the annual budget alignment of academic staff should not be expected to reveal how this staff is used. If reflection of the plan for resource utilization is not taken seriously, this argument is correct and staff counts taken from budgetary data are meaningless. But the budget should be the financial counterpart of the educational plan, and, as such, it is the only official record of planned staff deployment. Staff counts must be taken from it. If such staff counts are not meaningful, the fault is with the formulation and application of the budget and not with the counting procedure.

It has also been suggested that FTE staff counts be based on activities or specific assignments. Thus, teaching and other assignments or activities would be used to calculate full-time-equivalents. Such calculations would reveal staff utilization rather than staff availability. If five faculty members were assigned to a department, the fact that there were only twelve or fifteen hours of teaching to be done would not mean there were fewer than five FTEs in the department. Neither could it be taken to indicate that three hours of teaching per week constituted a full load. It is therefore important that there be some way of relating staff counts to assignments as much as to departments.

In addition to including as variables academic rank and organizational unit to which assigned, basic data on academic staff should include sex and age. Considerations of equal opportunity require the former, and questions of expected turnover due to retirement, staff benefits, and staff vitality require the latter.

Salaries are basic institutional data used for internal analyses as well as for external reporting. Data on average salaries by academic rank and on average annual increments by rank are important for comparison within the institution and with other institutions. The data may reveal that special effort toward salary adjustments is needed in respect to different academic ranks. Emphasis on youth and building for future excellence may require special attention to the salaries of instructors and assistant professors, while emphasis on established quality and the career status of senior staff may require special attention to the salaries of full professors.

The average salary of all instructors needs to be interpreted carefully because of its dependence on the mix of academic staff by rank. On the other hand, it does reveal the overall level of average salary support to academic staff and can be revealing when tabulated over a period of years. With a given amount of funds for faculty salaries, the decision to have fewer individuals at the higher ranks and salaries in order to pay more at the lower should be consciously made, rather than simply happen.

The number of faculty members working toward and the number on tenure need to be known as context for individual tenure actions. Unless tenure decisions are very carefully considered, a large proportion of the faculty with tenure can produce a situation in which the options for faculty development are severely curtailed. Predictions of a surplus of Ph.D.s in the academic market place in the 1970s should make colleges and universities particularly wary of this situation.

The quality of the faculty and, thus, the quality of the college or university are traditionally assessed in large part by basic data on highest degrees, granting institutions, publications, academic recognitions, professional affiliations and activities, and other experiences of individual members. Assessment alone makes it important that background data on academic staff be systematically maintained. All or much of the required data are collected somewhere in most colleges and universities. Some are collected on appointment forms. Some are recorded in recommendations for promotion or for tenure. Some are collected in the process of preparing annual reports. Indeed, faculty members frequently complain, and rightfully, about repeated requests for the same information.

Systematic collection in a central location is needed. Files can be initiated at the time of an individual's initial appointment and be maintained by an annual updating process. The establishment and operation of such a system of basic data on academic staff should not be undertaken lightly. Experience shows it to be complex and difficult. There are temptations to collect more information than it is feasible to maintain and to store it in uneconomical ways. Particularly for the larger colleges and universities, the solution is probably to utilize computer records for data that are likely to be called for repeatedly and to maintain file folders for those items that are infrequently needed or for which the retrieval capabilities of the computer are not required.

Staff counts made from the annual budget of a college or university should reveal in a general way the manner in which manpower resources are allocated to the primary functions of instruction, research, and service, and to the supporting and auxiliary functions. Such counts are often supplemented by specially collected basic data on the activities of the academic staff (Stecklein, 1961). Additional detail on academic staff is assembled for two basic reasons. First, the academic staff is the largest, in terms of financial support, and, most important, in terms of performing primary functions, component of the total staff. This fact alone makes it essential that the manner in which this resource is utilized be ascertained as clearly as possible. Second, the academic staff is a multipurpose staff. Professors engage in teaching, in research, and in service activities in ways and combinations that are not usually anticipated in the annual budget. In this regard they are different from other college or university staff, who serve individual functions which may be adequately identified by budget designations. In a few universities distinctions among instruction, research, and service are made in the annual budget for members of the academic staff. This procedure has considerable merit as a technique for recording the intended use of resources.

Information on activities of the academic staff is typically collected on a service report, faculty load report, or similar form. Such forms specify categories of activities, asking for estimates of time or effort devoted to each, and they may provide for indications of specific activities. Several basic questions are involved in the procedures used in collecting such data. What categories and subcategories of activities should be recognized? At one extreme, the categories can be limited to those of instruction, research, and service. The respondent can be asked to account for all effort, including committee work and administrative efforts in these three basic categories. At the other extreme, subcategories can be listed endlessly —undergraduate teaching, graduate teaching, thesis supervision, student advising, departmental research, sponsored research, and so forth. Some choice between these extremes is usually made. Activity reports need to be made in sufficient detail that important distinctions can be made, but the use of too many categories suggests, incorrectly, that fine distinctions can be made and gives the results an unwarranted appearance of precision.

What unit of effort should be used? One alternative is to ask respondents to record estimates of the average number of hours per week devoted to each category of activities. The hour data may be converted to percentages and thus provide both absolute and relative measures of effort. While there is little doubt that many faculty members, like other professional people, do spend more than forty hours per week on activities associated with their work, few could be expected to admit to occasions of spending less, and the tendency to exaggerate when reporting effort is often suspected in reports of this type. The usual procedure is to ask respondents to record a percentage of total effort for each category, with or without a suggestion that effort and time are equivalent. The percentage unit is straightforward and may be converted to full-time-equivalents.

Other types of units are possible and reasonable. If activity data are associated with courses taught, the credit hour unit bears consideration. If a faculty member engages in no activities other than teaching, a fifteen- or perhaps even eighteen-credit load may be a reasonable expectation. Thus, if teaching is only part of the full load, it would be reasonable to associate credit equivalent units to nonteaching activities. The use of these units would be consistent with the formal granting of released time for a nonteaching activity and can be used in a manner that recognizes differences in teaching assignments. Thus the load of a three-hour-per-week lecture to five hundred students (worth three credits) could be recognized as worth four activity units, and the aggregate of three smaller sections of the same three-credit course could be worth fewer than nine units to the instructor responsible for them.

Who should make the reports, and what should the basis of them be? Traditionally, activity reports are completed by individual faculty members who are asked to estimate the relative amount of time they devote to each of several categories of activities. The results are influenced by each individual's perception of what is desired and perhaps also by his guess about advantages that might accrue to giving one or more categories more weight than the others. An alternative is to ask the department chairmen to complete or at least to share directly in completing the report. This procedure can be expected to produce more consistent information because fewer individuals are doing the reporting and because those who are may be expected to attend closely to whatever instructions and guidelines are provided. It clearly relates the requirement of activities reporting to the management of resources, and it may stimulate discussion between faculty and chairmen on the definition of the specific responsibilities of an assignment.

Should specific activities be described on the form? Although it is not possible to give much of a statistical treatment to specific activities such as courses taught, number of advisees, titles of research in progress, names of committees, and service activities, descriptions which serve to substantiate the extent of efforts reported for them should at least be a matter of record. This method may be the most convenient for assembling needed information on the activities and accomplishments of individual faculty members and, by aggregation, for departments. If this is the case, care must be taken that the same information is not requested in other contexts—for example, for recommendations for promotion, for the annual department report, or for use in connection with proposals for research grants. Every effort should be made to see that each datum collected is so defined and filed that it can be used for every other purpose to which it is relevant.

For faculty members in instruction and departmental research units the task of defining and reporting public service activities can become difficult and irritating because numerous discrete activities of limited duration and fine distinctions are involved. A foreign language professor is called upon to translate a letter in Russian received by the governor. A science professor is called by a newspaper reporter to explain or comment on some recent research finding or unusual physical phenomenon. This may lead to a brief appearance on television. A professor of speech gives numerous high school commencement addresses, receiving only token honoraria. An economics professor does extensive consulting and earns more from this source than he is paid by the university. What is public service? When does it change to personal gain? Which of these items are of legitimate concern to the university? Can one expect to obtain conscientious reports on such matters, given the flexible nature of the professor's job? He can always claim that he read term papers on Saturday and Sunday to make up for highly remunerated consulting done on Thursday and Friday.

For the individual whose primary assignment is in a public service area, the reporting of activities in quantifiable terms may be somewhat distasteful and time consuming but not really unmanageable. In this connection it may be noted that, under the leadership of the Federal Extension Service of the United States Department of Agriculture, each state has developed a comprehensive State Extension Management Information System (SEMIS) designed to provide basic data for planning, programming, accomplishment, and evaluation of the entire range of extension activities. The systems developed within the several states are based upon a common framework (EMIS) of data collection and reporting (Systems Development Corporation, 1968). The central component of each SEMIS is a daily activity report employing a system of codes, which is submitted by each member of the extension staff. This report is keyed by means of the coding system to a program inventory and to program plans. The SEMIS efforts can be expected to generate appreciable amounts of basic data on extension activities for those colleges and universities that engage in federally funded extension programs.

Should activity reports for members of the academic staff reconcile with the budget? The report of the faculty member who is appointed to a single department and paid from the salary budget of that department is a simple budget item. The case of the faculty member paid from more than one account is not so clear cut. Should two or more forms be completed in his case? In some cases budgets serve merely as records of planned expenditures rather than records relating planned expenditures to separate functions or programs. In these cases, the activity reports cannot be expected to be related to the budget. But even for carefully devised and program-oriented budgets it may not be possible or feasible to attempt to anticipate all variations in the multipurpose efforts of the academic staff. Thus, it may not be reasonable to expect that activity analyses will be completely consistent with budgeted divisions of labor. However, in terms of staff covered and total counts of staff, the two sets of basic data should be reconcilable.

How valid and reliable can activity analysis data be? Faculty members are often reluctant to complete activity reports not only because they are unsure of the consequences of them but also because they are uncomfortable in making the necessarily subjective decisions required. Some department chairmen are similarly uncomfortable. The reporter and the user alike must understand that subjective estimates are involved and that the resultant data can be no more sound than the judgments that go into the original reports. Some, but not all, errors are random and self-adjusting in aggregations of data. If the data are viewed as honest estimates by individual faculty members or, perhaps better, as resource allocation estimates by the chairmen and not as absolute verities, they can have considerable validity for a number of purposes.

In considerations of manpower available to institutions of higher education, employees other than the faculty often receive scant attention. In budget planning, requests for new faculty positions are preeminent; considerations of the staff required to support the work of the faculty often appear to be afterthoughts. It may actually be easier for a faculty member to acquire a typewriter than to acquire the clerical support he needs in order to most fully utilize his competencies.

Basic data on administrative and support staff are as important as basic data on academic staff. For purposes of institutional research, management, and planning, they may be less extensive. The basic personnel data required by personnel policies, fringe benefits, and personnel development programs need not be discussed here, but any information generated in the operating process is potentially useful in institutional analysis. Personnel officers do engage in institutional research required by the programs for which they are responsible and they should continue to do so, but their records should be kept so that they are compatible with other files and can readily be interrelated with them.

From the standpoint of institutional research it is important that meaningful categories of administrative and support staff be developed and defined. At one level it is not always simple to distinguish academic staff from the other categories of employees. Is the director of the physical plant a member of the academic staff because he was once a professor of engineering and retains that title? Meaningful distinctions are made in terms of the educational requirements of a position and the nature of the responsibilities it entails. The terms *administrative, professional, technical, clerical,* and *service* suggest the distinctions required. Because of the wide variety of specific job titles used, such categories are basic to meaningful accounting for these types of personnel. The definitions of these categories are basic to considerations of career development, aiding in establishment of combinations of education and experience by which individuals in these categories can improve themselves to attain reclassification and higher salary levels.

As with the academic staff, head counts and full-time-equivalent counts are essential basic data. At least two special problems arise with counts of these categories of staff. One is that the turnover of subprofessional staff is typically sizable. Procedures for developing staff counts need to recognize this situation while analyzing it with the aim of minimization where possible. A second problem is hourly and irregular payment of part-time staff. Head counts of such employees may be misleading, and full-time-equivalent counts are difficult to develop. The budget allocations for these types of staff may provide the most useful approximations of their numbers.

Once meaningful categories and procedures for counting administrative and support staff have been developed, other types of basic data on staff can be collected and analyzed. Salaries and salary increases are as important to staff members as they are to faculty, and they deserve as careful study. Furthermore the needs for offices and other types of space for staff cannot be overlooked in projections of faculty needs.

A specific analysis that some colleges and universities have found useful is a department-by-department comparison of the ratio between administrative or professional staff and clerical and other support staff. For academic departments, the equitability of clerical support for faculty among the different departments is a recurring and legitimate concern. A single faculty-to-clerical ratio does not provide a satisfactory answer in terms of work loads, but, as with most other forms of institutional research, it can draw attention to the problem and provide a basis for other considerations to be brought to bear.

Finance. Each financial transaction, from the appropriation of state funds to the purchase of a supply of paper clips, produces basic financial data. Records of income received are used to prepare statements revealing resources available for application. The budgeting process results in allocations of funds and staff for use in the areas of instruction, research, public service, and support programs, and in accompanying basic data on resource allocations. As funds are spent, accounting records present basic data accumulated by account number. Monthly and annual reports of expenditures present further accumulations of data. In the broadest sense, all basic data collected in the accounting processes and in the regular and ad hoc reports which result from them are institutional research, for they contribute to understanding, operating, and improving the institution. Publications on program budgeting and cost effectiveness analysis for colleges and universities focus special attention on basic financial data (Systems Development Corporation, 1968; Ward, 1969; and Williams, 1966).

The regular collection and reporting of basic financial data are properly functions of the chief fiscal officer and consequently need not be treated extensively here. The concepts and details of business and fiscal administration and data handling are thoroughly presented elsewhere (American Council on Education, 1968).

Offices of institutional research do, however, draw upon the basic fiscal data. As has been repeatedly emphasized, the manners in which the data are collected and recorded need to be appropriate to the special research efforts of these offices. Despite the fact that an employee's salary may be budgeted, paid, and recorded without reference to his full-time equivalency or to his academic rank or title, these data elements are clearly essential to institutional analyses and should be recorded in the fiscal records. Expenditure reports almost always report total salaries paid, but the portions paid to faculty or academic staff are not always available. The not uncommon practice of using single account numbers for the total institution for such items as travel, telephone, publications, and staff benefit expenses makes it impossible to calculate total costs for individual academic programs.

Accounting systems used by colleges and universities are increasingly being organized in ways which allow budget and expenditure data to reflect the application of funds to institutional functions. The familiar budgeting and accounting categories of instruction and departmental research, separately budgeted research, extension and public service, and those for the several supporting functions illustrate this development. However, even functional budgeting and accounting cannot be expected to fully reflect resource allocation and use in terms of programs and functions. Activity reports can be helpful in associating academic salaries with the various functions to which academic staff contribute effort. Other expenditures more difficult to trace are allocated on various bases that are subjective or at least somewhat arbitrary. For purposes of cost analysis, there are no alternatives to the use of arbitrary bases (Cavanaugh, 1969; Miller, 1964).

The difficulties involved in the use of basic financial data to answer questions about the institution can be seen in the context of research. What is the level of research activity in a major university, and how does this level compare among the several schools and colleges? First to be considered may be the separately budgeted research that takes place in specially designated organizational units, for which the needed data are readily available. Most, but not all, research units can be associated with the several schools and colleges. The difficulty here is that not all schools and colleges have organized research units. If there is a college of agriculture, the policy may be to account for as much as possible of the agricultural research effort in the context of the Agricultural Experiment Station. Similarly, research may be accounted for by engineering experiment stations and bureaus of business and economic research. But there may be no way to account for the research of the arts and science departments. Moreover, the research effort in a college of business without an organized research bureau may be as extensive as a comparable effort accounted for by such a bureau in another university. Thus, to the totals for the organized research units must be added amounts for departmental research in order to obtain totals by which the schools and colleges may be compared. Activity reports for members of the academic staff paid from the instruction and departmental research budget can be used to estimate the proportions of academic staff salaries devoted to departmental research. The estimates obtained in this manner must be carefully considered because of the interdependent nature of all the activities of the academic staff. Similar ways should be found to associate other expenditures with research activities.

Expenditures for sponsored research can be included in research totals. Separate financial data on externally sponsored activities can be obtained readily because of the requirements of the sponsoring agencies. One difficulty that may arise is an absence of distinction between data on sponsored research and data on other sponsored activities. Some colleges and universities report all expenditures for sponsored activities as sponsored research when, in fact, some of the sponsored projects are instructional and others are of a public-service nature. These distinctions need to be made. Another problem arises when the accounts used for sponsored research are not associated with schools and colleges or departments. If the point of view is that sponsored research merely provides funding to individual faculty members, this situation may exist. The principles of accountability and financial control require that chairmen and deans share responsibility for sponsored activities and that the basic financial data reflect this responsibility. In other words, good management requires that it be possible for expenditures for sponsored research to be summarized by school and college.

All of this discussion is based upon the assumption that budget and accounting records reflect actual activities. Faculty members with split responsibilities must have split appointments. If a faculty member who is engaged in sponsored research or research for a separately organized research unit also teaches courses, the financial records need to show it. The teaching loads of a departmental faculty may be significantly lowered (and the research effort overstated) when full-time research personnel teach undergraduate courses, lead graduate seminars, and direct dissertations. Budgeting, accounting, and auditing cannot be properly done unless such transfers of resources are a matter of record. With the availability of computers, college and university officers cannot reasonably argue that university operations are too complicated to relate financial resources to the activities supported and to consequent products.

Facilities. The physical facilities of a college or university constitute a central and expensive resource. The decision to commit funds for a new building is certainly a major one. This decision must be based upon basic data on existing facilities and their utilization and upon the uses projected for the new building. Basic data on existing space are required for its assignment, operation, and maintenance; for evaluation of the space with regard to its use, and for decision-making involving renovation or the planning of new construction as alternatives.

The Space Analysis Manuals Project of WICHE has published a field-review edition of a set of six space-analysis manuals (Dahnke, Jones, Mason, and Romey, 1970). The existence of these most comprehensive manuals and of other publications (Bareither and Shillinger, 1968; Osso and Roberts, 1968) makes it unnecessary to undertake an extensive discussion of facilities data and its uses here. Almost certainly the WICHE manuals will become authoritative statements.

The most fundamental type of basic data on facilities is included in the inventory of existing facilities. This inventory contains information on buildings and rooms. The information on each room includes the type of room, the organizational unit to which it is assigned, the institutional function for which it is used, and the square feet of space and number of stations it contains (Osso and Roberts, 1968). The inventory data may be summarized to reveal the physical facility resources of the institution on a number of dimensions.

A second type of basic data on facilities describes utilization. Studies of the utilization of classrooms and related instructional space are common, and assumptions concerning the proper relationships among students, staff, and other characteristics of programs can be applied to use of other types of space (Dahnke, Jones, Mason, and Romey, 1970). For analysis of classroom utilization, data from the facilities inventory (type of room, square feet, and number of stations) are combined with data from the schedule of classes and data on the numbers of students registered in the classes. The fact that the data are from several sources again points up the importance of consistency among the several types of basic data. If the facilities inventory has been developed from architect's blueprints, for example, it is unlikely that the room numbers in the inventory correspond with the numbers painted on the doors and used in the schedule of classes.

Data on facilities inventory and on space utilization are used in combination with program plans and associated planning standards for long-range facility planning and for specific planning in respect to new buildings. The availability of funds is a very real constraint when planning the construction of a specific building. The single most important aspect of facility planning must be the institution program plans. The basic quantitative data are essential, but secondary. Renovation of existing buildings must be weighed against new construction. Space vacated when a new building is completed must be considered. Since many segments of the institution are affected by building changes, interrelated effects should be considered in program plans.

For too long, the term *planning* as applied to colleges and universities has meant campus or facilities planning. Space cannot be efficiently planned or effectively used in the absence of academic plans. In some instances a state legislature (or donor) provided funds for a specific building, the funds were accepted, the building was built, and only then was consideration given to the uses of the building and to the impacts of these uses on other institutional facilities. Perhaps—but only perhaps—in the absence of an academic plan for the institution this was the wisest way to proceed.

The necessity for academic planning to precede or at least to accompany facilities planning is illustrated by an actual experience. In the absence of a central review mechanism, an engineering building was built at a major state university and the teaching laboratories were designed to accommodate twelve students each. The upper limit thus imposed on laboratory section sizes affected the operating budget needs of the engineering program. It is not necessary to argue about the desirability of small sections, but the decision should not have been left to the architect and his advisors from the school of engineering. Shortly after this building was completed, the university created a central facility-planning mechanism giving responsibility for the academic program to a chief academic officer who inherited the implications of new construction for his academic operating budget.

Basic Data Information System

In one form or another and in one place or another, considerable basic data exist in any college or university. More often than not, however, data are not handy when needed and not completely understood when handy. How many times has an administrator or a faculty committee sought an item or tabulation of basic data only to find that a special and time-consuming effort was required to retrieve it? How many times has the data provided been so qualified that its use has been discouraged? And how many times has it not been exactly what was needed?

In response to these considerations, institutional research offices at a number of colleges and universities have developed institutional fact books, which are intended to be and in fact become authoritative compilations of frequently referenced basic data. Some of these fact books are annual publications of current data on a limited number of items. Others are loose-leaf notebooks containing data for each of several years on numerous items tabulated separately for each academic department with appropriate totals. The form adopted depends upon the anticipated distribution and use of the information included, the availability of the basic data to be included, and the resources available for undertaking what can be an effort of appreciable magnitude.

Appendix B presents the table of contents for a fact book developed at one university for distribution to school or college deans and to selected central administrative officers. Most of the data in the tables of this loose-leaf presentation are ten-year trends. The book is revised annually by deleting the data for the earliest year and adding the data for the most recent. New tables have been added in successive editions in response to requests from the users of the data. An appreciable effort was required to assemble the initial fact book volume, and the efforts required for the annual revisions are not trivial. The fact that these efforts continue is evidence of the acceptance and usefulness of the compilation as an authoritative source for this university.

In addition to the value of having a comprehensive and authentic set of basic institutional data available in fact-book form, the process of assembling the data produces side benefits. First, this process enables at least one person in the institution to become thoroughly familiar with the several sources for or repositories of basic data that exist in diverse locations within the institution. He discovers the forms in which the various types of data are kept, the manners in which they are produced, and the definitions which lie behind each item. This type of expertise is invaluable to the college or university as basic data is called upon for various purposes. A second side benefit of the process is that inconsistencies in existing basic data are discovered. This knowledge can lead to efforts to increase consistency. Finally, gaps in the array of basic data are discovered, and attention is devoted to finding ways of filling them.

The first fact book for a college or university will very likely be prepared by hand. There may be merit in storing the contents in computer records, particularly if data for past years are included and the compilation is updated annually by the addition of current data. Computer storage permits the data to be retrieved and reported in variable formats. Eventually it may be possible to devise ways of updating fact-book computer records from other computer records which result as by-products of program, personnel, registration, and financial transactions. When this happens, a basic data information system exists.

The existence of the computer makes possible, at least conceptually, the collection and storage of complete sets of basic institutional data in forms which allow rapid access and facilitate institutional analyses calling for consistent data of several different types. The terms *comprehensive data bank* and *integrated management information system* suggest generation of data as an automatic by-product of routine program, student, staff, financial, and facility transactions. Automatic updating of records may be viewed as the goal of efforts to refine basic data within a college or university.

Realism requires recognition that this goal will never be fully attained. The task of developing and maintaining a truly comprehensive and integrated basic data system is too large, and the degree to which it would ever be utilized is unlikely to justify the resources that would be required for it. It is, however, a worthy goal and one to be approached over time by means of carefully established priorities based upon intended and potential uses of the data in the system. Experience and logic both reveal that the undifferentiated goal of developing an integrated management information system leads to frustration and wasted effort more often than to results. A useful approach is to identify a unified set of purposes for the information system and to base the development of the system on it. If the selected purpose is a significant one, the system that develops can be expected to serve other purposes as well.

The need to complete questionnaires, specifically the comprehensive HEGIS package of the Office of Education, has led some colleges and universities to refine their collections of basic data, thus contributing to the development of information systems. The source of their activities may be regretted, but the result has not been altogether unfortunate.

An appropriate purpose for development of an information system is facilitation of decision-making in regard to resource allocation. If resource allocation is viewed as a component of the long-range planning process, additional meaning is given this purpose. When the approach to long-range planning and resource allocation appropriate to the institution has been identified, the system can be designed to provide data needed to serve this approach and the problems of decision-making that follow from it. In accord with the established approach to decision-making, data elements and derived data can be defined, and methods for collecting, storing, processing, and reporting the data can be devised. Considerations of basic data cannot be allowed to determine the approach to resource allocation, but the process of developing an information system with resource allocation as the focus can contribute to the specification of a resource allocation rationale and to the points in it where data can appropriately be brought to bear.

It has been repeatedly stressed that basic data should be generated from the regular routines of operating the institution. Interaction between operating procedures and data collection makes this relationship more than a one-way street. The process of refining the basic data can lead to improvements in operating processes. For example, a key element of basic data on physical facilities is the number of student stations in each classroom. When this item of data is systematically recorded, it can be used in classroom scheduling. Similarly, the collection of basic data on courses and sections approved for offering and on sections actually taught may require a computer record for each course that has been approved. This record can be posted each time courses are offered. Reports from it can provide information useful to the deliberations of the college or university curriculum committee. Using the course record, the committee can keep course offerings current with demand and can institute refinements in the scheduling process.

The concept of an analytical information system is appealing. A system in which accurate, consistent, and complete sets of basic data are produced automatically, stored conveniently, interrelated readily, and available as needed is certainly to be sought by any college or university. It cannot be arrived at easily even on a limited basis because so many components of the college or university are involved and because it depends so heavily on day-to-day operating procedures which cannot be interrupted. Because of their responsibility and concern for providing and using basic data, those responsible for institutional research must be centrally involved in the effort to achieve a comprehensive system.

Bibliography

American Council on Education. *College and University Business Administration*. (Rev. Ed.) Washington, D.C., 1968.

BAREITHER, H. D., AND SHILLINGER, J. L. *University Space Planning*. Urbana, Ill.: University of Illinois Press, 1968.

CAVANAUGH, A. D. *A Preliminary Evaluation of Cost Studies in Higher Education*. Berkeley: Office of Institutional Research, University of California, 1969.

DAHNKE, H. L., JONES, D. P., MASON, T. R. AND ROMEY, L. C. *Higher Education Facilities Planning Manuals*, preliminary field review edition. Boulder: Planning and Management Systems Division, Western Interstate Commission on Higher Education, 1970.

FARMER, J. *Why Planning, Programming, Budgeting Systems for Higher*

Education? Boulder: Western Interstate Commission on Higher Education, 1970.

HENLE, R. J. *Systems for Measuring and Reporting the Resources and Activities of Colleges and Universities.* Washington, D.C.: National Science Foundation, 1967.

LAWRENCE, B. *Compatible Management Information Systems,* technical report 1. Boulder: Management Information Systems Program, Western Interstate Commission on Higher Education, 1969.

MC GRATH, E. J. *Memo to a College Faculty.* New York: Teachers College, Columbia University, 1961.

MILLER, J. L. *State Budgeting for Higher Education: The Use of Formulas and Cost Analysis.* Ann Arbor: Institute of Public Administration, The University of Michigan, 1964.

National Center for Educational Statistics. *Definitions of Student Personnel Terms in Higher Education.* Washington, D.C.: Government Printing Office, 1968.

The National Task Force. *The Continuing Education Unit: A Uniform Unit of Measurement for Non-Credit Continuing Education Programs.* Raleigh, N.C.: North Carolina Department of Administration, n.d.

OSSO, N. A., AND ROBERTS, C. T. *Higher Education Facilities Classification and Inventory Procedures Manual.* Washington, D.C.: National Center for Educational Statistics, Office of Education, U.S. Department of Health, Education, and Welfare, 1968.

PETERSEN, D. F. "An Analysis of Grading Practices." In G. N. DREWRY (Ed.), *The Instructional Process and Institutional Research.* N.p.: Association for Institutional Research, 1967.

RUML, B., AND MARSISON, D. H. *Memo to a College Trustee.* New York: McGraw-Hill, 1959.

STECKLEIN, J. E. *How to Measure Faculty Work Load.* Washington, D.C.: American Council on Education, 1961.

Systems Development Corporation, *Extension Management Information System (EMIS); Data Definition.* Falls Church, Va., 1968.

WARD, R. C. *Mr. President . . . The Decision Is Yours . . . Deal Out the Dough.* Lexington, Ky.: College of Education, University of Kentucky, 1969.

WILLIAMS, H. *Planning for Effective Resource Allocation in Universities.* Washington, D.C.: American Council on Education, 1966.

CHAPTER 5

Studying Environment

F. Craig Johnson

❧❧❧❧❧❧❧❧

In simplest terms, school is a place where people learn. This chapter deals with studies of place and people. In the minds of Americans, the campus green has a romance and nostalgia associated with burning leaves and Saturday's heroes. Sentiment fancies the campus as a cloister free from political realities of everyday life. Broken windows, bayonets, and burning buildings crack this image of tranquility, jar taxpayers, and threaten the credibility of higher education.

Journalists and television commentators relate campus unrest to national and international trends. The political campaign of 1970 required office seekers at all levels to make statements of their positions on campus unrest. These statements were taken to reflect a candidate's general position on a permissive society, on drug abuse, and on law and order. Within a decade national attention

100

had shifted from Sproul Hall Plaza to a grassy knoll at Kent State, where, in the aftermath of tragedy, students, faculty, and administrators strained to keep down political activities. Fearing the university would be permanently closed, the president and students were wearing buttons to show their sincere wish to see the university remain open. At many institutions, however, the campus remains a platform for political comment.

The shift from an educational environment to a political one causes growing concern (Smith, 1969). Kruytbosch and Messinger (1970, pp. 10–11) observe:

The institutional implications of a norm of permissiveness toward partisan politics on the campus are clearer; the obstacles to establishment and defense of such a norm are clearer too. The power and depth of societal forces over which the university has little immediate control manifest themselves in a variety of ways—from opinion poll results condemning student "violence" and professional and administrative "timidity" to the introduction of countless measures in local, state, and federal legislatures aimed at "controlling campus disorder."

Purposes and Objectives

Public concern has focused attention on studies of university environment and on the relationship of this environment to institutional purposes. Self-study of its environment requires an institution to inventory its purposes. Sources of broad statements of purpose include local, state, and federal legislatures, state boards, trustees, and executive officers. Specific program objectives are stated by college deans, department chairmen, and faculty.

Brumbaugh (1960) pointed out the need to relate policy statements to efficient use of instructional space, curriculum organization and development, and determination of teaching load. Administrators need to know how policy statements shape the educational environment and when to recommend revisions in policy suggested by modifications in educational process. It is an operational necessity for administrators to understand institutional purposes as a part of the total environment. Different policy-setting agents play different roles in determining purposes of a specific institution. A look at some of these roles may be helpful in understanding how both external and internal agencies shape the university environment.

Although many new institutions of higher education have been established within recent years, none has started with complete freedom to determine its own goals or purposes. State constitutions; legislation; court decisions; administrative rules, regulations, and decisions; and opinions from the attorney general's office have contributed to a legal environment for both public and private higher education. Public institutions conform to the legislative plenary authority over education, and private schools must file incorporation papers with state authorities. State policies on education are indirectly referred to in statements of purpose prepared by individual institutions and are directly relevant when public institutions prepare justifications for funds at the request of state legislatures. The actions of courts and regulatory agencies, such as the Civil Service Commission and the Civil Rights Commission, have made deep inroads into the human element of the institutional environment. Inevitably these changes in the environment require a modification of statements of purpose and practices of institutions (Johnson, 1969). The following examples show how legal policy can affect the human elements of the environment.

Executive Order #11246 on Equal Employment Opportunities requires a university to hire all personnel including faculty according to a plan filed with and accepted by the Department of Health, Education, and Welfare. The racial and sexual characteristics of the human element of the university environment have in this case been established by an external political agency. In several states, laws have been proposed to require faculty to be in their classrooms for a specific number of hours per week. Review of admissions policies by the courts has resulted in preventing public universities from denying admission or from segregating classrooms, libraries, or dining facilities solely because of race. Thus, the human element—faculty, students, and service personnel—must qualify by meeting standards developed by external policy agents.

Institutional research offices often must coordinate planning efforts with efforts of statewide governing boards. The state coordinating boards play their major role in the budget process and use their discretion in the allocation of capital outlay expenditures.

State boards try to translate purposes and goals of institutions into a physical environment conducive to the accomplishment of those goals. Coordinating boards must consider the environmental needs of several institutions. Within a state system, some campuses may be multipurpose and have graduate as well as undergraduate programs. Others may have upper-division and graduate programs only. Still others may serve experimental purposes such as the development of new curricular and housing approaches. Others may be located in cities or other special environments which become important in a total plan of the environment. In planning facilities, says Schwehr (1962), there is "a problem of envisioning, designing, and perfecting an environment for the students and faculty which stimulates and perpetuates the learning process."

When Schwehr (1966) addressed members of the Association for Institutional Research, he pointed out that, in dealing with state control boards, "most of the persons concerned are busy at a different full-time position or are legislators concerned with many facets of the state operations. For these people the explanation of methodology and project needs must be of an 'overview' nature." Overview may take the form of a two-page summary on enrollment projections, space considerations and deficiencies, and availability and comparison of funds. Using Wisconsin as an example, Schwehr (1966, p. 88) illustrates the different roles played by several policy makers as they plan a campus environment: "The board of regents is concerned with meeting the needs of each individual institution. The state coordinating committee for higher education is concerned with the broad picture of education for the state as a whole. The building commission is concerned with all state agencies and is responsible for recommending to the legislature a statewide building program with appropriate funds."

These external agents of university policy play a critical role in determining the major resources of a university. Capital outlay and salary account for most appropriated funds for higher education. Institutional research provides assistance in inventory of resources and in reporting to external agencies the utilization of the environment that can be provided by them.

It is not easy to classify boards of trustees, regents, or governors as internal or external agents. Some serve a single campus which has a great deal of autonomy, while others serve many campuses for a state system. Whatever their constituency, they hold the corporate power of the institution. They appoint a president who serves at their pleasure without benefit of tenure or civil service law. The extent of influence of trustees on environment depends more or less on how active a role they play in the decision-making process. Hartnett (1970) reports on responses of 4200 trustees to an eight-page questionnaire. He concludes that "in general, trustees prefer a 'top down' form of institutional government, often preferring to exclude members of the faculty even from those discussions having to do with academic program of the institution. Yet the trustees themselves shy away from direct decision-making except when it comes to selection of the president and to matters of financing, the physical plant, and external affairs" (p. 67).

Trustees are most active in broad policy concerns of the environment and not with program details involving the educational process. However, like state control boards, they play an important role in the environment to the degree that they concern themselves with buildings and human resources.

Statements of institutional purpose made by law, board actions, or administration speak to university goals or purposes. Program objectives stated by chief academic officers, deans, chairmen, and faculty are most likely to state educational or subject matter objectives. Thus, a constitutional statement that institutions of higher learning shall "preserve and teach the cultural heritage of the state" becomes the basis for a program objective for "the development of methods for analyzing human behavior in the classroom and laboratory." The public is bewildered, occasionally, to learn that the state university is conducting research on dreams, sex, and medieval pond culture. It is hard for people to relate such activities to a goal such as preserving the cultural heritage of the state.

University administrators have been exploring program budgeting and other management techniques which require them to translate statements of purpose into programs. Six-year growth projections and total cost implications are calculated. One benefit of this process is that it forces an examination of department programs, college purposes, and institutional goals. Even complex universities find surprisingly little overlap in specific program purposes unless an effort has been made to combine programs. Typically they find a vast array of purposes not particularly related to department or college goals and little that adds up to university goals. To accommodate this array, some bland cover statement is developed which excludes no program and which charts no clear direction for the university as a whole. Institutional research can design studies which look at faculty, student, and administrative perceptions of goals and priorities. A study by Gross and Grambsch (1968) is an example.

The solution to the problem of diverse program objectives lies not in clearer writing of objectives, for writers of these statements know how to write clearly. The task is to reconcile the program of the college with the goals and objectives of the university. Meeting this obligation is a great concern for administrators, who are often caught in daily crises and can give too little attention to the independent directions which programs take when left untended. Institutional research can help administrators by studying the consistency between academic decisions and the degree to which these are perceived as relating to instructional goals and priorities.

Resources allocated for university building and personnel are an environmental component shaped by forces inside and pressures outside the institution. Because registrars tabulate data on environmental elements such as room units and sizes, special labs and other unique instructional space, student enrollment, class section size, faculty, and credits taught, they can describe the environment in detail. The office of institutional research plays one of its most valuable analytical roles when it relates environmental data to educational processes and evaluates the consistency shown with educational objectives, instructional goals, and purposes.

Making Objectives Operational

In studying the university environment, institutional research helps others to make objectives operational. The researcher uses analytical tools to show significant effects, clarify relationships, and expose consequences. Class size may be related to teaching methods which in turn may produce significant learning responses. Using this information the researcher can describe consequences of operations for both the university environment and the educational process.

Those who ask institutional researchers to design these evaluations should understand the basic nature of the questions which instructional researchers ask and the nature of the questions asked of them. In general terms administrators want to know what various programs are doing, which programs are exceptional, what special problems exist, and what cost implications are involved in changing an environment or process. The researcher has few absolute standards to apply. He is forced by the nonmeasurable nature of the university value system to ask questions which provide only relative answers. When evaluating statements of purpose and objectives, for example, he may ask whether operational definitions used at various administrative levels are appropriate to those levels. It would be as inappropriate for state legislatures to prepare performance objectives for teaching chemistry as it would be for chemistry teachers to claim they were "preserving the cultural heritage of the state" when they asked students to prepare sulfuric acid.

An example of some appropriate operational statements may be useful. A board of trustees might state, as an institutional goal, student assumption of responsibility for their own learning. The board would probably not develop guidelines and would leave the interpretation and implementation to the president. Operationally, the president would have the power to approve incremental dollars only for new programs designed to increase student responsibility for their own learning. Vice-presidents and deans, operating through the college and committee structure, would review programs to see how more responsibility for learning could be placed on the individual student. Departments might recruit new faculty members on the basis of experience with individualized instruction and might establish guidelines for credit by examination. And, finally, faculty members might write very specific course objectives indicating to students what they were expected to achieve on their own and what would be achieved by means of lecture, laboratory, or class recitation. Careful analysis would need to be made to determine whether the objectives were internally consistent and whether they were consistent with the broad policy statement of the board of trustees.

Criteria need to be established if objectives are to be evaluated. In developing criteria, the following guidelines may be helpful. First, objectives should facilitate communications between and within levels. As noted above, objectives must be stated at appropriate levels of operational specificity. It is also important when stating objectives to pay particular attention to the verbs used. Input objectives involve verbs such as *provide, establish,* and *create.* Process objectives involve verbs such as *generate, identify,* and *demonstrate.* Output objectives generally describe performances in gerund forms such as *yielding, resulting,* or *producing.* Clearer communication of objectives results if special care is taken in using appropriate verbs.

Second, objectives should consider long-range and short-term feasibility. *Time frame* and *planning horizon* are terms used by the systems analyst to estimate the feasibility of certain operations. Those involved should be able to accomplish program or personal objectives in a reasonable length of time. A chairman of a history department, for example, may find it difficult to evaluate departmental contributions of faculty members working on books if their endeavors are expected to continue for two and a half careers.

Third, objectives should be adaptable. Systems designers frequently develop meta-systems to keep original systems responsive to changing needs. Change of input objectives causes change in process objectives and vice versa. An input objective providing language laboratories in all classroom buildings may need to be modified, for example, if it is shown that students study more effectively in their dormitories. (Self-study should facilitate updating of objectives as well as examining them.)

Fourth, objectives should reflect characteristics of the environment including curriculum (such as liberal-arts, professional, and graduate), type of control (such as private, public, and church-related), race (such as predominantly Negro or nonracial), sex (coeducational or single sex), and region served (such as community, state, or city). Specific objectives involving student input to the environment should reflect relevant environmental phenomena such as size of the student body, a policy relating to transfer students, loan policies, graduate and undergraduate distinctions, housing services, and employment placement services. Objectives relating to faculty and staff should include applicable indications of staff recruitment, salary levels, leave policies, teaching loads, teaching reward systems, and university governance. Objectives on curriculum should indicate new programs, off-campus instruction, basic education, independent learning, graduate-assistant training, and special programs such as ROTC. Research objectives should include characteristics such as balance between pure and applied research, freedom of faculty to investigate and inquire, publications of faculty research, and criteria for evaluating research. Service objectives should indicate publication of books and literary magazines; procedures established for provision of consultation, speakers, exhibits, and group activities for students; procedures for provision of service to community and state; and policies specifically relating to continuing education and extension division. Objectives which delineate the internal management processes of the institution should take into account characteristics of staff, auxiliary enterprises, physical facilities, and finance. Inventories of these characteristics can be found in the basic data used by institutional research.

Fifth, objectives should consider behavioral, social, and mechanical interaction. Some objectives are stated with performance or behavioral verbs. An example is: Students who graduate should to be able to *discuss* historical roots of current social issues. Other objectives, input or process, may require social or mechanical terms: Faculty and students *interact* and *establish* informal relationships in a forum that allows for orderly transmission of the culture. Buildings are *built* to create an atmosphere conducive to learning. Interaction of behavioral objectives with social and mechanical objectives produces the ultimate changes in behavior that shape and reshape the environment.

Sixth, objectives must have implications for policy. However objectives are stated, they must have implications for the policy of the institution and its purposes. Institutional researchers can conduct systematic studies of policy implications of specific objectives once a framework of objectives and a means of evaluating performance on the objectives have been established. Conflicts between objectives and policy may prohibit people from meeting institutional goals. This problem arises when, for example, institutions undertake program budgeting and are still restricted by existing external policy relating to personnel classification and to object codes which virtually prohibits shifting people or auditing expenditures related to programs. Policies for tenure and promotion may seriously limit faculty incentive to engage in curriculum reform or instructional improvement. Inconsistencies between objectives, policies, and performance are basic concerns of institutional research and systematic self-study.

Physical Environment

Fuller (1966) states that the planning sequence for construction of new buildings is typically the following: "Once you know what funds you have, then you know the limitations of size you have in building the facility. When you know the size of the facility you know how many faculty you can put into it. Once you know the number of faculty the building can accommodate, you know how much room is left for students, and, finally, you hope you can adjust your curriculum to this building which you have now planned."

Fuller goes on to point out that inputs of curriculum, students, faculty, and facilities should be considered as a part of planning. Studies need to be made of teaching models, class size, class level, use of technology, faculty work loads, space needs of faculty, interrelationships of instructional and research space, and scheduling and cost implications for alternative learning modes. Institutional research should be able to relate the building, students, faculty, and facilities to learning objectives.

The architecture itself often sets the tone of the environment. The Gothic towers of the University of Washington with its campus axis oriented toward Mt. Rainier present a sharp contrast to the low moderns of Florida Presbyterian opening to the Gulf of Mexico. Enchanting as these environments may be, they provide little insight into the academic climate or program of the institution. Architectural design reflects administrative rather than academic concerns. As was noted in the Hartnett study, trustees are interested in buildings, grounds, and finances more than in the academic program. Careful study is needed on how the academic requirements can be reflected in architectural designs. Faculty members are often consulted as to how much space they need. Typically their requests total more than is available, and compromises made at a higher level result in assignment of space that does not always conform to academic needs. All concerned with the building process need a clear set of program objectives and alternate plans for implementing objectives according to institutional priorities. While institutional research and self-study can help to clarify the objectives and provide models for estimating cost of alternatives, frequently political concerns prevail.

Regardless of who makes decisions, planning an academic environment today requires careful cost effectiveness analysis. In the years ahead, it is fairly certain that a quality-of-life component will have to be added to this analysis. A principle discovered in industry can be applied to the design of higher education environments. If an oil line breaks, a petroleum company can be sued for destruction of environment, and the probability of this occurrence must be part of the cost effectiveness equation. Assumption of possible liability must also be realized in institutional planning. Clark (1968), in describing dormitories as cultural disasters, says, "One cannot understand those places, the standardized locations that tear life apart, without understanding the administrative definition of the situation that decides their form. And one cannot understand the unhappiness of students in these places if we continue to think of a dormitory as an educational residence. The modern dormitory is more like a bedroom suburb, with its radical separation of human activity, than it is a Left Bank. Students flee dormitories for a very simple reason; they cannot live in them." Many universities are now feeling the impact of empty dormitory space. Self-study should be devoted to quality-of-life considerations.

Clark goes on to relate convenience in university environment to coordination between academic and administrative policy. He suggests that selective inconveniences should be built into the environment and that all should feel involved as they bump into each other:

Given the American setting—particularly parental and student expectations—let us establish several dicta: (a) No campus is efficiently organized unless a student can have daily contact with the professor. (b) No educational structure is effective that does not put the administrator in those lounges, cafeterias, and hallways where his path will intersect those of the professor and the student. (c) No campus has an appropriate distribution of influence unless student and various nonfaculties feel themselves among the franchised. Only through personal encounters do we maintain on a campus the sentiments that support order among free individuals. Without the cultivation of informal situations that build the norms of caring, we turn it all over to the deans, the cops, and the courts.

Administrative convenience does not always facilitate academic functions. Since learning is a sporadic process, a match between individual student needs and an optimum environment is perhaps an unrealistic objective. Studies of the environment should periodically assess the possibility for these interactions to occur and identify specific practices which inhibit them.

Mason (1966) captures some problems associated with the form and function of the environment. "Proverb 1: Form should follow function. . . . Proverb 2: Educational planning should precede physical planning. . . . Proverb 3: Educational facilities should be flexible. . . . All these proverbial propositions add up to a recognition that the institutional system of facilities forms a matrix that contains and constrains (more or less loosely) the complex process of interaction and communication composing the functions of colleges and universities."

Part of the environment is the plant, and, consequently, the program must fit into it. As the program expands or changes, the plant needs to respond. As the plant expands, the program accustoms itself to it. Occasionally this interaction produces one more staircase going nowhere just for show.

Internal needs alone do not shape the environment. The Educational Facilities Laboratory (EFL) says that there has never been an effective physical plan to meet the realities of instructional life in the cities. "Nowhere," states an EFL report, "have we created the new organic urban campus, and, at the moment, nowhere has a college or university made a firm commitment to do so" (Rovetch, 1969).

External considerations can overpower internal objectives.

New York University serves as an example. The university maintains two separate campuses, one in the pastoral red brick colonial tradition and the other in the heart of Greenwich Village. The rural campus invokes nostalgia, and the city campus invokes crisis. Administrators at the university report that some of the best faculty members prefer to teach on the city campus, "where the action is." The university continually faces the problem of defining the goals and objectives of each campus to fit the learning desired and to accommodate the faculty.

When studies of the plant and program as they respond together to internal and external forces are conducted, a complex design is required. Simple proverbs and heuristics are not enough to meet the pluralistic institutional goals. A study designed by Astin (1955) looked at aspects of the administrative environment (rules and regulations), the classroom environment (instructors, students, and organized classes), the peer group environment (non-classroom activities with other students), the physical environment (location, climate, and living quarters), and the college image (school spirit, concern for individual student, and permissiveness). Astin developed correlations to show the interaction of these environments and suggested eight topics for institutional research and self-study. He stated that studies of the diversity of environment "should eventually yield information that will enable the administrator to maximize those educational outcomes which he thinks desirable, either by making appropriate alterations in the institutional environment or by changing his administrative procedures so that students are most likely to benefit from the particular environment selected" (pp. 130–131).

Typically, research on the environment has focused on student perceptions. Pace, Stern, Clark, Trow, and others have discussed the environment and the institutional "press" which is treated in the final section of this chapter. In 1970, the Educational Testing Service developed an Instructional Functioning Inventory for faculty use. This service has also developed scales to reflect the following environmental characteristics: intellectual-esthetic, extracurriculum, freedom, human diversity, concern for improvement of society, concern for undergraduate learning, democratic governance, meeting local needs, self-study and planning, concern for advancing knowledge, and concern for innovation and institutional esprit (Peterson and others, 1970). Results of applying these scales are meaningful as they relate to instructional goals and objectives. Characteristics of the institutional environment can be related to the responses of faculty members as well as to student responses.

A master plan is generally suggested as the best way to develop a building program for a campus. The more directly the plan incorporates academic purposes and objectives, the more useful it is in institutional research. However, realities of state appropriations, vagaries of federal programs, and the ability of medical science to extend the life of some of the most promising alumni make it difficult to maintain the priorities. The cold logic and quiet order of the situation room are far removed from the noise, smell, and panic of the battlefield. Emotions and training are tested. Human elements involved in planning new buildings test the strongest of men.

Problems, priorities, decisions, and pressures can be illustrated by the following example of a major institution that decided to build a new administration building. The architect designed a building five stories high with presidential offices on the fifth floor, vice-presidential offices on the fourth, middle management on the third, and student services on the second and first floors. The logic and order were unassailable. But the president decided he did not want to be all alone on the fifth floor and would rather be down on the fourth floor surrounded by people he worked with every day. This decision not only reduced the available space on the fourth floor but increased competition among other officers to be close to the president. All offices were scaled down in relation to the size of the president's office, which had already been much reduced by his own decision. Many staff assistants found themselves in strangely shaped long and narrow offices.

Functions carried on in administration buildings are fairly straightforward. When the plan is complicated by laboratories, theaters, cyclotrons, and data-processing equipment the problems mount. Planning and control of a physical environment are a widely shared responsibility. Research can suggest academic consequences of administrative decisions, but the final decisions are political, not quantitative. One finds it amazing that buildings get built at all.

Human Elements

The preceding sections on institutional purposes and objectives and physical environment have attempted to describe the arena in which institutional research and self-study are conducted. Studies of environment are commonly restricted to the physical limits of a single institution. If the research goes beyond a single institution and involves several institutions, then it is more legitimately research on higher education and not institutional research. The next sections deal with the human elements encountered by institutional research in conducting environmental studies. For each element, examples of general references and specific issues are presented.

Administrative Officers. Personnel records contain data on title, salary, source of funds, background, and experience of administrative officers. In the case of faculty members serving as administrators, contributions to a discipline and rank held in an academic department are also recorded. Studies of trustee characteristics have been conducted by Rauh (1959), by Hartnett, by Langan (1968), and by Boyer (1968). Studies of biographical characteristics ask how the sex, race, religion, age, and income of trustees compare to the distribution of these characteristics among the students of the institution. Summaries of trustee opinions on academic freedom, authority, and loyalty are described. Activities of the trustees are enumerated. The issue involved in these studies is the representativeness of the trustees for the environment which the institution is trying to establish. A legal issue is involved in lay control of church-related schools. There is continuing interest in the number of trustees who are black or female.

Presidents, vice-presidents, and deans must be especially sensitive to the environment. Duryea (1962) illustrates the need for this sensitivity when he points out that the environment helps the administrator do the following: limit the area in which administrators can exert effective leadership, determine in general the decisions which are made, determine the manner in which decisions are made, predict the consequences of decisions, and decide what types of faculty and administrators to attract. It would not be in the best interest of an institution to propose excellence in the undergraduate program and then to recruit faculty with background and experience in graduate instruction and basic research. Administrators are also selected to some extent on the basis of their own academic background and interest. If vice-presidents sit in executive session, some people feel they should represent all disciplines or professional schools in the institution. Studies are sometimes conducted to determine the representativeness of various administrative officers by background and training. Questions can also be asked about the equitability of appointments, salary, and tenure for administrative personnel. Assessment of the quality, experience, and background of administrative officers is of continuing concern to faculty and students. Many universities have adopted procedures which require faculty and student approval of any principal administrative officer. Universities tend to remain ambivalent as to whom they want in these roles—scholars, who will bring prestige to their offices, or managers, who will bring technical skills. More and more college presidents are selected from management ranks of industry and government, and they tend to recruit vice-presidents with managerial skills rather than with academic distinction.

Faculty. Basic data on faculty include department, rank, age, sex, salary, degrees, institution of degree, date of initial appointment, honors, publications, and other distinctions. Studies of these characteristics ask whether there is reasonable representation of race, sex, or institutions from which degrees were granted. As noted previously, the Office of Health, Education, and Welfare has begun to probe deeply into the question of representativeness by race and sex. The Women's Liberation Front and other pressure groups are asking whether women are equally represented in the university population, whether they are receiving the same salaries for the same job done, and whether promotion rates are comparable to those of men. The question of whether the faculty is being inbred is a continuous one. Studies are also conducted on the suitability and training of faculty in relation to the goals of an institution. Particularly in the applied sciences, faculty members who have been well trained find that within a short time their training is obsolete. Since, by this time, they are tenured, it is difficult to find suitable places for them.

Several studies of faculty as environmental input were reported to the Association of Institutional Research (Bagley, 1966, pp. 59–80). Religion of applicants for positions in denominational colleges, collection of faculty data for administrative purposes, faculty retention and attrition, the faculty market, primary assignments of faculty, and professional competence were considered.

Some consideration should be given to the quality of publications and consequent reputation of faculty as an element of the environment. In their book on small-group research, McGrath and Altman (1966, pp. 81–83) point out that faculty research in a local university environment has ties with an extrauniversity community having its own values and norms. Rank, salary, and reputation are measured against the pervasive production values, "publish or perish" and "money is power," which operate nationally. The problems of the reward system and how it operates are left for other chapters. At this point it is only noted that one measure of the environment (reputation of faculty) is a product of the larger environment of values held by faculty themselves. Faculty members, too, must conform to the environment they have created.

Staff and Service Personnel. Most staff and service personnel have their salaries, benefits, and promotion schedules standardized through a union, civil service, or some career service plan. The market for available talent is generally a local one and competition is with other state agencies, private industry, or local businesses. Personnel officers concern themselves with questions of the equity of salaries and benefits within the university as well as the responsibility for maintaining a salary schedule that will keep the institution as a whole competitive with local markets. Institutional research does not generally get involved with personnel. However, studies of efficient use of personnel and appropriate skills or services can be very worthy of institutional research. Often an efficient department secretary will be delegated responsibility and authority far beyond the job description for the position held. Secretarial and clerical help in departmental offices who assume tasks delegated to them during the registration and advising period have a marked influence on how students perceive the environment. The use of technicians to support research and instructional programs, particularly in the sciences, can be studied as part of the environment. If one looks at the same discipline (chemistry for example) across institutions, one finds a wide variety in the use of technicians. Institutions which do not allocate technical support carefully in respect to job descriptions and levels of responsibility may create an environment in which research cannot be carried on efficiently.

The promotion or advancement policy for service and staff personnel needs to be studied routinely to see whether practices follow policy. Morale problems result when staff members are re-classified to higher-paying positions while doing essentially the same work as others who must demonstrate additional skills before being advanced. This procedure adversely affects the environment.

Students. As with faculty studies, many descriptive reports on students can be prepared from data in master student files. Reports on the number of students by level, grade point average, and sex are generally prepared and distributed by the registrar. For the purpose of self-study, it is necessary to understand the student as part of the environment. The admissions policies and practices establish the quality of the student. Again representativeness in respect to race, sex, and attitude is important to the university environment. If the institution wishes to train only highly selected students, then one set of standards is applied. If the institution has as its charge providing an education to the working man's son, a broad range of ability can be tolerated. Broader ability ranges require educational programs that are broader, more expensive, and less efficient.

The environment can be studied to determine whether the university is providing a sufficient cultural and social life. This problem is acute for institutions located in a rural setting. A cultural environment needs to be created to retain quality faculty, and a social environment needs to be created as a safety valve for pent-up emotions of students.

A study of the peer environment is reported by Astin (1968), who says (p. 15):

From the point of view of the prospective college student, the stimuli provided by his peers may represent the most significant aspect of the college environment. The potential impact of the peer

*environment becomes apparent when one realizes the great variety
of roles the student and his classmates can play with respect to each
other: friend, competitor, advisor or confidant, sexual partner,
intellectual companion, and so on. Thus, insofar as sheer variety
and frequency of personal contact are concerned, no other source
of stimulation is likely to rival the student's peers.*

The frequency of these interactions, their patterns, and the needs for
the university to reinforce them are all subjects for studies for
institutional research and self-study.

Administrators, faculty, staff, and students form the human
element of the campus environment. Each contributes to change
and is changed by interacting. Secretaries who greet the public
and interact daily with faculty, administrators, and students need
to understand the purposes of the campus as well as the policies
that guide the people for whom they work. Faculty and students
interact in classrooms, of course, but facilitation of informal dialogue is becoming critical for mutual trust as an antidote to campus
unrest.

The orchestration of the environment is difficult because
freedom is a commonly held value. Sentiment is disdained. Ivy,
song, and ceremony have become objects of ridicule by some students and faculty. Discipline and profession traditionally com-
manded more faculty loyalty than did the institution, but the
institutions are under attack. When buildings are bombed or students are shot, faculty and students alike are accountable for their
failure to act for the institution. We in research must understand
the human element of our environment, or we have lost it all.

Responses to Institutional Press

The term *press* was developed by Murray in 1938. It is
concerned with the degree of need satisfaction provided to people
by their environment. Pace (1962) applied this concept to colleges
and universities: " 'Press' is found in the characteristics, pressures,
stresses, and conformity-demanding influences of the culture." Pace
and Stern have developed instruments to measure need (Activities
Inventory and College Characteristics Inventory) and the environment (College and University Environment Scale). These instru-

ments are administered to students in much the same way the Institutional Functioning Inventory is administered to faculty. Typically universities such as Princeton (Previn, 1966) and Minnesota (Brodie, 1967) administer the environment scale to entering freshmen to determine their perceptions of the campus environment. Norms have been published and individual institutions can see how they compare with other institutions having similar purposes. There have been some criticisms of the Pace and Stern inventories (Riesman, 1954), but these inventories are the best-known instruments associated with research on campus environment.

The work of Clark and Trow (1964) on the subcultures of the university is equally well known. The four subcultures defined are academic, collegiate, vocational, and nonconformist. The academic subculture is characterized by high identification with the college and great involvement with ideas. This subculture conforms to intellectual values. The collegiate subculture also identifies with the college but has little concern for intellectual values. The vocational subculture is not concerned with ideas and does not identify with the college. There may be a high degree of identification with a profession or with some individual faculty members who represent that profession. The nonconformist subculture is very much involved with ideas but does not conform to any group norms and has virtually no identification with the college itself.

This scheme for looking at the university environment is a useful one because it contrasts the environment of a given institution with the environment of other institutions having similar controls, purposes, or geographic locations. A state university, for example, may be surprised to find that well over half its students fall into the collegiate category until it recognizes that students in state colleges have a high tendency to associate themselves with the collegiate group (64 per cent in a study of five state colleges). The nonconformist group is always small, but it has become extremely active. Ethics become involved in studies designed to identify nonconformist students. These studies conflict with institutional values. The university is considered to be an environment in which people can explore their ideas freely without censorship. Attempts to identify students who have activist tendencies may lead to a kind of repression that is not consistent with institutional values.

Subcultures do not refer to types of students, but they refer to groups with which students may identify. An individual student may associate with one of these peer environments for a time and then move on to another group.

Special environments have been structured for students with similar interests. Stickler (1964) describes some of these plans. He states that the rationale for these special environments includes an attempt "to saturate a single area with all known learning tools"; that Stevens College developed "an innovational scheduling scheme to provide independent study"; that the University of Pacific and the University of California, Santa Cruz, devised a plan "to grow smaller as they grow larger"; and that the University of Michigan attempted "an on-the-job training program" at the Dearborn campus. These designs meet political, financial, and personal considerations.

Free universities are another response to the need for different environments. These institutions allow students to offer courses under faculty supervision. This response to student needs can be evaluated in terms of institutional goals, but it is difficult to do so where a clear definition of teaching has not been made. If all the faculty member does is sign the report card at the end of the term, leaving instruction to others, it is difficult to assign responsibility for that instruction.

The cluster program is another response to student needs. Students, upon entering the university, are grouped. Small groups given the same courses and housed together in dormitories generally build social and academic relationships. An extensive evaluation of this kind of program has been conducted at Florida State University.

Black studies programs are emerging in response to the needs of minority groups. These courses have the same kinds of problems as free universities do. Should they stand alone, or should they be integrated into the rest of the university curriculum? Who should offer the courses? What should their emphasis be? In some instances black studies programs have produced changes within the university environment. Roberts (1964) observes, "The fact that blacks have been able to produce changes in the institution to make it more responsive to the needs of blacks has a chain reaction. Many white students are beginning to protest the education they are receiving."

Change mechanisms can be built into the academic structure of the university program. The Educational Development Program at Michigan State University (Dietrich and Johnson, 1967) is an example. Self-study has been viewed as another mechanism (Ianni, 1965). Crookston and Bleassen (1962) suggest a procedure for change in the college setting through the student affairs office. Special counseling programs are established to help modify the environment at some institutions. The changes are slow. Tradition is highly valued as is appropriate for an institution charged with the preservation of a cultural heritage.

The university environment can be studied at many levels. School Environments Research presents some six hundred abstracts of studies linking human behavior to the environment. The Educational Facilities Laboratories, sponsor of the project, has supported many other projects and is one of the major sources of reports on the environment. At a less technical level Hodgkinson (1970) examined the basic environmental data of over 3600 colleges and universities from 1941 to 1970. Data on type of control, sexual and racial composition, geographic location, and size were collected from the *U. S. Office of Education Directory, Part III.* An additional questionnaire was sent to a sample of institutions to explore other environmental values. Openness, effectiveness, and modernity were characterizations of the environment expressed on the questionnaire. Forty-six tables and over 150 pages of text described the environment in what Clark Kerr calls "the most extensive study of change in higher education in the United States."

These and other references are good background for those involved in institutional research or self-study. Specific institutional studies ask whether the environment is consistent with the goals and purposes of the institution. The representativeness of trustees and of administrators needs to be reflected in the faculty and students. Student needs and environmental press can be investigated. Faculty values as part of the environment and value change in respect to environment should be investigated.

The lack of understanding of the environment can lead to empty dormitories, to inability to predict consequences of actions, to a breakdown of "belonging" that diminishes respect for responsibility and order, to reduced support from those who see the university as swaying from its purposes, and to other symptoms of campus unrest.

Bibliography

ASTIN, A. W. *The College Environment.* Washington, D.C.: American Council on Education, 1968.

BAGLEY, C. H. (Ed.) *Research on Academic Input.* Cortland, N.Y.: Association for Institutional Research, 1966.

BOYER, E. L. "A Fresh Look at the College Trustee." *Educational Record,* Summer 1968, 274–279.

BRODIE, R. J. "University Is a Many Faced Thing." *Personnel and Guidance Journal;* 1967, 45, 768–775.

BRUMBAUGH, A. J. *Research Designed to Improve Institutions of Higher Learning.* Washington, D.C.: American Council on Education, 1960.

CLARK, B. R. "The New University." *The American Behavioral Scientist,* 1968, *11*(5).

CLARK, B. R., AND TROW, M. "The Organizational Context." In T. M. NEWCOMB AND E. K. WILSON (Eds.), *College Peer Groups: Problems and Prospects for Research.* Chicago: Aldine, 1964.

CROOKSTON, B. B., AND BLEASSEN, W. W. "An Approach to Planned Change in a College Setting." *The Personnel and Guidance Journal,* 1962, *40,* 610–616.

DIETRICH, J. E., AND JOHNSON, F. C. "A Catalytic Agent for Innovation." *Educational Record,* Summer 1967, 206–213.

DURYEA, E. D. "The Theory and Practice of Administration." In G. P. BURNS (Ed.), *Administrators in Higher Education: Their Functions and Co-ordination.* New York: Harper and Row, 1962.

FULLER, W. E. "Implications for Institutional Research in the Planning of Inter-University Facilities." In C. H. BAGLEY (Ed.), *Research on Academic Input.* Cortland, N.Y.: Association for Institutional Research, 1966.

GROSS, E., AND GRAMBSCH, P. V. *University Goals and Academic Power.* Washington, D.C.: American Council on Education, 1968.

HARTNETT, R. T. "College and University Trustees: Their Backgrounds, Roles, and Educational Attitudes." In C. E. KRUYTBOSCH AND

s. l. MESSINGER (Eds.), *The State of the University*. Beverly Hills: Sage, 1970.

HODGKINSON, H. L. *Institutions in Transition: A Study of Change in Higher Education*. Berkeley: Carnegie Commission, 1970.

IANNI, F. A. J. "Appraisal of Changes in Education." *North Carolina Association Quarterly*, 1965, *40*, 180–187.

JOHNSON, G. M. *Education Law*. East Lansing, Mich.: Michigan State University Press, 1969.

KRUYTBOSCH, C. E., AND MESSINGER, S. L. *The State of the University*. Beverly Hills: Sage, 1970.

LANGAN, M. O. "Catholic College and University Trusteeship" Unpublished doctoral dissertation, State University of New York at Buffalo, 1968.

MC GRATH, J. E., AND ALTMAN, I. *Small Group Research*. New York: Holt, Rinehart, and Winston, 1966.

MASON, T. R. "An Inverse Relationship: The Uses of Facilities for Institutional Research." In C. H. BAGLEY (Ed.), *Research on Academic Input*. Cortland, N.Y.: Association for Institutional Research, 1966.

PACE, C. R. "Methods of Describing College Cultures." *Teachers College Record*, January 1962, 267–277.

PETERSON, R. E., AND OTHERS. *Institutional Functioning Inventory Preliminary Technical Manual*. Princeton, N.J.: Educational Testing Service, 1970.

PREVIN, L. A. "Reality and Non-Reality in Student Expectations of College." *Journal of Psychology*, 1966, *64*(1), 41–48.

RAUH, M. A. *College and University Trusteeship*. Yellow Springs, Ohio: Antioch Press, 1959.

RIESMAN, D. "Book Worms in the Social Soil." In *Individualism Reconsidered*. New York: Free Press, 1954.

ROBERTS, V. "Minority Interests in Value Change and Power Conflicts." In W. J. MINTON (Ed.), *Value Change and Power Conflict*. Boulder: Western Interstate Commission on Higher Education, 1964.

ROVETCH, W. "Architecture for the Urban Campus." in G. K. SMITH (Ed.), *Agony and Promise: Current Issues in Higher Education 1969*. San Francisco: Jossey-Bass, 1969.

SCHWEHR, F. E. "Planning Educational Facilities," *Journal of Experimental Education*, 1962, *31*, 140–144.

SCHWEHR, F. E. "Problems in Planning Educational Facilities on an

Interinstitutional Basis." In c. h. BAGLEY (Ed.), *Research on Academic Input*. Cortland, N.Y.: Association for Institutional Research, 1966.

SMITH, G. K. (Ed.), *Agony and Promise: Current Issues in Higher Education 1969*. San Francisco: Jossey-Bass, 1969. See especially MORGENTHAU, H. "Student-Faculty Participation in National Politics"; BLOLAND, H. "Politicization of Higher Education Organizations"; BIRENBAUM, W. "Lost Academic Souls"; OSTAR, A. "Higher Education and National Policy."

STICKLER, W. H. *Experimental Colleges*. Tallahassee: Florida State University, 1964.

CHAPTER 6

Studying Teaching and Learning

F. Craig Johnson

⁂⁂⁂⁂⁂⁂⁂⁂

In many circumstances where outcomes are difficult to assess, study and analysis can be applied to processes of education to determine whether they are consistent with desired outcomes and whether they satisfy agreed-upon criteria for effective operation. When desired changes in students are not apparent, the processes and operations of the institution should be investigated to determine whether they have been properly planned in relation to the changes desired.

This chapter deals with the processes and operations of the institution. Among these are classroom instruction and learning and the consequent duties, selection, rewards, and responsibilities of faculty; curriculum planning; student records and services; administration; and the decision-making process. Topics for institutional research or self-study are suggested, references to the literature of higher education are cited, and significant problems and issues are discussed. Because these processes and operations happen concurrently within an environment, outcomes may become part of other processes or operations, making it difficult to confine any discussion exclusively to one subject. The outputs of a curriculum revision committee or of an admissions office are inputs to the instructional process.

Classroom Instruction and Learning

Administrative and supporting offices of the institution provide numerous services which enable faculty to teach and students to learn. Courses and sections are scheduled, faculty are employed, instructional aids are purchased, computer facilities are maintained, students are placed at appropriate academic levels, and evaluations of instruction and student achievement are conducted. The registrar's office, office of the deans, media centers, computer services, and testing offices perform some facilitative services and assist the faculty in performing others. These offices maintain their own records and frequently conduct studies of their own operations and of research especially relevant to their records of procedures. A designated office of institutional research may serve as a consultant to research efforts, directed toward facilitating instruction, or research may be conducted quite independently of an office of research. Certainly the concept of institutional research covers studies concerned with instruction, but a specific office cannot and should not attempt to handle studies which can expeditiously be done by others. Studies directly conducted by institutional research should examine the effect one operation has on another, the combined impact of all operations on the educational process, and the compatibility of the process with institutional goals. For example, a carefully done cost study may be based on a model which requires determination and assignment of expenditures for such services to the appropriate instructional units.

The registrar's office schedules courses and sections in response to departmental requests for classrooms. Class hour, number of seats, and special facilities are included in the request. Computerized registration, including some form of preregistration, has automated much of the routine decision-making. Departments still have many problems arising out of preferences in hours for courses, numbers of students per section, and classrooms located conveniently near faculty offices. Students still have difficulties in registering for required courses on schedule and in making out a program which uses their time efficiently and recognizes their personal obligations. Personal requirements and preferences defy simplicity and efficiency of operation. A full account of the responsibilities of a registrar is stated by the American Association of Registrars and Admissions Officers (Stout, 1954).

Many colleges and universities have tried to apply open scheduling, especially in science courses. Postelthwaite, at Purdue University, used this technique for large laboratory sections of a beginning biology course. Many independent study applications have been made, and audio-tutorial carrels (Postelthwaite, n.d.) are becoming common on many campuses. Flexible scheduling of laboratory space requires the instructor to specify desired learning outcomes and then to adapt instructional patterns and available space to objectives. Students seem to enjoy the freedom to learn at their convenience and to spend as much time in the laboratory as they need to meet the stated course objectives. Supervision of these programs creates new administrative problems. Laboratory supervisors must be provided more hours of the day and more days per week. Cost effectiveness studies need to be made to determine the proper training program for supervisors, the best balance of responsibilities between faculty and supervisors as measured against laboratory objectives, and the appropriate qualifications and pay for supervisors.

An office of research can work with the registrar in conducting space utilization studies. At most universities, space standards are established and modified to fit special conditions. Special studies may include an analysis, by class level and class hour of credit hour production, an analysis of the effects of class hour on course grade point averages, or an analysis of the instructional facilities by department, hour, and type (general, special, and laboratory). Typically, these analyses reveal that the available space is used at about one-third of its capacity (based on a forty-hour week). Unwillingness of faculty members or full-time students to elect classes held early in the morning, after four o'clock, or on Saturdays results in tight scheduling of courses at premium hours.

Two problems concerning use of facilities need to be studied. The first is the current use of existing facilities, and the second is the projection of new facilities. Studies of existing facilities may include a comparative analysis of actual class size and recommended class size by type of instruction or an analysis of a computer scheduling model on classroom space utilization. Either study would ask whether utilization fits an established standard or model. Once present utilization has been established, the problem of space projection can be addressed. Utilization and building design studies need to use historically compiled data on recommended class size and actual class size at a specific institution to design adequate facilities for that institution. To estimate the number of assignable square feet needed for auditoriums, classrooms, teaching laboratories, research laboratories, offices, theaters, and athletic areas, projections are needed of enrollment, class hour volume, and faculty and staff needs. These projections should be made with consideration for the objectives and anticipated outcomes of the instructional, research, and service programs. In a basic space-planning volume by Bareither and Schillinger (1968), the authors claim that their numeric method of space assignment, by virtue of its pragmatic analytic process, is acceptable to faculty and departments. They claim that even faculty members with grossly exaggerated ideas on the amount of space they require find the systematic relationship of space to educational needs and objectives a satisfactory way to establish standards.

Faculty staffing of the instructional program involves study of quality in faculty and teaching assistants, proper section size, and equitable instructional load so that judgments can be made. The purposes and objectives of the instructional program must be considered in issues pertaining to financial resources. The larger the section size, the larger the faculty salary can be. One may fear that if sections get too large, the quality of instruction may suffer although there is no research support for relating class size and quality of learning. A further complication arises in that the quality of faculty is measured only in part by the quality of instruction.

Research output and other factors must also be weighed in making assessments. The faculty output is as difficult to measure as it is to control.

Instructional quality can be measured in several ways. The quality of the instructor can be evaluated by peer group judgments of publication quality, significance of research projects, and general scholarship. Faculty and teaching assistants can be rated by students on their course organization, classroom procedures, and concern for students. Finally, faculty-student interaction can be evaluated by relating student rating of faculty to faculty publications, student achievement, and student perceptions of faculty roles. (For a summary of several techniques, see Eble, 1970.)

The issue of section size "is not seen to be abating: 205 books, monographs, and articles [were] devoted to the problems from 1900 to 1932" (Bosely, 1963), and current interests in accountability and program budgeting will increase the interest. Studies of section size problems are uneven in quality, and some are of questionable validity. The position that small sections are better has not been documented, but most faculty members continue to prefer small classes and to accept larger ones only as forced to do so by scarce resources. It would make more sense economically and educationally if small section instruction were used only when essential to accomplish its objective and large sections were used where course objectives do not require faculty-student classroom interaction. In large section courses where presentation of information without discussion is the object, completely unabridged material may be recorded on audio or video tape or on the printed page and distributed to students. B. F. Skinner put it this way, "Any teacher who can be replaced by a machine should be."

Decreasing instructional loads of faculty and teaching assistants are becoming a major concern. If collective bargaining wins the day, teaching loads may decrease even further. Stecklein (1962) presents the following questions for study of faculty work load: "Who is to be included in the study? What kinds of questions are to be answered by the collection of faculty load data? How are the data from the report forms to be analyzed? How should each faculty member be asked to report his work load—in terms of hours per week, per quarter, or per semester, or in terms of his total working time spent on each of the kinds of activities? When is the best time to distribute the faculty load study forms? How long a form can a faculty member reasonably be expected to complete?" Faculty members resist the idea of being assigned specific duties and instructional tasks beyond six to twelve contact hours per week. In work load studies, faculty time reported averages fifty to sixty hours per week, with about 70 per cent of time consumed by counseling, paper grading, and preparation associated with instruction. Faculty reports, however, have been thoroughly discredited by repeated abuse.

Standard institutional studies include departmental analysis of faculty contact hours, credit hours, and percentage of time devoted to noninstructional duties; analysis of teaching load related to faculty rank and class hour; and analysis of faculty morale as a function of type and level of instruction. Such studies can serve as bases for estimates of the equitability of instructional loads among departments and colleges. Some insights can be gained into the roles departments play in establishing standard faculty teaching loads. A dean was asked the definition of a normal teaching load by one of his department chairmen. The dean replied, "If you tell me one faculty member meeting five students three times per week is a full-time load for prestigious scholars in your discipline, I'll accept your professional judgment. If, as time goes by, your faculty does not produce like prestigious scholars, then I want them back in the classroom." The paths to prestige and ignominy are unequivocally delineated, but, in state supported institutions, legislators do not accept a really low teaching load regardless of productivity in research.

Measures of work load must be considered in relation to both the outcomes of the work and the original objectives of the assignments. To accomplish this measurement, the procedures for assigning faculty work loads must be explicit and clearly relevant to the expected results. An auditor once asked a chairman, "I see you have a Professor Smith listed as teaching one three-credit course per year. What does he do the rest of the time?" The answer, "Just a second, I'll ask him," did not please the auditor at all. Nor would it please students or the public. It would not please all faculty members, many of whom carry extra loads because some of their colleagues pursue personal interests and hobbies and ignore their professional responsibilities.

Various faculty work load models can be built for allotting time for the several functions of instruction, research, service, and professional development. In a frequently used pattern the basic element is instruction. An initial assumption may be that a full load for faculty with no nonteaching duties is fifteen student contact hours per week. If two hours of preparation time are allowed for each contact hour, a forty-five hour week results. Loads are reduced for research and service, and for intensive professional development activities. Each reduction of teaching load should be based on some other assignment. Faculty and chairmen can discuss work load assignments periodically to see whether objectives are being met. Records and analyses of these discussions furnish auditability to a system for assigning faculty efforts.

An alternative procedure assigns certain weightings or units to each type of faculty activity and adds these figures to approximate an agreed-upon total. A three-credit course, for example, could be equated to twenty units. Five courses, assuming no other assignments at all, would be a full load, or one hundred units. An individual might, in a given quarter, have forty units of instruction, twenty units of committee or administrative responsibility, and forty units assigned for research.

Both faculty members and administrators are concerned with the use of faculty work load data. Doi (1960) sets some useful guidelines on who should examine the data and who should take action on them. He suggests that work load data should be collected on a continuing basis and that each dean and department head should be apprised of the uses to be made of the data. They should be informed of the kinds of questions they will be asked when they appear before the president's budget committee with requests for additional staff members or additional funds.

Teaching loads can be based on number of credits taught, number of contact hours, levels of instruction, number of students, and number of different preparations required. Specific procedures and policy issues are detailed in two publications of the American Council on Education (Bunnell, 1960; Stecklein, 1962). Institutional research can address itself to some policy issues. Should, for example, the same criteria be applied to all faculty, or are there factors which suggest that instructional objectives can be better met if each department establishes standards for its own discipline? The instructional portion of a faculty work load can be established in terms of relatively fixed units (such as credits, student credit hours, or contact hours). Other tasks associated with instruction are difficult to assess and weigh. Curriculum planning, grading, and advising can be time-consuming processes. In graduate departments, directed independent study, thesis direction, and oral and written examinations require extra hours. If a research program is associated with graduate instruction, time must be allowed for guiding research and publication. Some departments have heavy service commitments requiring faculty members to spend considerable time off campus consulting with industry and government representatives. All faculty spend time in committees and in performing administrative duties. All these noninstructional faculty duties and responsibilities need to be guided by university policy based on certain assumptions about a normal teaching load. For example, if a faculty member teaches off campus, the question of an overload salary should arise. If faculty members consult within the state university system or with other state agencies, the question of payment for consulting should arise. The question of additional employment outside the university should also be a matter of policy if such employment interferes with university responsibilities. For implementing policies on teaching load, a study of uniformity in interpretation and enforcements is appropriate.

Another major problem for study in public universities is the relationship of faculty to other state employees. There is no counterpart to a professor in state government, and civil service personnel policies do not have much direct application to faculty. State legislative committees and auditors question the unique role of faculty on occasion, but they seem satisfied if faculty activities are reconciled with university purposes. Self-studies and institutional research can be designed to facilitate this reconciliation and to help establish the credibility of faculty work load assignments.

The typical issues about wages, hours, and working conditions as negotiated by unions do not quite apply to faculty members. The salary distribution usually exhibits variations on a disciplinary basis, and comparisons are made from institution to institution. Financial security and fringe benefits can be evaluated as a part of an institutional study. Ingraham (1965) surveyed fringe benefits and concluded:

The most important compensation of the faculty member is the opportunity to do pleasant and useful work under conditions that make him effective and to live in a community of scholars without incurring economic hardships for either himself or his family. . . . Capital S for salary is a very good way to pay people. By means of salary, the greatest degree of freedom is given to the individual to use his compensation in the way he wishes. It maximizes liberty. By means of salary, the clearest decision as to merit or competitive status may be made; however, unless administrative decisions are wise, this may not be a blessing.

Yet salary alone seldom provides complete satisfaction. Tenure policy and practice, academic freedom, and promotion policies should be reviewed regularly by faculty committees. As part of this review, exit interviews can be held routinely with faculty who have terminated their contracts. New faculty can also be interviewed to see whether the commitments (actual, implied, or inferred) made to them at the time of employment are actually met. Criteria for establishing faculty performance need to be understood by both the individual faculty member and by those who are performing evaluation. Student evaluations of teaching effectiveness should be a regular part of the evaluation process. Attraction and retention of highly qualified faculty are concerns for all institutions. Faculty development can make a maximum contribution to higher education if faculty are hired to meet the specific goals and purposes of an institution. Studies can be designed to determine departmental practices in hiring faculty and to reveal criteria employed in faculty selection. Faculty can be interviewed to determine their understanding of their role in serving the goals and purposes of the institution.

Decisions concerning scope of course offerings, class size, and the like should remain the domain of the faculty, providing their decisions are consistent with available resources. It should be the responsibility of the faculty to keep course proliferation and unnecessary small classes to a minimum, but it is unlikely that the faculty will do so unless recurrent study and the application of specified criteria bring pressure to bear.

Data on faculty load should be made available to various faculty self-study groups engaged in examining curriculum problems and changes, but no prescribed standards applicable to all fields should be specified. Rather, faculty work load should be examined within the framework of the total curriculum, the objectives of that curriculum, and the strictures imposed by the discipline and by the students and faculty attracted to it.

Instructional aids and resources need to be studied as a part of classroom instruction. Reisman and Taft (1969) made a careful analysis of criteria for evaluating audiovisual systems. The first criterion established is effectiveness. To determine the degree to which one medium is more effective than others, media are ordered by rank and an ordinal scale is applied to several items of equipment. This procedure produces a relative measure of the effectiveness of certain media. Procedures are provided for establishing other criteria including versatility, ease of operation, accessibility, cost per unit per user per year, technological viability (possible obsolescence), physical durability, maintenance ability, multipurpose use, and attractiveness. Criteria are assigned weighting factors, and utility curves are developed. A scheme like this can be applied to testing the feasibility of technological solutions and to establishing the suitability of instructional objectives. However such analyses do not account for student attitudes toward instruction or for the amount students learn from different media. Most research finds no significant difference in learning, but it does indicate that some students find media of help with problems in organization of material, motivation, and review for examinations.

Computer science courses train students in the programing, operation, and use of complex scientific equipment. Yet, on many campuses offering these courses, computers serve research and administration while instructional uses receive low priorities. The problems of maximum utilization of campus computer services, the cost of leasing lines for off-campus services, and the optimum balance between research and instructional uses are important issues for institutional research. Carefully planned use of existing aids to instruction may be the only solution to increasing instructional cost and diminishing revenues.

An issue basic to the educational process is definition of a credit's worth of instruction. Traditionally, credits have been associated with a fixed amount of time (one hour per week) and the amount of learning is flexible (grades of $A, B, C, D, E,$ and F). Open scheduling patterns, credit by examination, individualized instruction, and other innovations allow, instead, fixed learning (completing course objectives) and flexible time. These new processes challenge traditional evaluation. Test item statistics which measure students against their peers give way to performance testing. Students are allowed to proceed at their own pace and may complete college in one-half or one-fourth the time normally required. Accelerated college programs, however, can create problems in assessing fees, in assigning dormitory space, and in providing services based on an assumption of fixed time. Institutional research must be aware of the implications that changes of instructional procedures have for the total perspective of the institution.

Admissions, too, poses problems. Standards are often established by faculty committees which try to attract students whose abilities are suited to the instructional objectives. Formally, admissions officers enforce these standards, but, informally, the freshman chemistry instructor, the housing officer, the football coach, and others determine who is eligible to attend the university. The admission process slips rapidly from a de jure system to a de facto one. Admissions practices need constant review.

Once a student is admitted, he may fall victim to rigid requirements and unfair placement processes. For example, students with good backgrounds in foreign languages are often placed in advanced sections rather than having the language requirements waived. Prospective students soon receive word not to excel in placement examinations, and beginning sections then become skewed with advanced students picking up an easy A grade. Minority students from deprived backgrounds with different cultural values are often admitted to an institution under an exception rule but are not provided with needed remedial work. Inflexible policies such as these fail to give the less well prepared student the attention he needs and prevent the better-prepared student from taking courses in fields that would challenge him.

Evaluation of instruction and of student achievement needs to be conducted within the context of institutional goals and the consequent evaluation of desired outcomes. The grading system and practices associated with it are continuing studies for institutional research. Evaluations are made of grading innovations such as the pass-fail option. Inequalities in grading may be observed and reported. Greater selectivity in students is often accompanied by more rigorous grading by the faculty. Occasionally a department, college, or nonacademic unit asks for assistance in studying academic performance of fraternity and sorority pledges. Special attention is often directed to graduate student performance and to graduate school evaluations of undergraduate student performance.

Changes in classroom instruction are interrelated with other processes in institutions. Shifts in scheduling have implications for the physical plant, admissions standards affect housing, and changes in course requirements can cause many alterations in a department and can greatly modify work loads in other departments. Sophisticated simulation models could be used to show the implications which change has for the whole institutional process. Even without such models, the financial implications of curriculum changes can be explored by institutional research. If this is done, sufficient time should be provided for study before the change comes up for approval.

Curriculum Planning

Governing boards generally delegate responsibility for the curriculum and its planning to the faculty. Faculty committees establish courses, credits, prerequisites, and course content. Policies are established to govern the number of credits required for a degree, the academic areas to be included, and the number of credits to be distributed among subject matter areas. Several policy issues are central to the work of curriculum committees: Should all students be required to obtain a general education by taking course work in the humanities, social sciences, natural sciences, and liberal arts? Should all graduate students be required to master a foreign language? Should students be required to demonstrate skills in writing and speaking? How much mathematics should be required of all students?

Problems arise when professional programs such as engineering are added to the curriculum. Requirements for certification or licensing create needs for additional courses, and unless the number of required general education courses is reduced, students must add as much as an extra year to the baccalaureate program. Small colleges and universities that do not offer professional programs are faced with other perplexing problems if they believe a general education is desirable. For example, a small liberal-arts college for women may feel the necessity for a chemistry department even though there are no chemistry majors. Chemistry is expensive to teach, and without majors it is difficult to attract qualified faculty. But without a chemistry department, the general education program appears to be incomplete.

Brown (1965) did a study that focused on another problem of curriculum expansion found at many smaller universities. He reported that universities with enrollments only one-fourth that of the largest institutions studied typically offered about one-half as many courses. If all courses offered were taught (seldom the case) and section sizes were equalized throughout the school, smaller classes would result in higher instructional costs. To a certain extent, this does occur. Yet, if smaller institutions reduce the number of courses they offer, students may look to other universities that can meet their special needs. The balance of the curriculum is an essential economic fact of life for an institution, and continuing research is needed to monitor the curriculum process and the implications of committee decisions.

Curriculum review should be a regular process. The number of courses in each discipline should be examined. Program objectives should be clearly stated and used to evaluate curricula. Course descriptions in the catalog should be reviewed to see whether they present accurate descriptions of course content. If a university changes its calendar (to quarter, trimester, or semester from some other system), the number of credits per course must be adjusted. Credit values for laboratory contact hours should be examined regularly to ensure equitability of effort across the institution. The costs of excessive laboratory hours in uses of instructional time and special facilities should be considered, too.

The procedures used by faculty to restudy curriculum and courses vary widely. Tradition usually guides the final action unless a systematic and logical analysis of content, instructional method, and objectives is specified at the outset. Use of the computer may be beneficial in elaborate studies such as an analysis of student course selection patterns. Very complex studies may involve a complete review by faculty committees of the total university curriculum. (Examples of such studies include University of California, 1966; Michigan State University, 1967.)

For studies on accrediting, regional associations provide procedural outlines. Offices of institutional research may be involved in collecting data and in analyzing these studies, but typically they are not involved in the decision-making process. In analyses, several aspects of the curriculum need to be considered. Judgment needs to be made on the representativeness of the content, the efficiency of sequences, the distinctiveness and distribution of courses, and the suitability of content to current problems. The judgments need to involve both educational and economic consequences of decisions about the curriculum. Unless care is taken, for example, an entire perspective, such as ecology or urban studies, may not be represented in the curriculum. Prerequisites that are not essential or that are unrelated to student abilities and competencies may result in inefficient sequences which do not challenge better students and which provide little opportunity for less well prepared students to advance. If the distribution requirements do not meet student needs or if courses are not related to current problems, free universities, black studies programs, and other curricula are established. These may nicely supplement the existing program, but they may also detract from it. In analyzing data for curriculum committee decisions, institutional research needs to point out these educational and economic implications and to relate the curricular actions to the goals and objectives of the university programs.

When new courses and curricula are being considered, several economic factors are important. The feasibility of new courses must be evaluated to determine whether properly qualified faculty members are available or new faculty members must be hired, whether adequate space is provided for or planned, whether equipment or special classrooms have been approved, and whether the new courses constitute needless duplication of existing ones. Too often, the cost of new courses is not made explicit at the time of new course approval. Subsequent budgets require additional funds to support hastily approved curricula. A system for review and approval of all cost implications for new courses should be designed. During periods of rapid expansion or when new colleges and universities are being established, review is often overlooked. Long-term commitments are made and much potential curriculum flexibility is lost.

A final problem in curriculum planning is the interrelationship of the departmental major and the general cultural offerings. Departments in large complex universities are allocated resources based on the number of students taught in their courses. Large courses serving nonmajors provide the revenue to hire faculty, but the added faculty may be used to teach added undergraduate and graduate major courses while graduate assistants staff the nonmajor courses. Carried to extremes, this procedure creates a distortion in the priorities of the institution. Furthermore, courses failing to satisfy the needs of nonmajors may give rise to duplicate courses in other departments, thereby limiting the number of courses students can take outside their major department. Institutional research and periodic self-study can call attention to the abuses of departmental rights to control their own programs.

Many of the issues involving the undergraduate curriculum are discussed by Dressel and DeLisle (1969). Special attention is given to undergraduate curriculum requirements in the liberal-arts colleges and universities, to provisions for individualization, to comprehensive patterns, and to unusual program developments. The conclusion of their study is that relatively few universities have made extensive use of available curriculum devices and procedures to reduce or eliminate traditional requirements in order to provide necessary flexibility.

Student Records and Services

In a limited sense, the inputs to higher education are high school graduates and the outputs are alumni. While college students are part of the educational process, they must be admitted, registered, graded, tested, advised, placed, housed, cared for when they are sick, and entertained and disciplined when they are well. These aspects of institutional life need to reflect educational goals and objectives. If they do not, it is difficult to distinguish the college experience from military service or penal servitude. Those responsible for educational institutions need to review institutional processes to see that they match and contribute to educational purposes.

The admissions policy of an institution determines its size and character. In the previous chapter, roles played by governing boards, legislatures, and coordinating state agencies were discussed. In this chapter the emphasis is on specific admissions functions and responsibilities. Faculty committees should establish criteria for admissions and should advise the admissions officer or agency on policy matters. The committee should be clearly identified and the policies widely published. Policies should deal with the use and weighting of secondary school records and test scores, with qualifications for transfer students, and with criteria for credit, transfer, suspension, dismissal, and withdrawal. Policies also should be defined and procedures developed to cover the award of financial aids, scholarships, loans, and work assignments. Hills (1964) suggests topics for studies of admissions policies, including achievement tests as predictors of college success, use of biographical data in evaluating student applications, adjustment of high school grades based on differences among high schools, simplified prediction formulas, and cutoff scores. Admission of disadvantaged students creates special problems which should be dealt with compassionately but with honesty and forthrightness. In order to optimize the admissions procedures, Hills suggests that universities decide on their objectives and honestly state them so students and counselors know what each college wants to do with what kind of students.

Curricula, policies, and expectations should be conveniently and accurately presented so that the student who knows what he wants to study can select a suitable college which meets his interests and needs. Prediction tables giving probabilities of various levels of performance associated with various levels of aptitudes should be made available for large groups of colleges in a conveniently useful form which carefully eliminates many possible avenues of error. Information on campus culture, subcultures, campus influence on students and other factors should be made widely available to be used by students in forming their value judgments of colleges. Colleges should organize and present information on financial aid programs including scholarships, loans, and work opportunities so that no student is denied an education for lack of funds. Counselors should be trained to help students use this information to make rational decisions about college entrance. Institutional researchers should be aware of and sensitive to these matters and should launch studies when malfunctions are apparent.

The records and reports maintained on students need to be reviewed to determine whether they are complete, accurate, and void of unnecessary duplication. Records need to be secure against loss or use by unauthorized persons. The records maintained on students are the basic data for most institutional research and self-study. Studies of curriculum, section size, course enrollments, student credit hours, and cost effectiveness depend on accurate data from the registrar. As institutions move to automated systems, the efficiency, accuracy, and flexibility of student record files should increase. Additional safeguards and definite policies are needed to protect students from unauthorized use of data.

The testing program requires special monitoring. Cumulative information is needed on students as they progress through the educational process. The student grade reports provide some information to counselors, but additional data are often collected on special aptitudes, skills, and attitudes which help students plan careers. The office of institutional research conducts studies using standardized tests like the Graduate Record Examination to compare students at one institution with students nationwide. The ACE student information form or the ACT student profile section provide useful information if carefully studied and widely interpreted. Cautiously used, predictions of grades may be helpful in planning student programs. Testing programs are also useful for placement, especially in determining advanced standing. Computers are being used widely in testing programs (for a review see Woods, 1970), and feasibility, effectiveness, and security of results are being studied.

The cost, organization, and effectiveness of testing programs should be evaluated regularly, especially in the age of the computer. Large volumes of data can be manufactured, and reams of paper can be produced containing such extensive tables that no one ever finds the time to assimilate and use them. Curiosity for information often exceeds capacity for utilization. A university that offers credit by examination either internally or through an external standardized program needs to be concerned about the compatibility of the standards, the equitability of use among academic units, and the accuracy of the records kept. An analysis can be made of the academic success of those students who satisfy requirements by previous courses and of those who receive course credit by examination.

The advising and counseling done by all institutions should provide individual attention to the educational, vocational, personal, social, and spiritual needs of students. Shaffer and Martinson (1966) describe the work of student personnel services in detail. Special counseling should be available for gifted, handicapped, and foreign students. Routine studies should be made to evaluate the coordination and qualification of counselors and advisors. Special studies can be made to determine student opinions about the advising and counseling they receive. These studies may reveal changes in behavior because of different approaches to counseling or to setting (such as residence hall or clinic). Efficient procedures for approval of individual academic programs need to be established and evaluated. If programs are standard and electives minimal, as they tend to be in professional schools, evaluation can be relatively simple. Advising procedures for freshman and for transfer students with special needs for counseling and advising beyond normal review and approval of their programs may require complex evaluation. The suitability and availability of counselors for each of many student problems require skillful coordination. Large numbers of counselors need inservice training, and programs for this training need periodic reevaluation. Where graduate students are used as dormitory counselors, there is a problem of variety in background and skills. Special training is needed in regard to the rules and regulations of the institution as well as the elements of providing guidance for students.

Academic advising presents special problems for institutional research and self-study. Faculty are often disinterested in academic advising because instruction and research offer more favorable rewards. Moreover, they are usually given little help in acquiring the knowledge necessary to perform well as advisors. Faculty and student opinions on coordination of counseling and the qualifications of counselors should be analyzed to see whether the total counseling and advising efforts are meeting students' needs.

Financial aid to students needs to be evaluated to see whether there is a coordinated program of scholarships, financial aid, and loans. The number of students receiving financial aid and the full extent of that support should be known, especially for each sport in the intercollegiate athletic program. The extent to which support for athletics differs from other forms of support should be subject to faculty policy review. All funds used for athletics and for the academic programs of athletes should be subject to regular review. The athletic conference standards for financial aid provide some guidelines, which keep aid equitable among institutions. Within an institution, studies need to be made to prevent exploitation of athletes and lowering of academic standards.

Student placement officers coordinate employment for students while in school, keep resumes on file, and set up interviews with prospective employers. This service may be provided by the university for all students or by colleges (usually professional schools). The cost and effectiveness of these offices are of constant concern. Since they have close contact with the public, the public relations values need to be examined. Representatives of government and industry form lasting impressions of a university based on their experience with the placement office. A recruiter who at one institution has had to wait for tardy interviewees finds it a pleasant contrast at another institution when he has only to push a call button for the next interviewee to appear. A study of recruiter impressions and judgments may be useful in assessing the value of a placement service to an institution. Student reactions to the service can also be obtained and matched with impressions of business and industry representatives.

Institutional environment factors play a major role in studying the needs for health and medical services. Residential campuses in remote locations need major medical facilities whereas commuter campuses in major cities need only first-aid and referral capacity. The coordination of medical facilities needs with other counseling services can be evaluated. General availability of medical care service records becomes a critical problem as institutions move toward master information systems. While these new record systems greatly facilitate and improve the service to students, they may be misused and infringe on students' constitutional rights. Because the quality of medical care requires medical judgment, specially trained teams are needed for evaluation. Appropriateness of the medical care to the environment and students' rights to privacy are matters for institutional evaluation.

On many campuses residence halls have been the major problem. Halls have customarily been built using cost effectiveness criteria which ignore the quality-of-life component. In loco parentis has since been replaced by open halls as students would not live in them otherwise. Yet universities remain responsible for controlling aspects of residence life—maintenance, fire and police protection, attractive meals served at competitive cost, and activities to occupy students' leisure time. The current exodus of students to apartments requires universities to study their total housing problems both on and off campus. Research may include an opinion survey on the type and nature of living conditions expected by students and parents covering such topics as academic freedom, on-campus and off-campus conduct, student government, and nonacademic services.

The activities within a residence hall and those available on the campus generally are designed to meet the educational, social, and cultural needs of students. Each activity can be evaluated against these and other standards. Most universities occasionally review activities to see how many students participate and whether students who participate in them meet satisfactory academic standards. Moral standards within the last decade have shifted, and students have gained freedom in their conduct and expression. Student demands have also resulted in student participation in activities directly related to instructional objectives. An evaluation can be made to determine whether these activities add to or detract from the educational purposes of an institution. If political activities, for example, help students to understand the political process and thus to meet an objective of their academic program, the activities may be appropriate and perhaps even worthy of academic recognition in terms of credit toward a degree. Political activities designed to destroy the educational institution, however, are not appropriate.

Once academic objectives are clearly stated, students, faculty, and administrators can evaluate each activity in terms of those objectives. Value judgments can be obtained on the representativeness of interest and taste for a single activity or for a group of activities. Student fees should support numerous activities; if athletics receives a major part of student fees, there may be an inequity which needs study. Issues concerning off-campus speakers, student publications, and protection of student rights as well as other questions of freedom and responsibility consume many hours of faculty and administrative time. The role of student government is not always clear in these matters, and true student opinion is difficult to collect. The extent of support for extremist positions is difficult to assess. Institutional research and self-study can provide some objective measures of student perception of the degree to which campus activities meet their needs.

Nonacademic discipline presents a complex and perplexing problem. Legal position and due process need to be observed. A locus of authority is elusive. A study may not be able to decide issues of discipline, but it should be able to draw the issues clearly. The educational soundness of disciplinary policy can be determined in respect to institutional purposes. The legal rights of students cannot be dealt with so simply.

Administration

The work load of administrators is somewhat easier to establish than is the work load of faculty. The duties of college administrators are described by Blackwell (1966). Most administrators keep regular office hours, fit into organizational charts, and have job descriptions that fit them into a hierarchy of a line and staff organization. Wittmer (1968) concluded from his study of historical data that the complexity and size of university administration has not kept pace with increases in faculty, student body, institutional income, and developments in secular society. The work load of administrators has increased along with pressures from students, taxpayers, and alumni. Many administrators return to the classroom and the laboratory in preference to enduring the battle of continued responsibility with diminishing resources. Salary and fringe benefits for administrators should be evaluated to see whether policies make faculty reluctant to serve in administrative positions. Administrators' perceptions of their roles and the purposes of the educational program need to be reviewed routinely. If administrators do not see how their tasks relate to the educational mission, dissatisfaction can grow. The administrator who sees his responsibility within the context of institutional goals can provide the most effective service.

Morgan (1968) suggests five topics for research on the decision-making process in higher education. They are: "(1) What are the principal decision structures that exist within university organizations? (2) What kinds of decision rules determine which structure will respond to specific problems? (3) How are new decision rules formed in response to solving new kinds of problems? Do the new problems actually lead to the development of new structures or just to modification of the old? (4) In what manner, and how frequently, do the university's several structures interact with one another? (5) Do the decision structures of public universities differ significantly from those in private universities?" Studies of the decision-making process in higher education have received little attention in the literature.

Operationally, the formation of administrative policies and procedures begins with the department. Students take courses in the department. Faculty are hired by the department. Courses and rooms are scheduled for instruction by the chairman of the department. The department serves as a basic political unit for representation on the academic senate. Budgets are developed by departments, and resources are allocated to departments. Expenditures are made in terms of departmental budget numbers. Research projects are administered by departments or institutes, and contractual arrangements with outside agencies are generally originated at the departmental level.

Each decision made by the department is subject to review at various administrative levels. Studies of the review departmental actions receive are appropriate topics for institutional research. If the matter is essentially one of curriculum, it rests with the faculty in the department, with some policy review by the university curriculum committee. If it is a matter of contracting with other state or federal agencies, policies are established at the level of a board of regents. Personnel and salary actions are reviewed by the Civil Service Commission, the Civil Rights Commission, or state personnel offices to determine whether equal opportunities are being provided for minority groups and whether qualification standards are being met.

The Decision-Making Process. Platt and Parsons (1970) present both a theoretical orientation toward and a review of the decision-making process in higher education. They describe the academic value system, the social organization, and the influence process. They conclude that influence is used more than power and that faculties tend to be associational. In their teaching and research, they operate as individuals, but they work through committees in departmental matters. This associational decision-making process has implications for institutional research and self-study. The process itself may be studied, and other university problems may be subjected to study in terms of the process.

University policies on goals, the means to pursue these goals, and the role of university government establish administrative procedures. Administrators need to review present and past procedures to see whether they are consistent with institutional goals, and institutional research can facilitate a systematic approach to this review process. Research can reveal patterns of organization, authority, and influence that show relationships of structure to goals. It can analyze the satisfactions expressed by those who support the institution to show relationships of social service to goals. It can examine the role of students in decision-making and the procedures used to handle student demonstrations to relate values to goals. Finally, it can explore moral and political considerations in the use of authority to relate rights to goals. Additional subjects for research involving administrative procedures are suggested by Lunsford (1970). Specific studies which may be made by an office of institutional research could include analysis of university committee assignments, application of an intercorrelation matrix to determine the influence and power of university authority, or a study of faculty perceptions of their social service commitments. Faculty members in some academic disciplines (sociology, psychology, economics, and political science) have begun to do research in these areas and could be interested in institutional problems of organization and governance. Patterns of organization under current study in various institutions should be brought to the attention of those responsible for the decision-making process. Studies need to be made of both faculty and student involvement in decision-making.

Problems in communicating institutional research were the subject of the 1969 annual forum of the Association for Institutional Research (Wright, 1970). The institutional researcher as communicator, communicating with state agencies, communicating within the institution, and communication of policy were major topics involving the decision-making process. Many techniques were suggested for conducting research on decision-making and for communicating research results within the university.

The argument is often made that because education is a process, only studies of process are appropriate to it. Obviously this position is wrong, for ultimately processes must be judged by their results. The process of education is carried on within an institution that is given resources and is expected to perform certain social missions. Institutional research and self-study are concerned with the evaluation of the institution as it accomplishes its academic functions. This evaluation needs to measure the internal consistency of purposes, functions, and accomplishments.

Bibliography

BAREITHER, H. D., AND SCHILLINGER, J. L. *University Space Planning.* Urbana, Ill.: University of Illinois Press, 1968.

BLACKWELL, T. E. *College and University Administration.* New York: Center for Applied Research, 1966.

BOSELY, H. E. "Class Sizes and Faculty-Student Ratios in American Colleges." *The Educational Record,* 1963, *43,* 148–153.

BROWN, H. S. "The Pattern of Curriculum Expansion in the University." *College and University,* 1965, *40,* 185–193.

BUNNELL, K. (Ed.), *Faculty Work Load.* Washington, D.C.: American Council on Education, 1960.

DOI, J. "The Use of Faculty Load Data Within an Institution." In

K. BUNNELL (Ed.), *Faculty Work Load*. Washington, D.C.: American Council on Education, 1960.

DRESSEL, P. L., AND DE LISLE, F. H. *Undergraduate Curriculum Trends*. Washington: American Council on Education, 1969.

EBLE, K. E. *The Recognition and Evaluation of Teaching Effectiveness*. Salt Lake City: Project to Improve College Teaching, 1970.

HILLS, J. R. "Admissions Procedures That Make Sense." In *Research in Higher Education: Guide to Institutional Decisions*. New York: College Entrance Examination Board, 1964.

INGRAHAM, M. H. *The Outer Fringe: Faculty Benefits Other Than Annuities and Insurance*. Madison: University of Wisconsin Press, 1965.

LUNSFORD, T. F. "Some Suggested Directions for Research." In C. E. KRUYTBOSCH AND S. L. MESSINGER (Eds.), *The State of the University*. Beverly Hills: Sage, 1970.

Michigan State University. *Improving Undergraduate Education: The Report of the Committee on Undergraduate Education*. East Lansing, Mich., 1967.

MORGAN, W. E. "The Study of University Organizations." *The Journal of Higher Education*, 1968, *34*(3), 144–151.

PLATT, G. M., AND PARSONS, T. "Decision-Making in the Academic System: Influence and Power Exchange." In C. E. KRUYTBOSCH AND S. L. MESSINGER (Eds.), *The State of the University*. Beverly Hills: Sage, 1970.

POSTELTHWAITE, S. T. *The Auditorial-Tutorial Approach to Learning*. Minneapolis: Burgess, n.d.

REISMAN, A., AND TAFT, M. I. "A Systems Approach to the Evaluation and Budgeting of Educational Programs." In R. H. P. KRAFT (Ed.), *Strategies of Educational Planning*. Tallahassee: Educational Systems Development Center, 1969.

SHAFFER, R. H., AND MARTINSON, W. D. *Student Personnel Services in Higher Education*. New York: Center for Applied Research in Education, 1966.

STECKLEIN, J. W. *How to Measure Faculty Workload*. Washington, D.C.: American Council on Education, 1962.

STOUT, E. M. "The Origins of the Registrar." *College and University*, 1954, *29*, 415–418.

University of California. *Education at Berkeley: Response of the Select Committee on Education*. Berkeley, 1966.

WITTMER, D. R. *The Rise of Administration in Higher Education*. Madison: Board of Regents of Wisconsin State University, 1968.

WOODS, E. M. "Recent Applications of Computer Technology to School Testing Programs." *Review of Educational Resources,* 1970, *40* (4), 525–539.

WRIGHT, P. S. (Ed.), *Institutional Research and Communication in Higher Education.* Berkeley: Association for Institutional Research, 1970.

CHAPTER 7

Evaluating Outcomes
of Instruction

Joe L. Saupe, Paul L. Dressel

ᑲᑭᑲᑭᑲᑭᑲᑭᑲᑭᑲᑭᑲᑭ

Institutional research includes the collection, organization, and dissemination of factual material, but unless this leads to evaluation and subsequent improvement of processes or results, the data collected usually have but limited impact. It is possible but highly improbable that evaluation can deem a process and its results the best possible. Evaluation is inevitable in making choices. The issue, then, is adequacy of the evidence upon which judgments are made.

Resistance to formal evaluation indicates unwillingness to reexamine evaluations which have already been made and enshrined in procedures congenial to those involved in executing them. Institutional research committed to evaluation in reference to purposes and objectives and concerned with economy, effectiveness, and equity in the processes employed in attaining these purposes and objectives is, to many faculty members and administrators, a disturbing and

151

unpopular venture. Their resistance may not be entirely recalcitrant or averse to criticism and to change; it may be based on idiosyncratic assumptions, values, or goals irrelevant to broader educational goals and or on concerns about effective allocation of limited resources. The professor who refuses to teach classes larger than ten or fifteen students because he finds satisfaction in intimate contacts with small groups of students exemplifies this pattern. Evidence of lower costs and equally effective learning in larger classes is irrelevant to this professor; furthermore he may have a different although perhaps not clearly explicated concept of effective learning.

Institutional research on institutional accomplishment is both essential and difficult. While much data collection, analysis, reporting, and utilization is carried on within an institution for purposes which are marginally related to the accomplishment of its purposes, a major thrust of research on the institution must be to determine how well it is accomplishing its purposes and to suggest how purposes might be more fully achieved. As higher education and individual colleges and universities have grown in recent decades, the enterprise has become more expensive and more prominent and has attracted increasing numbers of critics from both within and without the institution. It has become almost impossible for a college or university to remain complacent about its functioning. In the decade of the 1970's, perhaps more than ever before, the evaluation of institutional accomplishment is an essential continuing function.

The evaluation of accomplishments is difficult for several reasons. A principal difficulty is that college and university purposes are so imprecisely specified, as a rule, that evaluation remains ambiguous; ambiguity is increased when changes are made in the purposes under scrutiny. Meaningful evaluation of accomplishments can proceed only on the basis of ongoing purposes and objectives that provide the evaluator with relatively unambiguous indications of what to look for as indicators of accomplishment or its absence. To say that a purpose is "to produce the educated man" is insufficient; to say that a purpose is "to produce college graduates" is precise, but simplistic.

Meaningful purposes and objectives for higher education almost always have a long-term dimension which renders evaluation difficult. That education is "preparation for living and learning" is an accepted, though imprecise, statement. But even were it given more precise meaning, judgments about accomplishments could not be made until later in the lives of the recipients of the education; even then the influence of experiences other than the education under evaluation would be difficult to estimate. Even in the case of professional education, with the possibility of assessing professional performance and contribution, the intervention of time between education and assessment creates difficulties. In any case, at the time an assessment is completed, the implications apply to an educational program which has certainly changed in the interim. An adequate evaluation of a four-year undergraduate program based on behavioral changes would require more than four years, but many decisions about resource allocation cannot be postponed for four years.

Another difficulty arises in evaluating programs on the basis of ultimate results. Most programs of any duration are a complex of experiences interrelated in various ways and to various degrees. It may be impossible to trace ultimate changes back to the impact of any part of a program. Lacking, as most educational evaluation does, elaborately controlled experimentation, it is impossible to determine what characteristics of a program determine its quality as measured by student change. Though changes in student behavior indicate program quality, they do not define that quality. Frequently we are driven in assessing program quality to proceed on the basis of assumptions or hypotheses which assert that given program characteristics produce desired behavioral changes.

Despite the difficulties, there are approaches to the evaluation of institutional accomplishment that can provide information useful to the institution as a basis for improving its performance. This chapter is devoted to consideration of such approaches and of other factors involved in institutional evaluation. Three program areas—instructional, research, and service—are examined to suggest ways in which their quality and accomplishments can be assessed.

Institutional Purposes and Objectives

Higher education has become a complex enterprise with a diversity of functions and purposes. The central function common to all colleges and universities is the education of students in degree-oriented programs. Research and associated scholarly and creative activities are pursued in most colleges and universities in response to a second function and set of purposes and objectives. External service programs are guided by a third set of purposes and objectives. The three basic purposes—generation, transmission, and application of knowledge—justify the existence of the university. Finally, the several institutional programs that exist to provide supporting services to the three principal functions have purposes and objectives.

Instructional Programs. Instructional programs have purposes and objectives at several different levels. At one level are institutional purposes which suggest or indicate the range, type, and levels of academic programs to be offered. The accepted purposes of community colleges dictate that they offer some combination of general academic and vocational programs at the freshman and sophomore levels. Specialized undergraduate institutions offer a range of undergraduate programs that is restricted by institutional purpose. Universities may offer a wide range of undergraduate, professional, and graduate programs, but the range and levels of these programs may also be subject to some restrictions on the basis of institutional purpose.

At another level are educational objectives which are common to groups of programs. Specific academic programs or majors have unique objectives related to the subject or professional field at each program level. In addition, there may be general education objectives common to all undergraduate programs. Foreign language objectives stating facility and research competencies may be common to all programs leading to the doctor of philosophy degree.

Institutional purposes and academic objectives may indicate the types of students which specific programs of the institution are designed to serve. Purposes can lead to open-door admissions policies or to special programs for students from disadvantaged backgrounds. Selective colleges and universities base admissions standards on assumptions or evidence about the types of students who are able to achieve institutional academic objectives. Other institutions have purposes leading to the admission of a heterogeneous student body; public colleges and universities defend to their state legislatures the admission of nonresident students on the basis that heterogeneity has educational benefits.

Concerns about efficiency and effectiveness can lead to specification of optimal numbers of students for individual programs. Thus, the number of students for which each program is designed can also be conceived as an additional dimension of total program balance. Further specifications for individual programs may indicate the expectations the college or university has for the activities of graduates. The purpose of a professional program may be to prepare students for immediate employment. For other undergraduate programs, preparation for graduate study may constitute an overriding purpose. At the graduate level, preparations for college teaching, research, or other types of future positions may entail competing purposes which deserve reconciliation. It may even be reasonable to specify as objectives the percentages of degree recipients expected to enter various types of employment and to base development of programs on such objectives.

Research Programs. At least three distinguishable types of purposes guide research and the other creative and scholarly efforts of colleges and universities. First, and perhaps foremost, faculty research has as a purpose the enhancement of teaching programs. In this sense research must contribute to the accomplishment of objectives of instructional programs. Several more or less generally accepted assumptions that provide the basis for this fundamental purpose of research in the college or university are: faculty research creates an environment of inquiry which is conducive to learning; students learn by participating in research; research activities provide stimulation to faculty which carries over into classroom teaching; and research produces knowledge to be taught.

A second purpose of research is the production of knowledge per se. While the production of knowledge through research can and is in other countries carried on elsewhere than in colleges and universities, major portions of this responsibility have been assigned to and accepted by higher education in our society. Through funding of research in colleges and universities, the federal government has been principally responsible for this development and for the appearance, at some institutions, that research has gained a higher priority than instruction.

Finally, some research efforts in colleges and universities have specific missions directed at community and social problems, thereby tying these efforts to the institution's external service function. The agricultural experiment stations of the land-grant universities are specific illustrations of situations in which research is directed toward the solution of specific problems more than toward the production of knowledge per se. Colleges of education provide faculty to conduct school-system surveys directed at the solution of local problems. In recent years colleges and universities have accepted the challenge to assist, through mission-oriented research, in solving problems created by urban life and by environmental pollution.

External Service Programs.   The external service programs of a university may include cooperative extension; continuing education; and institutes, centers, or other units which carry on consultation and research with various groups and organizations outside the university. More specifically, external service includes off-campus offerings of credit and noncredit courses, on-campus offerings of noncredit courses(usually in the evening), workshops and conference sessions, and research in consultation teams on a variety of social and community problems. The usual attitude toward external service programs is that they should be self-supporting although in fact the salaries, facilities, and other support for most of these programs are provided through the same funds that support on-campus activity.

College and university public service programs, too, are guided by purposes and objectives, and the accomplishments of these programs may be evaluated in reference to them. In the broadest sense, mission-oriented research, as described above, is carried out in response to public service purposes. Public service carries the expertise and competence of the college or university to the broader public. There are at least three kinds of component and associated purposes for this function.

A first set of purposes relates to national missions. Land-grant universities have been assigned the agricultural cooperative extension mission by law. Various federal departments experimenting with adaptation of the agricultural model to other areas of national concern have involved higher education in these efforts, and industrial extension programs have thus been directed toward applying the agricultural model to problems of business and industry. Title I of the Higher Education Act of 1965 is directed toward establishing community services and solving urban problems with college and university involvement. Additional legislation is almost certain to expand the range of extension purposes related to national life.

A second set of purposes underlying continuing education programs is carried out through courses, workshops, seminars, and other instructional experiences for professionals and other adults. Professional development and learning are now viewed as lifelong processes. Thus the purposes of continuing education are similar to those of traditional instructional programs except in respect to the acquisition of academic credits and degrees. Regular college courses offered for academic credit away from the college campus, as in evening programs, share certain of the purposes of continuing education, but they are perhaps better viewed as extensions of the degree-oriented function of instruction to special populations of part-time students.

Colleges and universities are increasingly assisting community groups in problem solving through education. Subject matter appropriate to problem-solving purposes can be derived from the nature of the specific problems for which group solutions are sought. In contrast, the purposes of continuing education are usually oriented to the subject matter needs of individuals. Thus, the ultimate purpose of programs for problem solving can be solution of community problems common to all. However, the approach must be through contributing knowledge to a group as a basis for the development of solutions within the group itself.

Internal Service Programs. Internal service programs support the achievement of the basic purposes of instruction, research, and external service, and the contributions of each supportive program can be evaluated on this basis. The number and variety of types of support programs prohibit a thorough treatment of them here, but brief references to a few are given to reveal how their objectives interact with those of the institution's primary purposes.

Educational service programs provide direct support to the primary programs. Although it may appear to students and faculty that the overriding concern of the library is keeping its holdings properly cataloged and shelved, its purpose is to contribute to learning, research, and even external service. Related educational service programs with similar purposes and objectives include audiovisual and computer services.

Student service programs provide conditions, activities, and support which contribute to an environment conducive to learning. Activities have unique purposes related to student development; the accomplishments of each activity can be evaluated on the basis of its special purposes.

The purposes of admissions and registration are also facilitative. And their purposes are perhaps best served when the necessary activities of these operations are carried out with maximum convenience and satisfaction to the student. The list of internal service functions could be extended to include the functions of general administration, financial affairs, development, operation and maintenance of the physical plant, and other processes and operations. All have purposes involving the instruction of students, the conduct of research, or the extension of the institution's expertise to the public.

Assessing Instructional Programs

The central objective of instructional programs is usually and perhaps most meaningfully expressed in terms of desired changes in behavior or growth of individual students. David G. Brown (Bloom and Hastings, 1970) suggests that behavior change or growth objectives can be grouped into the categories of "whole man growth" and "specialized man growth." Objectives in the whole-man-growth category apply typically to undergraduate programs and more specifically to the general education components of such programs. Thus, these objectives generally apply to all undergraduate students. Brown suggests that objectives in this category include increasing the student's ability to learn to feel (compassion, love, and concern), learn to retain facts, learn to think (employing logic and methods of analysis), learn to decide (employing philosophy of life, value systems, and methods of analysis), learn to act (doing, creating, and communicating), and learn to learn. Specialized-man-growth objectives, particularly applicable to professional and graduate education, also apply to the specialization component of undergraduate education. They are associated with individual educational programs or groups thereof. Brown suggests that they include increasing the student's ability to choose a career, gain admission to the next stage in career development (for example, medical school), develop skills needed to fulfill a career, earn a living for self and family, and fulfill society's new power needs (including discovery of talent). Brown's categorization of growth objectives may be compared with similar outlines suggested by others. Alexander Astin (Lawrence, Weathersby, and Patterson, 1970) distinguishes between cognitive and affective behavior objectives, and the two fundamental taxonomies of educational objectives make the same distinction (Bloom, 1956; Krathwohl, Bloom, and Masia, 1964). Brown's suggestions, however, appear to be particularly useful in suggesting approaches to assessment. His paper includes specific suggestions for each type of objective suggested above. The measures discussed in the following sections are included.

Student Testimony. Students may be asked by interview or questionnaire whether they are achieving or have achieved a stated objective by means of questions that may vary in specificity. Limitations to this measurement technique are obvious but, for certain objectives, alternatives to it are difficult to come by. When the arguments against and the available experience with the use of student testimony are fully considered, the conclusion must be that conscientiously sought student testimony on institutional accomplishment of objectives possesses significant validity.

Self-Reports of Behavior. In a similar fashion, students may be asked to report on activities and behaviors which are considered to indicate the achievement or nonachievement of specific objectives. They may be asked whether they have selected a career objective, and their responses to the question may be compared from freshman through senior years. They may be asked whether they plan to seek admission to a professional or graduate school program. They may be questioned on the number of books they have read voluntarily, the number of concerts they have attended, or the number and types of community service programs in which they have voluntarily taken part. This approach to measurement is straightforward; with meaningfully worded questions on relevant behaviors during limited periods of time and with conscientious student cooperation, the resulting evidence must possess considerable validity.

Test Performance. The most common method for assessing student accomplishment of cognitive educational objectives is by means of testing. Although the measurement of student accomplishment is the principal purpose of course examinations, the measurement of institutional accomplishment is an accompanying effect. However, meaningful institutional objectives are usually expressed in broader terms than those for specific courses; for this reason and because there are typically no criteria referents for performance, course examinations are seldom involved in institutional assessment.

Institutionally developed tests can provide valid measurements of the accomplishment of institutional objectives. Some colleges and universities have established proficiency requirements in communication skills and quantitative ability as prerequisites for graduation. Performance is judged by written tests based on standards which constitute institutional objectives; the percentage of students earning passing scores on first testing is evidence of institutional accomplishment.

A number of colleges and universities also use comprehensive examinations for measuring achievement of more pervasive educational objectives. Comprehensive examination at the undergraduate level may be administered to all undergraduates at a late stage in their program, or it may constitute a requirement of specific programs. In either case, while serving as an assessment of student learning in relation to objectives, such examinations also provide evidence of institutional accomplishment. Local preparation insures that they are relevant to institutional objectives. In another form, comprehensive examinations are common in graduate programs and, with the establishment of systems for recording student performance on them in relation to program objectives, these examinations can contribute to institutional evaluation.

In addition to institutionally prepared tests and examinations, standardized tests are also used. The Graduate Record Examination is a widely known illustration. An advantage of this examination is that national norms for comparison are available. A disadvantage is that it is developed on the basis of educational objectives which may not coincide with those of any individual college or university. For those students for whom the objective "to gain admission to the next stage of career development" is applicable, performance on national and professional school admissions tests (such as those available for law, business, and medicine) provides relevant evidence of accomplishment. Similarly, performance of graduates of professional school programs in passing professional examinations (such as bar examinations, board examinations for medicine, and C.P.A. examinations) for entry into professions indicates accomplishment of programs. Percentages of graduates who pass these tests are indicators of institutional accomplishment.

As is the case with other approaches to measuring accomplishment of objectives, technical problems are associated with the use of tests and examinations. The extensive literature available on topics in educational measurement makes it unnecessary to attempt to treat such technical considerations here. For example, because educational objectives typically deal with changes in behavior, the pattern of pretests and posttests is implied, and consequent difficulties of measuring behavior change using gain scores are appreciable. It is important, however, that technical problems and unattainability of reliable and valid measures not stand in the way of developing and using less than perfect indicators of accomplishment such as those suggested above. Conscientiously developed measures used with recognition of their limitations are superior to no attempt at evaluation at all.

Postgraduation Activities. Particularly for professional program objectives, information on the experiences, successes, and failures of graduates can be relevant. Such information is typically secured by means of an alumni follow-up questionnaire on which self-reports are requested. It is important that the information requested by this means be rigorously specified for relevance to program objectives. It is also important to remember that the program being evaluated and maybe even its objectives have changed since the graduates being surveyed were in the program.

To overcome the latter difficulty, at least in part, an exit questionnaire may be administered to degree recipients at the time of graduation. At this time, the graduate will be able to report on his plans for the immediate future and may be able to report on long-range plans. Both types of information may be relevant. A specific illustration of this approach is provided by the exit questionnaire administered to all Ph.D. recipients in behalf of the National Research Council. The information reported on these forms provides the basis for national compilation of manpower data on individuals granted the doctorate. Analysis of the responses on the forms by a university can also provide evidence of accomplishment in graduate programs at the institutional level.

Assessing Research Programs

There have been relatively few successful attempts to demonstrate the economic value of research. The research programs of the agricultural experiment stations over a period of years are often noted as one of the most successful research ventures in terms of apparent results. Some efforts have been made to determine the economic impact of increased productivity and improvements in varieties and breeds and to relate the gains to the expenditures but, in much of research, the gains really transcend any dollar evaluation. A new drug or antibiotic resulting from medical research may reduce the discomfort of many individuals or save many lives. A new insecticide may increase productivity or successfully suppress mosquitoes; the increase in human consumption or comfort may be significant but not easily priced. Thus a product may have significant impact which transcends economic benefits. As has been suggested previously, the evaluation of research is not a simple task if one moves beyond the counting of articles, books, or pages. Even among outstanding scholars in a field there will be disagreements about the significance of new research. But certainly the judgment of a group of widely accepted scholars is a more significant basis for evaluating research than the judgments of laymen.

As with instruction, it is possible by observing a research activity to make some judgments about how well it is organized and designed and how effectively it is administered. The adequacy of the equipment and the extent and effectiveness of its use reflect not only the availability of resources to purchase equipment but also the amount of care exercised in planning research and relating it to equipment needs.

In some ways, the research process can be evaluated by the quality and the extent of the support services provided. A chemistry department without a glass-blowing specialist has limited capacity for research. Special facilities are required for the care of animals used in research programs. Lack of separate research laboratories for various types of research does not necessarily mean that quality research is not being done, but it does suggest that whatever is being accomplished is being done under serious handicaps and that the research activities engaged in must be severely limited by inadequate physical facilities.

The impact of research on instructional programs has been touched upon in a number of ways. Obviously, graduate-level courses and graduate student research are closely interrelated with, perhaps almost completely dependent upon, the departmental research program. The involvement of faculty in significant research coupled with at least some minimal interest in training researchers shows some promise of quality in aspects of the graduate program even though there is no great interest in teaching. At the undergraduate level, the impact of research can be favorable or unfavorable depending on the degree of immersion of the faculty in research and on their extended interest in undergraduate teaching. Undergraduates can and do get a thrill out of contact with a productive scholar who is able to interpret to them with enthusiasm and clarity what he is doing.

Assessing External Service Programs

In some cases the evaluation of an external service program can be made quite simply by finding out if it actually does what was suggested; however the objectives of many of these programs are quite unclear. Workshops and conference programs usually originate in response to a request from an external organization. The substance of these sessions is often ill-defined, and behavioral objectives are often totally neglected. Therefore conference and workshop programs in continuing education centers are evaluated largely through numbers of conferences held, the number of people in attendance, and relatively crude indices of satisfaction on the part of those who attend. Success tends to be measured in terms of growing demand rather than product evaluation. However process evaluation does have some significance. If activities are well organized, if things move along efficiently, if people find the content of sufficient interest to merit remaining in the sessions, and if, on the whole, those who attend are satisfied and even excited with the experience, programs are clearly not failures.

Noncredit course offerings can also be evaluated on the basis of process evaluation. The facts that people come, pay their fees, continue to attend, and express some satisfaction seem to be evaluation enough for those charged with operating public service programs.

Process and Product in Instruction

If product assessment of instructional programs by recourse to behavioral change is seen as too difficult or too time consuming, it may be abandoned in favor of more immediate criteria such as the number (or per cent) of students completing various programs or the number of student credit hours produced by the instructional programs. Similarly, instructional support services may be evaluated by their immediate output. The admissions office can be evaluated on the basis of its success in bringing to the university the numbers and types of students which constitute enrollment targets by program. Counseling services can be reviewed by considering numbers and types of clients, sources of referrals, and student and faculty satisfaction. Libraries can be evaluated (quite inadequately) by considering numbers of volumes held, additions, size of professional staff, and circulation. Accomplishments such as satisfied enrollment targets and adequacy in resource circulation demonstrate that the functions assigned are being performed, but they say nothing about quality. By comparison, some judgments of relative efficiency can be made, but the fact that one department produced more student credit hours per faculty member does not speak to quality either. Relatively lower admissions office expenditures per student admitted is, likewise, no indication of how well the job is done.

Discussion of product evaluation necessarily involves the subject of criteria. Criteria can be organized in a useful way by viewing the university primarily as a purveyor of knowledge. Criteria can thus be developed within a framework for assessing instructional program quality according to six program variables or categories: program rationale, knowledge resources, transmission variables, research and scholarly activities, support resources, and operating characteristics.

Program Rationale. A quality program is first of all developed on the basis of clear and meaningful goals and objectives. The design of the program should be explicitly related to these objectives in such a way that it is apparent to students, faculty, and even outside observers that the work required and the experience offered in the program are related to the objectives and, indeed, require students to engage in activities which are prototypes or at least forerunners of kinds of behavior expected later. Departmental staff often argue that teaching and research activities are so interrelated as to be inseparable. To some extent, this may be true at the graduate level, but it is certainly not true at the undergraduate level and, all pleas to the contrary, a highly research-oriented faculty does not usually make a strong undergraduate faculty. Thus, departmental emphases and priorities must also be viewed in trying to judge the adequacy of the instructional program.

If the rationale for a program has been clearly thought out, this should be reflected in the details of the program design, in the catalog description of courses included, and in any related courses or experiences required of students. The success of a program in journalism obviously depends on numerous experiences for students to write and to receive adequate evaluations of their writing. Vague course descriptions indicate, at the very least, that students and advisors are being given inadequate help in planning student programs. Vagueness may also reflect lack of adequate planning or such a high degree of flexibility that there is no assurance that one course will be different from another similar one.

The appropriateness of a course or program to the kinds of students enrolled is another significant element of program rationale. Departments offering courses which serve students from numerous other fields may resist or simply be incapable of developing a course which interests nonmajors and provides experiences relevant to their development. Courses for majors, too, can be based on an unrealistic conception of a segment of student population.

Checklists or rating scales embodying goals, objectives, and details of program rationale can be developed. One can simply check the presence or absence of a particular item or develop a rating scale in terms of the extent of its presence or absence.

Knowledge Resources. This category raises the preliminary question of whether enough is known about a program area to justify its existence in a college or university. Premature attempts to gain stature for some vocational area by introducing a college curriculum in the field may produce a situation in which there is little more than a program title. One university some years ago introduced a curriculum in mobile homes only to find that there was not really enough substance to justify a series of courses in this field. At one time non-Western studies and black studies raised the same problem. Until an adequate base of knowledge exists, there is no justification for a program.

This, in turn, raises the question of faculty adequacy. While new fields may sometimes have to be generated by persons trained in traditional fields, this should be done only in the stronger universities. The new field of policy sciences may become a generally accepted discipline or field of study but, at the moment, the introduction of a curriculum for policy sciences would in most institutions raise serious questions about the adequacy of faculty available for the program. Beyond this, of course, there is a need to identify the various field subspecialties already reflected in course offerings, and to assure the presence of the minimal numbers of faculty necessary to cover these. In terms of neither the total work load nor the knowledge included is it feasible for one individual to offer a complete program. Any new graduate program must include faculty members who have been productive in research, and at least one or two of these should have prior experience in direction of graduate programs and student research.

Adequacies of library holdings, laboratory facilities, and equipment also deserve attention. In the case of new programs, there is a tendency to push to get underway, hoping that resources will follow instead of procuring resources over a period of time and then initiating the program.

Transmission Variables. This category includes all factors involved in the transmission of knowledge to students. It involves not only the presence of facilities and staff but also evidence of competency in the organization and use of these resources. A magnificent library is of little use unless the staff and the information retrieval procedures make the resources readily available to staff and students. Students must be adequately informed about programs in order to make wise choices not only in terms of present interests but also in terms of ultimate goals. If they are not, there has been a failure in the transmission of knowledge. Faculty skills in teaching and in use of educational technology need to be examined. Awareness of innovative methods for teaching and learning and active attention to innovation and improvement are key factors in appraisal of transmission.

Research and Scholarly Activities. No graduate program can be regarded as acceptable unless there is evidence of extensive research or scholarly activity on the part of the faculty. A master's-level program may not require a thesis of the student and it may not require research in depth on the part of faculty members. Even so, a faculty member would be inadequate if he were not engaged in some sort of scholarly activity which would keep him in the forefront of the thinking of his field. To some extent, research is also requisite for faculty who teach in undergraduate programs. While overinvolvement has its obvious difficulties, the faculty member who is not involved in scholarly activity is shortly outdated, and several generations of students may suffer therefrom. Direction of independent study certainly requires a faculty member capable of doing some independent work of his own.

It is often stated that the appraisal of research output is simpler than the appraisal of teaching. There is very little to justify this view. One can note the amounts of staff time assigned to research and to teaching. One can look at the numbers of credit hours or publications produced. To some limited extent, the journals in which articles are published are suggestive of quality, but the simple counting of publications is not revelatory of the quality of research. Furthermore, it does not indicate the extent to which that research is related to instructional activities of the faculty member. Research which is done primarily to develop a list of publications or to satisfy a peculiar interest of the faculty member may contribute little to knowledge and even less to the quality of instruction.

Support Resources. No program can be adequate unless it is provided with adequate physical facilities, financial support, and emotional commitment. Program support involves physical space, equipment for teaching, research, financial support for travel, consultation and the like, adequate secretarial, clerical, and technical support, and support from related academic departments. Less obvious but equally important is the extent of commitment to the work of the program by the administration and by the faculty itself.

Operating Characteristics. This last category involves some indicators which are sometimes regarded as evidence of quality although they are perhaps not as closely related to quality as some of the variables listed in preceding categories. In a sense the name of the category is an avoidance of some other catchall title, which might be more ambiguous. Program size is considered here. Although size is sometimes taken to be negatively related to quality, there is at least some critical mass that is necessary for effective performance, and failure to attain this somewhat indefinite critical mass would certainly suggest a lack of quality.

Closely related to size is the matter of growth. Obviously, a program that has been stabilized over a period of years does not reveal quality through growth, but a new program should demonstrate consistent growth for several years until it attains at least the critical mass. Failure to grow would, for a new program, suggest lack of quality.

Efficiency and productivity may be regarded as separate and conjoint indicators of program effectiveness and quality. Purposive and vital programs are usually efficient and productive, and purpose and vitality are certainly related to quality. Possible variables for measurement here might include such things as student-faculty ratios, degrees granted per faculty member, degrees per student enrollment, and average time to complete a degree.

These variables and the implied measures associated with them can be used in deciding whether a proposed new program is ready for launching. They can be applied to existing programs to determine how effectively they are operating. Through comparisons among similar units and through reference to specific indices such as student credit hour productivity per full-time-equivalent faculty member, guidelines for budget support can be developed. Some factors, such as degree production, may be considered as effects and related to costs in such manner as to produce a cost effectiveness analysis. This may be more meaningful than an attempt to project actual dollar returns and relate these to actual dollar costs in the classical pattern of cost-benefit analysis.

Measures and Quality Assessment

Although we accept behavioral change as the ultimate criteria in judging program quality, the difficulties and time involved in evaluation make it necessary to employ other procedures and criteria. In the preceding section, six categories of program quality variables and assumptions relating these to program quality were introduced. Many individual variables can be derived from this sort of analysis, and some have been suggested, but another critical step must be taken—identification of specific procedures by which measures of these quality variables can be obtained. Sources of evidence on quality variables include the operating record systems (which reveal enrollments, number of faculty, degrees granted, and data on finances), questionnaires or interviews with degree recipients (which can give some evidence on effects of phenomena such as space on behavioral change and graduate competency and can reveal student evaluations of program variables), and annual faculty reports on activity accomplishment and program evaluation.

For every program offered or proposed, there should be a detailed program statement including objectives, rationale, and program design. A proposal document should provide basic data on all important points, and scales for rating these can be developed. Any program statement should be structured to facilitate use of the material included. Ratings and judgments by outside consultants can be utilized. Specific program variables may be suggested, or consultants may, out of their experience, develop some of their own. If statement formulation is approached on a university-wide basis, what emerges is something approximating the nature of a detailed self-study carried on by each of the operating units in the university. If desired, crude judgments of relative quality of programs can be made by examining emerging materials. If more refined approaches are deemed necessary, summaries and rating scales can be used to obtain them. However, no set of categories or procedures can bring about uniformity among programs which differ as markedly as those of a university. There is no common set of criteria that can be used for all programs, and there is no single set of standards which can be applied to them all. If local standards are developed, they will have to be prepared for groups of programs with high degree of similarity rather than for all.

Ideally, national standards based on measures derived from reference groups composed of corresponding programs around the country should be used but, for most programs, explicit standards are not available. And where such standards are available (as is the case for library holdings, AAUP salary recommendations, or accrediting agency specifications), there may be good reasons why these are not applicable to a particular institution. When resources are not available, an institution may have to decide on an acceptable level of program quality in terms of its own goals and service area.

Program evaluation is, of course, carried out for purposes other than writing program statements. One of the most common purposes is establishment of the prestige of the institution. This purpose is accommodated through reporting the degrees, honors, and awards of the faculty; through indicating the wide range of programs available; and through publicizing the accomplishments of outstanding alumni. Evaluation and widespread reporting of the quality of an institution constitute a means to growth both in stature and in size. The reportage attracts students and helps to increase the selectivity of students accepted by the institution. In a more responsible sense, such evaluation may help in determining the relevance of the programs to social needs and, thereby, in documenting the responsiveness of the institution to society.

Another purpose is particularly important in a period of stress, criticism, and waning support. In this case, program evaluation includes cost-benefit or cost effectiveness analysis to demonstrate, across various levels of government and private citizenry, the economic significance of higher education in terms of the beneficial long-term effects on development of our society and our economy. In applying financial analysis to evaluation, one need not attempt to claim perfection or even the highest possible degree of efficiency. Above all, in attempting to carry on evaluation of accomplishments and programs, an institution should not become so obsessed with presenting a success story that it fails to discern inadequacies and undertake to correct some of the weaknesses which are exposed.

An ultimate question is placement of responsibility for quality assessment. Obviously, this kind of assessment is a broad and complex operation. It requires faculty understanding, acceptance, and support; it also requires effective relationship to the budgeting process so that those who carry out program evaluation and conscientiously apply the results toward apparent improvement are advantaged rather than penalized by their efforts and results. Those who make improvements can be penalized because of the failure of others to do likewise. This exigency creates need for the quality control concept frequently used in industry.

In one sense, program evaluation is an academic audit parallel to the internal financial audit carried on in most institutions. Indeed, it is useful to think of the academic audit and the internal financial audit as parallel and occasionally closely interrelated activities if one is to get the fullest benefit from the assessment of program quality.

Bibliography

BLOOM, B. S. (Ed.), *Taxonomy of Educational Objectives, The Classification of Educational Goals, Handbook I: Cognitive Domain.* New York: Longmans, Green, 1956.

BLOOM, B. S., AND HASTINGS, J. T. *Handbook on Formative and Summative Evaluation of Student Learning.* New York: McGraw-Hill, 1970.

HARRIS, C. W. (Ed.), *Problems in Measuring Change.* Madison: University of Wisconsin Press, 1963.

HAWKRIDGE, D. G., CAMPEAU, P. L., AND TRICHET, P. K. *Preparing Evaluation Reports: A Guide for Authors,* AIR monograph 6. Pittsburgh: American Institutes for Research, 1970.

KRATHWOHL, D. R., BLOOM, B. S., AND MASIA, B. B. *Taxonomy of Educational Objectives, The Classification of Educational Goals, Handbook II: Affective Domain.* New York: McKay, 1964.

LAWRENCE, B., WEATHERSBY, G., AND PATTERSON, V. W. (Eds.), *Outputs of Higher Education: Their Identification, Measurement, and Evaluation.* Boulder: Western Interstate Commission on Higher Education, 1970.

National Society for the Study of Education. *Educational Evaluation: New Roles, New Means.* Chicago: National Society for the Study of Education, 1969.

SAUPE, J. L. "Assessing Program Quality." In C. FINCHER (Ed.), *The Challenge and Response of Institutional Research,* ninth annual forum. N.P.: Association for Institutional Research, 1970.

SUCHMAN, E. A. *Evaluative Research: Principles and Practice in Public Service and Social Action Programs.* New York: Russell Sage Foundation, 1967.

TYLER, R., GAGNE, R., AND SCRIVIN, M. *Perspectives of Curriculum Eval-*

uation, AERA monograph series on curriculum evaluation. Chicago: Rand McNally, 1967.

WEBB, E. J., AND OTHERS. *Unobtrusive Measures, Nonreactive Research in the Social Sciences.* Chicago: Rand McNally, 1966.

WITTROCK, M. C., AND WILEY, D. C. (Eds.) *The Evaluation of Instruction: Issues and Problems.* New York: Holt, Rinehart, and Winston, 1970.

CHAPTER 8

Developing and Using Information Systems

Thomas Mason

❧❧❧❧❧❧❧❧

A central function of institutional research is the translation of complex data generated in the operations of a college or university into comprehensible information to serve the policy-making, planning, and governing processes of the institution.

In this chapter, the role of institutional research in the development of institutional information systems is discussed, and current movements in the application of modern management information systems technology to the field of higher education are reviewed.

The distinction between data and information is significant; Rosove (1967, p. 3) has drawn it as follows: "Information is an aggregate of facts so organized or a datum so utilized as to be

173

knowledge or intelligence. Information is meaningful data, whereas data, as such, have no intrinsic meaning or significance. Information is the concept relating data which are otherwise meaningless to some specified human purpose or objective." (See also Mason, 1970.)

An information system functions at three levels: (1) Data collection, storage, and maintenance. Elemental data are recorded and stored as representations of the transactions, events, activities, and inventories occurring in the operations of an organization, such as a college or university. (2) Data retrieval and reporting. Operating reports are generated at various levels of summarization and at specified time intervals to display the current status of a set of transactions, activities, inventories, or populations. These reports tend to be highly detailed and are used primarily in the control and management of a particular operation or activity. (3) Analysis and evaluation. Management information is created when the detailed operational data are interrelated, analyzed, interpreted, and evaluated in reference to the policy issues and decision problems facing the institutional administration. Analysis, interpretation, and evaluation require assessment of historical trends; comparison of similar data among components of the institution and with other institutions; and prediction of the costs, consequences, and feasibility of alternative policy options.

Institutional research is primarily concerned with the third functional level of the information system—with the processes of integration, analysis, interpretation, and evaluation. However, as electronic technology has greatly enlarged the capacity for economically capturing, storing, retrieving, and manipulating data, the importance of carefully designed elemental data collection and reporting systems has become a focus of interest and concern. The institutional research officer is a major consumer of operating data. He is responsible for integrating and interrelating data from various components of the operating systems, for example, for linking financial, student, instructional program, and faculty data. He therefore has major interests in the content, coding, file structure, and design of systems for gathering elemental data and reporting operating data. As a major consumer, the institutional research officer should be a participant in the planning and design of the institution's information system.

In some cases, institutional research officers have assumed administrative responsibility for the institution's information system and data-processing operations; but, in general, such administrative responsibility for a complex, technical enterprise is detrimental to the interpretive overview that should be the central concern of institutional research. The institutional research officer is in a unique position to see and understand the interrelationships between the various operating sectors—finance, student records, personnel, and facilities—that contribute basic data to information systems. Because of his position, he may take the lead in planning and coordination of information systems development for the institution, but the technical implementation of such a system probably should rest with others.

Uses of Information

Ideally, the design of an information system for a college or university should begin with a conceptualization of the decision-making processes at various levels of institutional administration. Who makes what kinds of decisions? What kinds of information do they need to assess decision-making options?

In reality, however, the decision-making and policy-forming processes, even in a relatively small college, are so complex, the numbers of institutional decisions so manifold, and the processes of decision-making so fluid that establishing a comprehensive description of decision-making processes is extremely difficult. Furthermore, the kinds of questions raised are constantly changing as new issues emerge. Information developed for one series of decision problems or policy issues may not be relevant when a new set of issues emerges. Nevertheless, the basic processes and operations of the college or university are organized and ordered into recurrent and regular cycles that require the continuity and consistency of information over time. It is in these regular cycles of policy development that the foundations of a computer-based information system may be built.

The most common and perhaps significant process of this type is the budget-making cycle. If the institution's budget functions as a short-range plan reflecting resource allocation decisions and policies, it comprehends and touches upon nearly every facet of institutional life in one degree or another. The budget-making cycle provides an excellent example of the complexity of planning an information system.

Typically, the budget cycle begins with the formulation of expected budget requirements for a fiscal year one, two, or even three years in advance. Usually the first question asked is: how many and what kinds of students will the institution serve in the projected fiscal year? Enrollment projections and their modification in terms of policy considerations are the starting point. The making of enrollment projections, frequently a responsibility of the institutional research officer, usually starts with a set of historical data regarding change over time of student demands on the institution. Extrapolations of historical enrollment flow by entry, and persistency of various classifications of students in the institution usually points up a series of policy issues and information requirements. How many qualified applicants can be expected? Do admissions policies need to be changed in the light of objectives such as increasing educational opportunities for minority and educationally disadvantaged groups? Are retention rates likely to change or to remain constant?

Frequently an initial set of enrollment projections leads to a revision of projected policies. For example, an analysis of revenue-cost relationships may suggest the desirability of expanding enrollment. After several iterations and revisions in the shaping of enrollment policy, a set of budget enrollment targets emerges. This leads to another series of informational requirements: what changes in course load distributions are likely to occur if the enrollment mix is changed? Changes in curriculum requirements, new program offerings, and shifts in student course demand may significantly affect the distribution of predicted resources. For example, many institutions in recent years have abandoned freshman English requirements and modified foreign language requirements, leading to a redistribution of course loads. The most difficult kinds of forecasting problems pertain to predicting consequences of shifts in student demand or changes in academic policies or programs. In many institutions a recent shift in student demand toward the social sciences, humanities, and arts has caused imbalances in the distribution of faculty resources which require time to modify. Some judgment has to be made of the impact of these changes, and the institutional research office frequently is called upon to provide historical information about course load, class size, and teaching load distributions as bases for judgment.

The conversion of projected teaching loads into faculty requirements involves review of instructional load policies and of the use of faculty time for the other programs and functions of the institution. Historical review of faculty course loads and comparison of teaching loads with other institutions may be required if some change in policy is contemplated. Typically, some set of norms on the direct teaching load of full-time faculty is used in making budgetary projections. These may be expressed as number of courses taught, credit hours of courses taught, contact hours of courses taught, or student credit hours per full-time-equivalent faculty. More frequently, however, simple student-to-faculty ratios obscure their component variables of teaching load and class size and leave it to the reader to search out the variations between subject fields and levels of instruction.

When a projected faculty requirement is derived for the given enrollment level and mix of the budget year, institutional officers must make some judgment as to whether anticipated resources can be expected to provide for it. If it does not appear that the projected faculty size can be realized, adjustments may be made either by increasing teaching loads or by reducing the projected enrollment size in the extent that control is possible. Neither of these alternatives, in fact, is easily controllable. Conversion of projected faculty requirements to dollar costs brings into play the need for comparative salary data in order to reach decisions about faculty salary levels. Interinstitutional comparison of faculty salaries is one of the most common demands on institutional research.

The foregoing example of the budget-making process has been carried far enough to illustrate the potential range and diversity of information desirable to aid in policy-making processes. Many more factors, of course, have to be brought into play, such as support staff, supply and expense, administrative costs, and physical plant costs. All of these, in themselves, invoke needs for a wide range of information and for analytical evaluation.

The nature and formality of information requirements varies with the size of the institution or, in larger institutions, with various levels of decision-making. In the smaller college or at the department level in a larger institution, the information flow is more informal and much more related to personal considerations. The department chairman is concerned with improving the status of the individuals that make up his faculty and with the prospects for recruiting additional faculty. In building his budget request, he needs information on planned enrollment size and expected loads on his department. He is concerned with implementing curriculum improvements. Frequently he advocates reduced teaching loads, lower class sizes, and, of course, increased support. Generally, the role of the department chairman in the budget-making process is that of an advocate (Dressel, Johnson, and Marcus, 1970, chap. 10).

The dean of a school or college has problems of a different order of magnitude. He faces the problems of justifying resource requirements and making resource allocations among a number of groups of faculty, departments, or divisions. The dean must have a grasp of the interrelationships between the various components of the programs under his jurisdiction and must judge the ways in which program changes in the projected budget year are likely to impact the various components. Although the information he needs is at a higher level of generalization, the dean frequently must deal with the detailed characteristics of each department or division program. He, too, must utilize a great deal of informal, personal information in making his judgments and in building the case for his resource requirements.

At the executive level of the institution, the chief academic officer and his colleagues start with an institutionwide point of view. They must evaluate the resource possibilities of the institution in the projected budget year. It is at this level that more formalized statistical data and analytical research are heavily utilized. As Russell (1967, p. 26) has pointed out: "An able executive will already be in possession of a considerable fund of information about any situation in which he is called upon to make a decision. But there is always the possibility that he may not have *all* the facts before him, and that some of his information may be unfounded or out of date. This is where institutional research comes into the decision-making picture." (See also Mason, 1967, for a commentary on Russell's paper.)

As the pace of change in higher education has accelerated and as institutions have grown more complex, the institutional research function has become more highly organized. The institutional research analyst may be viewed as an extension of the eyes, ears, and minds of the responsible officers of the university or college. Perhaps one of the more significant differences between the institutional researcher and those more heavily engaged in basic research in higher education is that the institutional research officer must operate as an integral although, hopefully, objective arm of the policy-making agents of the institution.

As a policy decision is taking shape, the information sought includes historical comparisons, comparisons with other institutions, established precedent, and the projected consequences of alternative policy approaches. The task of the analyst as a staff aid to the policy-forming agencies is primarily the ordering of objective information bearing on the decision problem. However, the task is not merely to convert data into information by integrating hard data about various particular functions into quantitative analyses and projections; the analyst must add a significant store of qualitative information not only about the issue at hand but also about the extremely complex political-social environment in which he is operating. In other words, he must add intelligent judgment to the harder sources of information we ordinarily think of as being produced in an organized management information system. The demand and craving for rational, objective information is his primary concern. He must sort out, from the massive complexity of events, transactions inventories, and histories, the meaningful relationships that bear on the issue at hand.

The role of the analyst is to help evaluate the context and content within which a decision will be shaped. He cannot assess all possible alternatives. He must quickly reduce the problem to the critical areas of conflicting possibilities. His evaluation of the unresolved areas of decision should operate within the range of values most significant in the decision context. He seeks whatever relevant data are available, assesses them in terms of the qualitative preferences prevailing in the policy-making environment, and builds an analysis using assumptions (clearly stated as such) where hard information is not available. The review of the assumptions as well as the results by the policy-making group provides the focus for the discussion and evaluation that lead to the agreement that becomes the decision.

Dissatisfaction with tenuous assumptions and unsubstantiated judgments can lead to constant demand for more and more hard information. As information problems recur, the analyst may be in the best position to identify a need for systematically recording some kind of data not currently being generated by an operational process. At this point he needs to take the responsibility for initiating consideration of an extension of the elemental data base to include the data needed for analysis.

As more sophisticated analytic methods are applied in colleges and universities, the need for new kinds of data to be generated and recorded (preferably in machine-readable form) becomes more pronounced. The various approaches to analysis, evaluation, and prediction coming into use in modern management can have significant influence on structuring the computer-based information system of the institution.

Structure and Analysis

Systems analysis and operations research, which were given their primary impetus by the application of scientific method and mathematical models to war and defense operations and planning, have had a profound impact on the emergence of contemporary management science. The application of these new techniques to higher education planning and management is still in its infancy but, in spite of its experimental stage of development, the movement to introduce the modern management science syndrome into the administration of higher education is having a powerful impact. The entire effort has been greatly stimulated by the rapid emergence of sophisticated computer technology, which permits the merging and synthesis of large masses of data and the manipulation of these data for analysis and prediction.

Much analysis, however, still is elementary and as old as human logic and rationality. As with all science, the analysis of a complex problem begins with an attempt to define that problem in concrete, operational terms. Many problems, if data reflecting the relevant components are available, are adequately informed by the relatively simple methods of tabulation, ordering, and summarization of data and by elementary descriptive statistics. However, in more cases than not, the data simply are not there at the outset; and the analyst is faced with the alternatives of constructing hypothetical substitutes to get around the absence of data or beginning the arduous and time-consuming task of digging out data from old records or dispersed sources that are not retrievable in machine-readable form.

Early data-processing procedures involved the continuous updating of card or tape files which entailed constant destruction of historical data. The data originally recorded on the cards may have been transcribed onto paper transcripts, personnel records, or financial reports and never conserved as machine-retrievable historical records. In cases where this has happened, historical analysis is greatly hindered. If, for example, a thorough analysis of the flow of students over time, with observations of attrition and retention rates, or academic performance of students of various characteristics were sought, six to eight years of data would have to be reconstructed from student transcripts. If a change in faculty tenure policy were being contemplated, historical data on the effects of current policy on faculty retention and turnover would have to be reconstructed from scratch.

Sometimes the available data are recorded in aggregates or in derived data elements which obscure the original elemental components. For example, the student credit hours generated in various subjects and at various levels may be recorded carefully over the years, but student course loads and trends in total credit hour consumption of courses and the distribution of enrollment (class sizes) —the component elements of the student credit hour construct— may have long since been lost and may not be reproducible without great effort.

The absence of complete data, especially in the case of a new and unique kind of problem, calls for the application of statistical sampling methods and for the approach of operations research which is designed to increase the rationality of decision-making in cases where information is absent and predictability is highly uncertain. One definition of operations research highly favored among its practitioners states that "operations research is the art of giving bad answers to problems to which otherwise worse answers are given" (Saaty, 1959, p. 3). A tentative search for a solution to a decision problem in operations research leads, at least, to more coherent definition of the essential data which should be built into the operating data system.

The development of computer simulation models has been one of the more exciting outgrowths of the emergence of operations research, systems analysis, and modern computing technology. In their applications of models to higher education, the work of Judy and Levine at Toronto, Herman Koenig and associates at Michigan State, and George Weathersby at the University of California has attracted widespread attention (Minter and Lawrence, 1969).

All of these studies reveal gross deficiencies in the kinds of machine-retrievable information used to drive models. As the review of the WICHE Planning and Management Systems program later in this chapter indicates, models are having and can have a major influence on the shape and content of the data base underlying development of an institutional management information system. The cost of developing a data base adequate to driving simulation models frequently appears to be prohibitive. At the very least, a great deal of time and effort is needed to reconstruct the data inputs required to drive them. However one benefit of the painful model preparation process is the capacity to subsequently use models to do work such as evaluating the information and data needs more cogently and judging the value of collecting, conserving, and utilizing certain kinds of data in the analytical process.

The institutional research analyst who is investigating and evaluating the use and utility of models should be in a position to judge the availability of data, the problems of developing data not currently available in retrievable form, and the potential costs of developing such data. To the extent that new management science techniques are likely to be adopted and utilized in colleges and universities, they serve as significant organizing inputs to the structure and design of a comprehensive computer-based management information system.

One of the major problems of any comprehensive management information system design is collecting data for which the use does not merit the cost of collection, storage, and potential retrieval.

It is almost impossible to judge what data of those generated in the day-to-day transactions and activities of the institution may be important at some future time. It is simply not feasible to collect all kinds of data in every possible form although this is very likely to be the result if an attempt is made to satisfy everyone. The analytic methods used by the institutional research analyst can help to identify priorities in the types of data that are most important for administrative decisions requiring interpreted management information. This judgment must come from experience in interpretation and evaluation, in evaluation of alternative goals, and in observation of the interplay of goals, objectives, and values with the decision- and policy-making processes of the institution, and thus from an understanding of the overall nature of the decision process of a college or university.

Interpretation and Evaluation

The creation of a comprehensive data base containing all the essential data elements reflecting the operations of an institution is the dream of most institutional researchers. The hazard of a rich data base is that it will produce large masses of data that cannot be communicated effectively into the decision-making processes without careful selection, summarization, and interpretation. The reduction of data into selective indicators of trends and relationships requires analytic interpretation of relevance and meaning in terms of a given decision problem. This means that the institutional research analyst must fully understand the nature and context of the issue or problem in order to select the appropriate data and to frame his analysis appropriately.

One of the fundamental tools of interpretation is comparison. By itself, the fact that 580 student credit hours were taught in the academic year by each full-time-equivalent instructor in English has little meaning except in reference to comparable indicators in other subjects within the institution. The figure may then indicate that loads in English are higher or lower than in other fields of comparable structure. More meaning is added if the figure is related to prior history, indicating that English teaching loads have gone up or down in recent years. Even more interpretive satisfaction is gained if comparison, on the same basis, can be made with English departments in other, similar institutions—a most difficult comparison to secure.

Frequently, the interpretation of a derived, composite indicator, such as student credit hours per FTE instructor, requires that it be analyzed in terms of its component parts. English may have the same number of student credit hours per FTE as history, but analysis may show that English has a higher teaching load in terms of credit hours taught in smaller classes. Further investigation may show that the reason for a higher average teaching load in English is the teaching by some instructors, of two or more sections of the same course. The analyst (or others participating in the decision problem) may interpret the teaching loads as qualitatively equivalent. Otherwise, an even more detailed investigation may be required to evaluate the distribution of individual faculty loads and the reasons for variation in class size. This, in turn, may invoke other qualitative considerations of equity regarding the allocation of faculty resources.

The foregoing example suggests the interplay between quantitative data and qualitative evaluation that is essential in the translation of data into information. It also points up the essential characteristic of an information system—that data must be capable of summarization into general indicators but, in many instances (when an issue or question about their meaning arises), the general indicators must be broken down into their elemental components. Summary and aggregation measures—essential for the reduction of masses of elemental data to comprehensible levels—must be structured to reveal, through comparison, significant differences. The explanation of these differences, however, often requires disaggregation back to basic data elements. The information system must be designed to permit in-depth analysis when issues or questions arise regarding the interpretation of general information.

The process of translating data into information sometimes involves the art of making assumptions. Only limited amounts of hard, quantitative data can be captured and recorded economically in a basic data system. Many factors important to a given decision problem lie in an as-yet-unrecorded future; and many dimensions are of a subjective or qualitative nature. As a result, interpretation and evaluation must rely on inferences and assumptions based on judgment and experienced intuition. The analyst, in communicating his evaluation of a problem, is supposed to identify and state such assumptions as explicitly as possible. The decision makers can then judge from their own experience the validity they will grant to the assumptions, modifying them if necessary.

Frequently disagreement over assumptions will lead (time and resources permitting) to special research into the issue to secure more data, more opinions and attitudes, or comparative information to provide a stronger basis for a given assumption. Often, this process will point up the need to record certain kinds of basic data in the course of operating procedures. An illustration involves the identification of ethnic background of students, faculty, and staff. Most institutions in the past were precluded, by law or policy, from asking and recording race or ethnic origin. The Civil Rights Act of 1964 and the growth of educational opportunity programs for minority students at last forced institutions to seek information on ethnic origin. Initially, gross assumptions had to be made. Then, to avoid the older legal restrictions, voluntary surveys asking students to record their racial origins were tried. Obvious inaccuracies (for example, and unlikely number of American Indian responses) and incompleteness resulted. Since then, with considerable concern over the conflicting legal requirements and the problems of security, many institutions have appeared to be planning to make race or ethnic origin a data element in student and staff records.

At the same time, near-violent controversies have accompanied the development of minority educational opportunity programs. During the more peaceful deliberations, hard data are sought on how many of what kinds of minority students are in the institution or are being recruited. Evaluation of programs requires that the students in them be identified. Many institutions have established as goals recruitment of certain portions of their student bodies from minority groups. Attrition rates have to be estimated to determine recruitment quotas. In the face of these issues, unverified estimates or assumptions are not satisfactory, and hard data are demanded, at least to settle quarrels over how many of what kind. A new kind of data element must be added to the system, and procedures for collecting, securing, and analyzing the data on minority populations and programs must be established.

Among the most important uses of assumptions are the estimation of the probability that some future state of affairs will occur and the evaluation of the desirability of that future condition. These uses of assumptions are the foundation of planning. Most decisions need to be evaluated in terms of possible future consequences. A single assumption about the possibilities of future states or consequences usually needs to be settled upon to make a decision or to agree on a course of action toward a goal, but the analysis and evaluation prior to a decision often must assess a number of alternative possibilities and attempt to estimate the costs and consequences of the alternatives.

The judgment of future probabilities and the evaluation of alternatives depend heavily on both historical and current data. Projection of the future usually is based on extrapolation of past trends; modifications reflect desired or expected changes. Building on information about past trends and existing conditions, the analyst seeks to find the relationships between component factors of the system he is working with by which he can evaluate the effects of future changes. For example, if the institution expects an increase in transfer admissions from community colleges and plans to hold admissions of entering freshmen constant, the analyst may predict changes in instructional costs and space requirements due to a higher proportion of upper-level students. Changes in the relationships may be hypothesized on the basis of alternative possibilities, and an evaluation of the alternatives may be made. The point is that analysis and evaluation usually must be grounded in the reality of current relationships derived from the institution's data base. Current relationships often are the only basis for judging an uncertain future.

To the extent that institutional goals and objectives are explicit and reasonably operational (which they rarely are), they serve to select and specify the alternatives to be considered. More often than not, however, consensus on goals and objectives relating to the problem has not been achieved. The analyst must be able to detect the general tendency in the policy-making environment in order to define the problem and select a manageable range of alternative assumptions. As the decision makers judge the assumptions he has made and arrive at a conclusion, they are implicitly accepting some set of assumptions as goals. In the process, the prevailing values in the decision environment become more evident. This kind of information, perhaps better called intelligence, is vital in the processes of institutional research if research is to effectively serve the governance of the institution. Intelligence items cannot be recorded in electromagnetic images for manipulation on a computer, but they are vital in translating data into information. A major and most critical part of an institutional information system is this kind of intelligence; but it depends, to an increasing extent, upon the development of a comprehensive data base for factual information.

Systems Design

The foregoing discussion has emphasized the function of institutional research in the translation of data into information needed in processes for developing the policies of a college or university. As the processes become more formalized in order to span larger organizational systems, the demand for quantified data increases. Communication in a large, diversified organizational system transcends the interpersonal subjectivity of a smaller group and depends more upon impersonal, objective data. The pluralistic nature of an academic community, although it is sustained and moved by a set of common purposes and unmeasurable values, is governed primarily through the allocation of resources. Resources can be quantified and, as the scale of the institution broadens, quantitative data become more essential to the control and management of resources.

In greatly expanding the capability of recording, storing, retrieving, and utilizing quantitative data, the revolution of computer technology has also expanded the dependence of decision-making processes on hard data. Accompained by the chaos typical of all revolutions, the computer has markedly changed the nature of higher education management in ways not yet fully understood, yet alone controlled (Rourke and Brooks, 1966; Caffrey and Mosmann, 1967). The promise and potential of a comprehensive data base capturing the recordable transactions, activities, and inventories of the institution's operations increase the reliance of decision makers on quantitative data. Sometimes, when issues involve essential values behind university functions, overreliance on quantitative data may actually be harmful but, in many cases, the resolution of policy issues can be expedited by availability of measurable facts. The demand for hard evidence as background for the shaping of resource allocation policy has been a major factor in the growth of institutional research.

As the earlier sections of this chapter have emphasized, the role of the institutional researcher in the organization, interpretation, and evaluation of data gives him a unique ability to participate in the design and development of an integrated information system. He uses all the operating data systems—student, financial, and personnel records—as sources of much of his research data. Since much institutional research involves the relationships between programs and resources, he must be able to integrate data from different operating systems with additional data collected in special studies. He should have an overview of all the operations of the institution and an understanding of their interaction.

The institutional research officer is concerned with the structure and content of the basic operating data systems—with the definition of data elements, the classification of data categories, the coding of recorded attributes, and the timing of data collection. Special attention must be paid to the data elements and coding by which different files can be linked together. For example, analysis of instructional costs would involve linking student course enrollment data with course attributes and characteristics, with personnel information on the attributes of instructors and with financial data. Consistency and continuity of the information system over time is of major concern to the institutional researcher because of his heavy reliance on historical data. Since changes are necessary and desirable from time to time, historical comparability is a special problem. While the institutional research officer cannot be involved in all the complex details and technical problems of systems development and programming, he should be consulted in the determination of the content and structure when a new system is being designed or when changes of existing systems are planned. In many cases, an officer responsible for an operating data system—the registrar, finance officer, or personnel officer—does not need, for his own purposes, certain data essential to institutional research; yet the data can be most appropriately recorded and processed in the course of routine record keeping. Other data not of direct concern to the operating officer may be extremely significant to the general institutional management, and the institutional research officer may be in the best position to identify these types of data and to insist that they are also included in the operating systems.

How much of the basic data needed by institutional research can be extracted from the operating systems? The institutional research office frequently must develop a set of integrated data files of its own. For example, at the University of Colorado the office of institutional research develops and maintains a set of files in which selected data obtained from a variety of operating systems are utilized along with supplementary data and special coding. One of the files contains combined course information. The original operating files contain the identification of each course and section, a breakdown of the enrollment in the course by level of student, the credit hour values of the course, and the time and place in which the course is scheduled. For each course, the office of research adds the instructor and his rank; a series of classification codes denoting department, school, or college; a coding from the Office of Education's *Taxonomy of Instructional Programs;* and a weekly contact hour value for each section. This file also contains an allocation of the instructor's salary and full-time equivalency. From the integrated record on each course, a diverse series of analytic reports are generated on instructional loads, salary allocations, class size distributions, faculty teaching load, unit costs, and instructional space utilization. Files containing student attributes and faculty characteristics also are maintained by the office for its continuing studies and for the extraction of data on specialized inquiries from national, state, and institutional agencies. These files permit the analysis of particular aspects of the instructional program and also form the basis for a comprehensive course load forecasting model. Much of the reporting to state and federal agencies is generated from these integrated institutional research data files.

In the process of linking data from different operations, the institutional research office frequently identifies inconsistencies in coding and must work with the operating officers to resolve such problems. If the building space inventory file contains building and room number codes which do not coincide with those used in the schedule of classes, the research office may have to construct a reference table to link the two files, or it may work with several of the officers to get the coding of the files on a common basis.

One of the major problems in developing an integrated information system is the fact that the various operations, in the development of their particular data systems, work independently of one another. Use of different programmers and systems approaches or development of systems at different times with different personnel can result in a hodgepodge of systems which inhibits creative integration of management information. Many institutions have centralized development and operation of their information systems, forming a single office of administrative systems where systems analysts and programmers are grouped in one agency serving all users. Chaney reports that while this sometimes has created problems of responsibility and many users are dissatisfied with their loss of control over their own systems, improved coordination of data systems can be achieved (Chaney, 1969a). (See also Chaney, 1969b.) The organization of advisory committees to oversee and coordinate the development of computer systems and to assist in the setting of priorities on systems and on systems development has become a common practice. The institutional research office can play a major role in systems coordinating groups by defining and explaining interrelationships among the various operations that contribute data.

Uses and Misuses of the Computer

The ability to store, retrieve, and manipulate by computer the large quantities of data generated in operating processes has extended the capacity of institutional research to provide a wider range of information, analyses, and projections. The comprehensive simulation models currently being developed would not be possible without the computer. Where only limited sampling and compilation of data were possible before the advent of sophisticated technology, much more detail can now be generated. Whole populations or the entire span of a given institutional operation can be covered.

The advent of the computer has not been without its disadvantages. The ability to use it has lagged far behind the technological capability of data processing. Frequently computer capability has been oversold and underutilized. Some data collected at considerable cost could have been more simply processed by hand or more economically acquired by sampling.

In some cases, processing of data by computer can lead to loss of understanding. When an analyst has to work directly in the environment in which the data are generated, he has a much better comprehension of the meaning, limitations, and significance of the data and of the qualifications that must be imposed on quantitative values. Black-box computing without adequate control checks can lead to grossly erroneous information. A programming error may cause dropping of records or miscalculation of some value and, without laborious checking against original records, there may be no way of knowing that the output is incorrect.

Electronic data processing systems require rigorous precision and uniformity in the structure, format, and coding of input data, and the programming of the computer requires precise logical definition of the operations to be performed. Rigor and precision do not guarantee accuracy or truthfulness. As the common saying in the data-processing business goes, "Dirty data in, dirty data out." Yet people seem willing to attribute a curious credibility to the output of the computer. When the user of the data must work with a programmer who does not fully understand the nature of the data or the relationships to be manipulated, much time, effort, and expense can be wasted. Careful evaluation should be made before the expense of programming a particular study on the computer is undertaken.

Institutional research studies often involve searches through original records, construction of tallies from lists, and extraction of information from operating reports. As has been argued earlier in this chapter, much of the information created by institutional research cannot be quantified or computerized for it involves communication of subjective values and evaluation of meaning. Sometimes meaning can be perceived and conveyed more effectively with a limited amount of selected data than with a large and complex mass of data such as the computer is all too capable of generating.

One of the promising and exciting aspects of computer technology is the potential for direct interaction between the analyst and the computer by computer terminal. Time-sharing systems, although still in their infancy and expensive to employ, permit on-line retrieval of data from machine-readable files; with the use of user-oriented languages, interactive manipulation of the data by the analyst becomes more immediate. The potential development of simulation models, which permit direct intervention for altering variables and obtaining a readout of the impact of the change on control variables, attracts much attention from institutional researchers. Such models and the accompanying technology required to drive them are expensive and limited in terms of what they can do, and this has restricted their use. Nevertheless, the alluring promise of on-line interaction with a comprehensive computer-based information system is a favorite topic of discussion among institutional researchers. The development of such systems has even become a major activity of some institutional research offices. (See the series of papers on the topic: "Synthetic Output by Simulation," 1968.)

Progress in Systems Development

As computing technology has evolved over the past twenty years, institutional administrators, registrars, business officers, and researchers have actively engaged in applying it to the management and operations of their institutions. The College and University Machine Records Conference was established in 1956 as an annual forum for the exchange of ideas, experience, problems, and dreams. The programs of the American Association of Collegiate Registrars and Admissions Officers, the National Association of College and University Business Officers, and the Association for Institutional Research have been substantially devoted to papers and discussions of information systems. Rourke and Brooks (1966, chap. 2) place heavy emphasis on the role of the computer in contributing to a managerial revolution.

A landmark study, under the leadership of the Reverend R.J. Henle of St. Louis University and jointly sponsored by the National Science Foundation and the National Institutes of Health, was begun in 1961 "to devise and test simplified, adequate systems of measuring and reporting financial, manpower, facilities, research, and other activities in colleges and universities" (National Science Foundation, 1967). The Henle report, issued in 1965, outlined the conceptual structure for an integrated data system—then hopefully described as a total information system—that still stands as a good model of information system organization.

In spite of these efforts, the development of information systems continues to fall considerably short of the technological potential of computer science. The change from second- to third-generation computers carried with it serious disruption and breakdown in the conversion of older systems. All too often institutions investing thousands in machinery have failed to make adequate investment in the personnel required to effectively utilize it. The oversell of the computing marketeers has greatly exceeded the performance capability of most users.

In the meantime, a new and powerful motivation for the development of comprehensive information systems has been emerging—the growing restriction on resources which has applied to both public and private institutions. Concern for strengthening the planning and management of colleges and universities has become a national movement. The end of the higher-education honeymoon of the past two decades is manifested in growing public and political demands for accountability in expenditures and for proof of the effectiveness of higher education. Between 1956 and 1969, national expenditures from current institutional funds rose from four billion to over seventeen billion dollars, while higher education enrollments were merely doubling. At the same time, competition for public and private resources was increasing—more money was also needed for defense, welfare, health, primary and secondary education, urban redevelopment, environmental control, and many other programs. The emergence of student unrest, occasionally resulting in violence, invoked a public and political reaction that furnished additional incentive for the tightening of financial support to higher education. Both the student movement and the public reaction have raised fundamental questions about the basic values and practices of colleges and universities. The spread and strengthening of statewide higher education coordinating agencies during the 1960's was symptomatic of the growing visibility and impact of the burgeoning costs of higher education and of the ensuing political demand for control and accountability.

Merger of these phenomena with the growth of new ideas in management science, organizational control, program budgeting, and cost-benefit analysis has given power to the movement to rationalize—and bureaucratize—the planning and management of higher education at institutional, state, and national levels. As political awareness of higher education has become more acute, a national movement to establish systems of control and accountability over the pluralistic, diverse, and previously self-regulating (or unregulated) higher education complex has taken shape. The development of systematic management information systems designed to support massive reorganization of the governance of higher education has become an imperative in the eyes of institutional, state, and federal administrators concerned with justification and rationalization of resource allocation in higher education.

WICHE Management Information Systems Program

Perhaps the most remarkable representation of interest in higher education management information systems is the Planning and Management Systems Program of the Western Interstate Commission for Higher Education (WICHE). The WICHE program emerged on the crest of a movement to develop an integrated institutional-state-federal structure of uniform information about the operations, costs, and outputs of higher education. The program has become, in fact, a national focal point of efforts to devise common systems for information communication and to develop new techniques for planning and management analysis in higher education.

The Western Interstate Commission for Higher Education emerged in 1953 as an interstate compact to provide for the exchange of students (particularly in medicine, veterinary medicine, and dentistry) among states that had certain programs and those that did not. WICHE was modeled on the Southern Regional Education Board (SREB); in turn, the New England Board of Higher Education was established on the model of SREB and WICHE. Subsequently, WICHE grew into several areas of interstate cooperation and exchange—mental health, nursing, higher education administration, library programs, and the like. Annual College Self-Study Institutes, in cooperation with the Center for Research and Development in Higher Education at the University of California, were originally aimed at stimulating the development of institutional research.

Perhaps because the western states have traditionally exchanged information and practiced comparative institutional analysis, and perhaps because statewide planning and coordination for higher education had an early start in the West (where expenditures for higher education relative to population always have been high), the need for common, compatible data systems for the exchange of information among institutions was more acutely felt. WICHE provided a neutral but interested base for dialogue between institutions and the increasingly powerful state agencies—institutions sensitive to the prerogatives and autonomy claimed by the academic community and agencies charged with the coordination of higher education development and the development of rationalized state systems for planning, resource allocation, and evaluation of the needs of higher education on a statewide basis.

At the same time, the federal government, particularly through the Higher Education Facilities Act of 1963 and the subsequent general higher education support programs, gave added impetus to the formation of state coordinating agencies. The organization of the National Center for Educational Statistics in the Office of Education and the development of the Higher Education General Information Survey clarified the need for uniform, consistent, and compatible systems of reporting data through the states to the federal level (Drews and Drews, 1969, and the critique by Baughman, 1969).

After more than a year of study and discussion by an ad hoc design committee composed of institutional and state agency representatives, WICHE submitted to the Bureau of Research a proposal titled "A Regional Cooperative Project among Higher Education Institutions and Coordinating Agencies to Design, Develop, and Implement Management Information Systems and Data Bases including Common Uniform Data Elements." As originally conceived, the WICHE project would be developed and tested with the participation of about twenty institutions in the western states and subsequently expanded to a national level. However, when the program was funded and organized in late 1968 and 1969, the Illinois Board of Higher Education and the State University of New York were added as participants to provide additional systems of a scale comparable to California.

By July, 1969, when the full-time staff had been organized and had begun to refine and communicate the objectives of the program, a growing chorus of voices from the rest of the nation had deepened into a roaring demand for participation in the development of the program. It quickly became obvious that, under federal sponsorship, the WICHE Management Information Systems program could acquire the potential to structure a national system for reporting and evaluation of higher education programs and expenditures. The federal-state alliance that had developed under the various higher education acts of the early 1960's was currently restricting the pattern for public resource allocation to higher education. The WICHE program was perceived by institutions, by state agencies, and by the United States Office of Education as a critical center for the development of a uniform conventional vocabulary and of a set of procedures for the reporting of information about the loads, costs, and outputs of institutions of higher education.

Early in 1970, the WICHE Management Information Systems Program (renamed the Planning and Management Systems Program) "went national" and immediately confronted the staggering task of building national consensus on the terminology and analytical procedures by which data are organized and information is developed for reporting to state and federal agencies. By early 1971, the WICHE program seemed well on the way toward becoming a national center or laboratory for research, development, and training in the contemporary technology of higher education planning and management, particularly in respect to information systems and analytical modeling.

The goals of the WICHE Planning and Management Systems Program are described as follows (Lawrence, 1971):

The rapid growth in size and complexity and the current demands for better accountability in higher education have highlighted the need for effective application of new management techniques in colleges and universities. In response to this need, a large number of institutions and agencies of higher education, with the assistance of WICHE, are seeking to develop new management concepts and techniques designed to assist in improvement of higher education institutional management, improvement of statewide coordination, and improvement of decision-making processes at the highest national levels.

The WICHE Planning and Managing Systems Program concentrates on two aspects of higher education planning and management: (1) The development of a common communication base for the exchange and reporting of program and cost data on a comparable basis. This effort involves the standardization of definitions of basic data elements and of procedures for aggregating, reporting, and analyzing data elements. (2) The development of analytical tools and procedures designed to improve program-planning and resource-allocating processes in higher education.

The projects concerned with the development of a common communication base involve development of the following aids: (1) Data elements dictionaries are designed to specify and define basic data elements associated with students, staff, courses, finance, and facilities. (2) A program classification structure is designed to provide a common taxonomy of the programs and activities of colleges and universities. The general program categories are Instruction, Organized Research, Public Service, Academic Support (for example libraries and computing), Student Support, and Institutional Support (for example administration and physical plant). This classification structure incorporates the *Taxonomy of Instructional Programs,* which was prepared by WICHE for the National Center for Educational Statistics (NCES) for use in the Higher Education General Information Survey. (3) A personnel classification manual (also being developed for NCES) is designed to provide a standard classification scheme for higher-educational personnel. (4) Higher education finance manuals are intended to develop procedures for aggregating institutional financial data for reporting in the Higher Education General Information Survey. (5) Cost-finding principles are concerned with developing standard conventions for allocating all costs to specified programs within an institution. (This project is intended to lay the foundations for comparable exchange and reporting of program cost information.) (6) Information exchange procedures establish common methods for producing comparable information, particularly on costs of instruction and costs per unit of output (for example, per degree). (7) Faculty activity analysis procedures are aimed at developing standard methods for analyzing faculty assignments, activities, and effort and at establishing conventions for allocating faculty resources to institutional programs. (8) Input-output indicators are intended to provide a taxonomy of the outputs of higher education, possible measures of these outputs, and methods of evaluation. (9) Information systems design manuals are intended to develop guidelines for the design, installation, and operation of information systems in higher education.

The analytical tools and procedures for program planning and resource allocation developed or planned in the WICHE Planning and Management Systems Program include the following: (1) Resource requirements prediction models are a series of computer models showing relationships between programs and activities and the resources required to support them. (2) Student flow models are designed to simulate the progression of students through an institution for predicting the distribution of student loads within the programs of an institution. (A state-level student flow model is being contemplated to aid in predicting the distribution of students among institutions in a state.) (3) Higher education facilities planning and management manuals are designed to provide methods of estimating facilities requirements and to aid in the allocation of existing facilities. (4) Facilities costs and capital financing procedures are designed to provide bases for estimating capital investment and plant operation costs, for analyzing the trade-offs between capital expenditures and operating costs, and for allocating capital and plant operating costs to institutional programs. (5) A higher education national indicators survey is designed to develop indicators (similar to consumer price indicators) for examining the impact of federal programs on the income and expenditures of colleges and universities.

The WICHE program also expects to carry out special projects for small college systems, statewide planning systems, and departmental management systems. A major sector of the WICHE effort is a training program, employing seminars and specialized training materials, in higher education planning and management systems.

The major problem confronting the WICHE program is development at the national level of a basis for consensus on many definitions, concepts, and procedures involved in the various projects. As of early 1971, some six hundred individual institutions and boards or agencies representing hundreds more were signed up for the various levels of participation in the program. The organizational structure that has been established to maintain communication with this large and diverse constituency is as follows: a National Advisory Panel, representing higher education associations, professional organizations, and national and regional compacts, which serves as a general sounding board; an Executive Committee, which controls the basic policies of the program, determines priorities, and advises the program director; an Advisory Council composed of representatives of institutions and agencies that are committed to contributory participation in the program, which is a general forum for communication with the participants; and a Technical Council, which advises the program staff on technical priorities and oversees the coordination of the various projects. (Each project has a task force of specialists drawn from institutions and agencies who can provide expert advice and assistance in the development of a particular effort.)

In spite of the difficult problems presented by consensus building and by reconciliation of the conflict between institutional autonomy and the emerging state-federal systems of control, the WICHE program is well started in furthering the managerial revolution in higher education. If it is able to fulfill its goals by developing common systems for exchange, reporting, and analyzing information about the programs and costs of higher education, the WICHE Planning and Management Systems Program will greatly aid the field of institutional research in its role of translating data into information to serve the policy-forming, planning, and governing processes of colleges and universities.

Bibliography

BAUGHMAN, G. W. "Critque." In C. B. JOHNSON AND W. G. KATZEN-
MEYER (Eds.), *Management Information Systems in Higher Education: The State of the Art*. Durham, N.C.: Duke University Press, 1969.

CAFFREY, J., AND MOSMANN, C. *Computers on Campus*. Washington, D.C.: American Council on Education, 1967.

CHANEY, J. F. "Data Management and Interrelation Data Systems for Higher Education." In J. MINTER AND B. LAWRENCE (Eds.), *Management Information Systems: Their Development and Use in the Administration of Higher Education*. Boulder: Western Interstate Commission on Higher Education, 1969a.

CHANEY, J. F. "Organizing for Administrative Systems Analysis Data Processing." In C. B. JOHNSON AND W. G. KATZENMEYER (Eds.), *Management Information Systems in Higher Education: The State of the Art*. Durham, N.C.: Duke University Press, 1969b.

DRESSEL, P. L., JOHNSON, F. C., AND MARCUS, P. M. *The Confidence Crisis: An Analysis of University Departments*. San Francisco: Jossey-Bass, 1970.

DREWS, T., AND DREWS, S. "HEGIS: A Report on Status and Plans." In C. B. JOHNSON AND W. G. KATZENMEYER (Eds.), *Management Information Systems in Higher Education: The State of the Art*. Durham, N.C.: Duke University Press, 1969.

LAWRENCE, B. "The WICHE Planning and Management Systems Program: Its Nature, Scope, and Limitations." Unpublished Manuscript, 1971.

MASON, T. R. "The Role of Institutional Research in Decision Making." In G. N. DREWRY (Ed.), *The Instructional Process and Institutional Research*. Athens, Ga.: Association for Institutional Research, 1967.

MASON, T. R. "The Road from Data to Decision Making." In *Proceedings of the Fifteenth Annual College and University Machine Records Conference*, 1970.

MINTER, J., AND LAWRENCE, B. (Eds.), *Management Information Systems: Their Development and Use in the Administration of Higher Education*. Boulder: Western Interstate Commission on Higher Education, 1969.

National Science Foundation, *Systems for Measuring and Reporting the Resources and Activities of Colleges and Universities*. Washington, D.C., 1967.

ROSOVE, P. E. *Developing Computer-Based Information Systems*. New York: Wiley, 1967.

ROURKE, F. E., AND BROOKS, G. E. *The Managerial Revolution in Higher Education*. Baltimore: Johns Hopkins Press, 1966.

RUSSELL, J. D. "Decision Making in Higher Education." In G. N.

DREWRY (Ed.), *The Instructional Process and Institutional Research*. Athens, Ga.: Association for Institutional Research, 1967.

SAATY, T. L. *Mathematical Methods of Operations Research*. New York: McGraw-Hill, 1959.

"Synthetic Output by Simulation." In C. FINCHER (Ed.), *Institutional Research and Academic Outcomes*. Athens, Ga.: Association for Institutional Research, 1968.

CHAPTER 9

Allocating and Utilizing Resources

Donald C. Lelong

Ⅽ𝔇Ⅽ𝔇Ⅽ𝔇Ⅽ𝔇Ⅽ𝔇Ⅽ𝔇Ⅽ𝔇Ⅽ𝔇

In this chapter, the terms *allocation* and *utilization* are sometimes used almost interchangeably. Literally, allocation implies assignment for specific purposes while utilization implies expenditure. In practice, the allocation of resources often assumes corresponding utilization, and utilization often implies that there will be subsequent allocations. This chapter deals with the combination of resource assignments and expenditure. Concern with the combined process speaks to the strategy of getting more out of institutional resources.

Since allocation implies assignment, it describes procedures by which high priority programs or organizational units get the larger pieces of the budget pie and low priority units or endeavors get smaller pieces, or no budget at all. Many people, including students, quickly become enthusiastic about participating in institutional priority-setting and budget-allocating reviews because these occasions afford an opportunity to wield power in behalf of particular educational value judgments. Fewer are enthusiastic about examining the utilization of resources once the allocation decisions have been made. Examination of existing structures requires analysis of the efficiency with which the units are expending the resources already allocated to accomplish ends already agreed upon. It is a more tedious task, demanding greater competence in educational administration; those participating are likely to tread directly on the toes of resource managers. However, diligent evaluation of the processes of education is likely to free more resources than is careful review of educational priorities. Any thorough analysis of institutional resources should cover both the allocation process and the utilization process as two aspects of the same objective.

Need for Efficiency

If higher learning symbolizes one of the better things in life, and if indeed the best things in life were free, then this book would not need a chapter on resource allocation and utilization. In fact, if this book had been written before the mid-sixties it probably would not have included a separate chapter on the subject. Why, overnight in the life span of higher education, have those in charge become so concerned about efficiency[1] in the allocation of institutional resources? Why do university presidents and their lieutenants now commiserate so earnestly about the dire need for management information systems, program planning and budgeting systems, and resource allocation models? One might conclude that the basic problems of managing the men, materials, and money of higher education have somehow changed. Actually, while the problems are the same as they have always been, rapid expansion of higher education, the sheer magnitude of the current enterprise, rising costs, and grow-

---

[1] The term *efficiency* is defined throughout this chapter to describe a relationship between inputs and outputs—namely, maximum output for a given input or minimum input for a given output. Organization theorists have tended to redefine the word to mean something less than cost effectiveness, which is actually a synonym.

ing public insistence that higher education be held more strictly accountable have exerted unprecedented pressure upon institutional executives to get the most out of their resources. The pressure has, in effect, replaced many of the scholar-presidents of yesteryear with chief executives interested in the techniques of scientific management. It has made many unreplaced scholar-executives sensitive to the rumblings about inefficiency in higher education and has caused all executives to consider more deliberately their responsibilities for effective resource use.

Probably the most persuasive issue in convincing colleges and universities of the need to economize and the accompanying need to examine resource allocation was the public concern over rapidly climbing expenditures on higher education through the sixties. More recently that concern has been reinforced by pressing social demands in other areas. Several factors pushed expenditures upward. A large part of the rise can be accounted for by the growing numbers in attendance. The desirability of a college education has been accepted as an article of faith by millions of parents and potential students who have witnessed the economic and social advantages it can bring. In fact most American families expect their children to go to college whether or not the family possesses the necessary financial resources (Campbell and Eckerman, 1964, p. 29). Since the passage of the original GI Bill in 1944, when we made our commitment to the goal of mass higher education, enrollments in higher education have increased six-fold. In 1940, 16 per cent of our college-age population attended institutions of higher learning, and 678 million dollars were expended in their behalf. By 1960, 33 per cent of our youths were attending colleges and universities and the cost amounted to 5.6 billion dollars. By 1969, 44 per cent were enrolled at a cost of 19 billion dollars (American Council on Education, issue 1, 1970, p. 70.6 and issue 2, 1970, p. 70.106). These numbers reflect not only a larger and larger population in the college-age group but also a continuous increase in the percentage of that age group continuing their education beyond high school. With 44 per cent of the pertinent age group in post-high-school institutions, the United States has not yet come close to the goal of universal opportunity for higher education. Nevertheless the progress is dramatic, and increases in annual cost of higher education stemming from student numbers alone would give sufficient cause for close examination of the price we are paying.

Expanding enrollments are by no means the only source of increased expenditures, however. The cost of higher education on a per student basis has also jumped markedly since World War II. Again the causes are several. The knowledge explosion and the concomitant demand for scholarly research have reduced the supply of faculty talent available for classroom instruction. Together, burgeoning student numbers and exploding knowledge have driven up the price of faculty service more rapidly than other prices in our economy. The flight of Sputnik I in 1957 impressed upon humiliated and frightened national policy makers the significance of leading the race for new knowledge and the commitment to research which the race required. (Actually Sputnik only accentuated an emphasis dramatically illustrated by the explosion of the first atomic bomb more than a decade earlier.) Teacher-scholars both led and followed the billions of dollars which were channeled into research activity. Fast-moving frontiers of knowledge in virtually all academic disciplines required conscientious faculty to spend more of their professional lives keeping up with the field, with correspondingly less time left for classroom instruction. As one sociology professor of twenty years' experience put it, "When I joined the university, twelve credit hours per term was the standard teaching load in sociology. Now the standard load is six, and I am working harder than ever." Another academician claims that "it's really just a matter of time before most of us fall behind, try as we will to keep up with all of it." Exploding knowledge has also exploded the nonteaching work load of the professor and has reduced his time in the classroom even if he is not engaged in and paid by a formal research project. The fact that qualified faculty members have been in relatively short supply over most of the past two decades has also permitted them to reduce their teaching loads.

The demands of the research establishment and of expanding enrollments upon a relatively inadequate pool of faculty talent have combined to produce perhaps the most significant impact on cost-per-student statistics. During the decade of the sixties, faculty compensation across the country increased by 78 per cent (American Association of University Professors, 1961–1970). During the same period consumer prices increased 27 per cent (U.S. Department of Commerce, 1970a, p. 344, and 1970b, pp. 5–8), and average family income in the U.S. increased 68 per cent (U.S. Department of Commerce, Bureau of the Census, 1970, p. 3). Clearly, the increased price of faculty—the largest single item in educational budgets, often combined with a reduction in teaching load—represents a major cause of rising costs. Some economists argue that the increased price of faculty service is at least partly offset by gains in productivity, but the validity of this argument must be based on the quality aspect of productivity in view of reduced teaching loads.

A third cause of increased expenditures, at least in four-year institutions, has been the heavier enrollments in relatively high cost upper-division and graduate programs. These have grown disproportionately to enrollments in the less expensive lower-division programs. Just before World War II, graduate students constituted 7.8 per cent of those enrolled in our four-year colleges and universities. By 1955 the representation had increased to 10.2 per cent and by 1969 it had increased to 13.8 per cent (American Council on Education, issue 1, 1970, p. 70.5). A number of cost approximations and state funding formulas place the direct cost of master's-level instruction at something less than twice that of undergraduate instruction; the cost of Ph.D. instruction is reported to be approximately three and a half times that of undergraduate teaching on a full-time-student basis. In any event, both the cost weights and number weights of upper-division and graduate education have undoubtedly escalated the average-cost-per-student figure in four-year and graduate institutions.

When the effect of higher cost per student is regarded in terms of several million students who are struggling (or being carried along) through the process of higher education, it is small wonder that so many people want to hold college and university administrators more closely accountable. As Governor William G. Milliken (1970, p. 8) of Michigan observed, "People are increasingly demanding to know how their children are learning, what they are learning, and why they are being taught whatever they are being taught. They are very clearly saying at the ballot box that they will not support higher taxes for education unless they get the answers and get them soon." Though the Governor was referring primarily to public school education, his sentiment comes into sharp focus in the actions of state and federal legislative groups in their appropriations to higher education. Appropriations requests have had to compete vigorously not only with the war in Indo-China but with other surfacing national crises—needs to eliminate poverty, to create equal opportunity for all races, and to stem the debilitating pollution of our environment. As the sixties closed, the annual rate of increase in state appropriations to higher education was falling. Unqestionably colleges and universities have been under the gun to show and tell what they are accomplishing with the billions entrusted to them.

Academic administrators have other reasons, quite apart from outside pressures, for wanting new and better methods of studying the allocation and utilization of their institutional resources. The multiversities, universities, and many of the colleges and junior colleges of 1971 hardly resemble their parents of 1941. Nor do the styles required for their administration resemble those appropriate before and during World War II. The sheer size of many contemporary campuses, in terms of students, staff, and budget, calls for new methods of making resource allocation decisions. Unfortunately, but apparently of necessity, the new modes emphasize analysis rather than personal rapport. Thirty years ago a university president could know a large portion of his faculty personally; today that is physically impossible. He could also maintain firsthand knowledge of the problems, ambitions, and shortcomings of most academic departments. That also is now physically impossible; the size and complexity of the institution preclude it.

In the large- and even the medium-size university, as the locus of decision on a departmental issue moves from the department to its college to the central administration, the decision inevitably becomes based upon a less complete and less personal understanding of all the factors bearing upon it. Decision makers in a central administration simply do not have the capacity to know and understand all the details of each situation. In the absence of familiarity, choices tend to be based more on objectivized, quantitative criteria. The resource allocation process becomes dependent upon organized, formalized knowledge rather than on informal, personal understanding. Budget officers find that they need statistics on teaching loads, class sizes, course offerings, curricular enrollments, mix of faculty rank, and salary levels. Such analyses become indispensable because of the sheer magnitude and complexity of allocative decision-making.

Further emphasis on the need for a systematic approach to allocation problems is provided by the leveling of enrollments in institutions accustomed to continual growth. Private colleges and universities probably suffer less from nongrowing pains than do public institutions simply because most private schools passed through adolescence long ago. Public institutions have reared almost an entire generation of administrators under the blessings and condemnations of growth. Now these people are finding that growth cannot be taken for granted. Increasing demands for university services present problems in great variety but the problems are generally of a sort which educators welcome. They are termed challenges in the cause of greater service. So when dictums of the state coordinating board, the creation of neighboring institutions, or other circumstances choke off the enrollment growth of a university, it faces a greatly reduced range of administrative choices. Reduced choices are aptly described in the 1969–1975 Academic Plan of the Berkeley Campus of the University of California. The master plan of the University of California places a ceiling of 27,500 students on Berkeley campus enrollment:

The prospects facing the campus in the ensuing decade are in direct contrast to the conditions which have pertained in the 1950's and 1960's. During the next ten years, the growth of the graduate student body relative to the undergraduate student body will cease. Enrollments will be stabilized at all levels of instruction. . . . the budgets which sustain the programs of the academic departments . . . will also be stabilized. In large part, the further progress and development of the campus will be subject to the constraints imposed by an inelastic resource base. This prospect introduces a new dimension [into the allocation process]. Previous campus plans— and derivative decisions concerning educational priorities and resource allocations—have been based primarily on enrollment capacities. Increases in budgets have been correlated with enrollment growth. When actual enrollments in a particular area of study have exceeded the budget estimates, excess work loads have been absorbed by the faculties concerned. . . . When enrollments have declined, or when planned estimates have not been realized, it has proved possible to use the excess resources thus made available to initiate new programs, or to achieve desirable upgradings of programs, or reductions in class size. In the future such adjustments will be difficult to accommodate. Growth—or improvement—in one area will mean retrenchment in another. . . . the prospect for the 1970's is a condition of some inflexibility in which new programs are initiated only when existing programs are reduced or terminated, and new appointments are made only when budgeted faculty positions are released by retirements, resignations, or terminations [Regents of the University of California, 1969, p. 4].

In short, growth offers a good opportunity to correct miscalculations and many other administrative errors. But when the size of the budget stabilizes, no one gets a greater portion unless someone gets less; that fact alone is enough to make administrators look longingly toward efficiencies which might free existing resources for new uses.

Climate for Efficiency

Textbooks describe economics as the study of the allocation of scarce resources to maximize given ends. But economies are easier to effect in some situations than in others; in higher education they appear to be extraordinarily difficult. Both the external setting and the internal environment appear to work against decisive, expeditious action. Resource allocation in higher education has at least two dimensions: kinds of decisions, involving the principles on which allocations are made in this sector of the economy; and levels of decisions, pertaining to all higher education, to state systems, to individual institutions, or to departments within institutions.

Since money typically commands the use of human services and material goods, the filtering of money through the entire labyrinth of federal agencies, state systems, and specific colleges and universities demonstrates great deployment of human and material resources. Decisions which channel money, men, and materials through higher education differ in nature from decisions which allocate resources to and within most American organizations. In our free enterprise system the majority of productive organizations are profit-oriented. The forces which guide the use of resources are relatively simple, direct, and easy to interpret. Business firms receive funds in rather close and direct proportion to the quantity and quality of goods and services they furnish. Purchasers usually buy the same sorts of goods and services over and over again at reasonably frequent intervals. They gain considerable experience and knowledge concerning the best buys, and they direct their purchases to the suppliers who give them the most for their money. In our mobile age, the family head is even likely to buy several houses (typically the largest family acquisition) over the course of his lifetime. In any event, what is bought by private parties in the marketplace is usually purchased by those who are going to use it, and they derive all or nearly all of the benefits.

This is not so with funds that flow to higher education; the circumstances of resource allocation are quite different from those of the marketplace. Forces which directly determine the availability of resources to higher education are greater in number, indirect in their impact, and difficult to interpret and reconcile. A college education is purchased once in a lifetime; a substantial part of the cost is usually paid by other than the recipient of the education; the college is almost never selected on the basis of firsthand experience with its services; and the outcome of the exchange—the education of students—is judged to be of substantial value not only to the recipient but also to society at large. All of these circumstances tend to prescribe a loose, ambiguous, and tenuous connection between the quantity and quality of higher learning provided by a specific institution and funds made avaliable to it. Compare, for example, the degree of control a man has over that fraction of his federal income tax dollars ultimately finding its way to the state university where his son is enrolled with the control he has over monies intended to purchase a new automobile. Automobiles are clearly sold in the marketplace for the private use of those who acquire them. Education is not a marketplace phenomenon but a social phenomenon.

While we direct the allocation of resources in the private sector through dollar votes cast in favor of suppliers who give us the best performance, we direct much of the funding for higher education through the political ballot box. The Congress and state legislatures vote appropriations with some knowledge of the general needs of higher education but without knowledge of the needs of specific institutions or of the aspirations of individual students. To a modified extent, basic policy decisions about the support of higher education are made in a similar manner by the large philanthropic foundations. Even though money paid for tuition, room, and board represents direct payment for services rendered, audible and definitive feedback from students on the appropriateness of the institution's resource allocation represents a very recent phenomenon. It cannot and should not be ignored by institutional administrators, but the recently loud voice of the student population is likely to conflict with reactions and directions from public officials; those, in turn, may well be different from the wishes of parents, alumni, and other private benefactors. Overstatement this may be; nevertheless the signals given to educational administrators with respect to best deployment of resources probably come through much less clearly and less promptly than those given the business firm attempting to respond to the needs of its customers. In higher education we are not at all sure what we are getting for our money; we don't really seem to know what we want, or who should pay for it; and it is not even completely clear who *we* are.

Three levels of decision-making channel support to and within higher education enterprises. At the top are those decisions which distribute funds to higher education in general. The most significant of these are actions taken by Congress, state legislatures, and perhaps a few of the largest eleemosynary institutions. At this level colleges and universities compete for funding with highways, national security, public schools, welfare programs, and a host of other social needs. Below this layer are decisions which assign funds to specific institutions. Again governmental units and major religious and philanthropic organizations play key roles but, at this level, students, by deciding which college to attend, also have a decisive impact upon the resources available to specific colleges and universities. Through gifts, corporate and noncorporate business firms as well as alumni and other private donors often affect materially the welfare of their favorite citadels of learning. Finally, decisions within the institutions—by the president, vice-presidents, deans, and faculties—distribute available operating funds among programs and departments. Students also participate at least indirectly in this final allocation by choosing fields of study, taking more than normal course loads, or staying on for graduate work. Outside forces also play a significant role in the internal allocation process to the extent that such forces make policy decisions affecting institutional operations and to the extent that the university accepts funds to perform specific tasks. Legislatures appropriate generous amounts for the college of agriculture or the medical school while starving the liberal-arts college. Federal agencies furnish matching money for highway safety research or the training of professional social workers providing that the institution also supports these efforts. More than one wealthy alumnus has altered both the curriculum and the health of his alma mater's operating budget for decades through a generous gift designated for a narrowly restricted purpose. Obviously the executives of higher education must be vitally interested in all three levels of allocation; this chapter deals largely with the last because it is most germane to the responsibilities of institutional researchers.

The institutional setting within which citizens of the academic community divide scarce resources to maximize given ends defies description. While it is enormously frustrating to some men, it shapes and hones others into skillful entrepreneur-administrators. Though order seems only vaguely discernible behind the curious processes and personalities of academia, some characteristics of the environment in which allocation decisions are made can be at least partially described. An obvious problem is lack of incentive for faculty members to teach more students and the accompanying absence of incentive for students to economize on the use of faculty time.

Tuition and fees are usually levied as a lump sum for full-time students and by the credit hour for part-time students. Package pricing prevents the student from allocating his fee monies to get the most out of them. Once he has paid his fee, the full-time student can typically take from twelve to twenty credit hours per term. He can usurp much faculty time or require little. In effect he pays the same amount to sit in a lecture course of five hundred as in a seminar of five—though the institutional cost of the latter might be a hundred times the former. He has no way to register the cost-benefit relationship of these instructional modes as does the consumer in the marketplace. (The student might indicate on a course evaluation that he prefers the smaller seminar to the large lecture, but that preference would be stated without regard to cost.) If, instead, the student were faced with differential registration fees representing different modes of instruction for the same course, he might well select a low-cost large lecture as an optimum allocation for part of his funds, saving high-fee tutorials for subjects in which he was most interested or with which he experienced the most difficulty. Under present tuition-pricing systems, there is virtually no way for students' fees to influence the distribution of instructional funds (except with respect to disciplinary field of study) in accord with student assessment of costs and benefits. Once the student has paid his tuition, he is free to take all the instructional service he can absorb, and he has no reason to economize on institutional resources. The typical college fails to employ any sensitive and reliable mechanism to measure student cost-benefit assessments of institutional resource allocation.

On the other side of the instructional exchange stands the professor, with equally little incentive to maximize the output of his instruction. Neither his salary nor his promotion depends upon it. On the contrary, both depend primarily upon his scholarship and possibly upon how well he professes but rarely upon the numbers of students exposed to his wisdom. His dependencies often convince the faculty member, quite logically, that teaching large classes, especially many of them, is dysfunctional—particularly if those classes are filled primarily with undergraduates. On the graduate level, he could argue the dysfunction of enrolling large numbers of graduate students as well as the even greater dysfunction of actually graduating them. The academic department serves its own self-interest, so the argument goes, by enrolling large numbers of graduate students, devoting as much time to faculty research as possible, and placing its better Ph.D. recipients in the best universities. The purely pragmatic department might well keep large numbers of graduate students both to help on research projects and to make sure that its better candidates are thoroughly prepared for employment interviews by prestigious universities. While the incentives extended to faculties in recent years have produced a prodigious volume of research output, they have tended to create a monolithic standard for

Institutional Research in the University

success, requiring shifts in the historical allocation of faculty energies. The monolithic standard has not provided much incentive to serve well the ever-larger student population.

Aside from the recent history of higher education, the economics of production seem to be somewhat alien to the academic temperament. Most faculties view with indifference or distaste the idea that an institution of higher learning must be production-oriented. The impact of that attitude cannot be overestimated; it pervades the entire environment in which resource allocation decisions are made. Many choose the academic life because it affords opportunity to pursue one's own intellectual bent free from the restrictions of the time-clock, production-line world. They regard with passion the time-consuming, laborious, and exhaustive examinations of their chosen subjects, paying little attention to the energies expended or the number of students affected. If a professor thinks about academic output at all, he typically thinks of quality, not quantity. One outstanding lecture is worth a thousand poor ones; one penetrating paper in a prestigious journal is worth many of lesser insight. Department chairmen, deans, and, to some extent, presidents espouse similar values and priorities. Quality is the password. It brings prestige among peers, and that represents an intangible reward as important to faculty and administration as money. Case after case can be cited in which the faculty member has accepted a lower salary or rank in favor of membership in a department or institution of greater distinction. In fact, faculty salary levels in the lower ranks are often not very attractive in outstanding departments and universities. It is regarded as an honor for a young man's resumé to reflect work in such esteemed company. To talk about output in other than scholarly terms almost categorizes one as gauche; quality and its accompanying prestige have been the coin of the realm.

Both faculty and administration have assumed that high cost and high quality are inevitably linked in lockstep. After all, professors need a great deal of time to keep up with (or occasionally advance) the knowledge in their fields. In addition, the basic technology of education largely precludes unsupported increases in quantity without counteracting declines in quality. At least that hypothesis is commonly held. Small classes and low student-faculty ratios are jealously guarded as hallmarks of excellence by institutions which can afford them and are assiduously sought by those which cannot. As long as face-to-face verbal communication between teacher and student remains the preponderant means of instruction in higher education, faculties will undoubtedly continue to insist that cutting cost means cutting quality. Bowen (1968, pp. 12–13) speaks to this point:

At the root of cost pressures besetting all educational institutions is the nature of their technology. . . . To be sure, educational institutions have benefited from some technological innovations. . . . But these developments have been sporadic and have had little direct effect on the productivity of the individual faculty member, who is, if you will, the principal "labor input" in the educational process. The microphone (or public address system) is perhaps the most important technological development which has affected the productivity of the teacher since the invention of the printing press, and no one would claim that this device has had an effect on output per man-hour in the field of education which is at all comparable to the effects of the major technological innovations in other sectors of the economy.

Among the most influential forces in the institutional setting are those which stem from the organizational structure and politics of resource allocation. Unlike the employees of most organizations, the majority of employees in a college or university are professionals of almost notorious independence of mind, who share with the administration major policy-making responsibilities. Faculty authority and responsibility in areas such as admissions, related academic standards, and curriculum formulation do not represent mere delegation of authority by the administration for the sake of decentralized management but evidence authority vested in the faculty either through the by-laws of the institution or through a long history of what might be termed academic common law. This means that departmental and college faculty bodies can and often do make decisions which have profound impact on the allocation of institutional resources—without analysis or even deliberate consideration of that impact. As any observer of faculty meetings well knows, faculty approval of a new interdisciplinary major in environmental studies is likely to be given with next to no knowledge of where the new student majors will come from, how existing programs and class sizes will be affected, or how the pattern of institutional program funding will be altered. These problems are regarded as of secondary importance and as the proper responsibility of the administration. After venturing that schools of social work tend to operate more like families than like production processes, one writer offers the following view of decision-making by faculties: "Decision-making authority is diffuse and uncertain. Although some commonly accepted school or university goals and objectives do exist, there appear to be none which effectively guide the decisions made by faculty. Inputs are unmeasured and unknown. The idea that scarce educational resources (or dollars) should not be wasted is not one which appears to play a large role in faculty deliberations" (U.S. Departments of Health, Education, and Welfare, Social and Rehabilitation Service, 1970, p. xiii).

Not only are decisions which significantly affect the use of resources often made with little consideration of the resource implications; many department chairmen charged with responsibility for effective resource use have little interest in the subject. While the chief administrators of academic departments may be elected or selected for a variety of reasons, pressures and opportunities offered by the office seldom motivate the incumbents to view their tasks in terms of effective resource allocation and utilization. Most chairmen consider themselves professors and scholars first and chairmen second. They judge their own performance by essentially the same standards as they judge performance by their colleagues, and they usually expect to hold the office for only a limited period of time. Though some department heads selected by the dean may try conscientiously to deal with his allocation problems, even those individuals are likely to have little control over the activities of their departments. They truly serve their departments and cannot long survive the displeasure of their colleagues. Only the rare chairman regards himself as a professional administrator pursuing an administrative career. Yet, collectively, these lieutenants of the academic army nominally control the largest single segment of most institutional budgets.

Thus, the climate in which men, materials, and dollars are deployed in the name of higher learning is at best insensitive to any need to economize. Stated institutional goals do not often serve as effective guides for resource allocation. The values and preoccupations of faculties have relegated economic problems to the fringes of deliberation. When questions of productivity are addressed, they are more likely to be answered in terms of the quality of academic production than the quantity. Crucial responsibilities are widely shared, and clearly assigned authority is correspondingly rare and weak. Fast and decisive action becomes difficult if not impossible. Incentives to economize on the use of institutional resources are few and far between—for both students and faculty. Finally, many of those charged with husbanding the resources of the institution regard the charge as only secondary to their scholarly pursuits.

Before leaving a discussion of the institutional setting, a word or two should be said about the relationship of institutional research to the resource allocation problem and to the climate within which the problem has to be solved. In essence, institutional research can and must bring an analytical approach to an environment which has not fostered analysis in the allocative process. Even though it is not always clear where the ultimate power of decision lies, the office of institutional research is typically charged, by common consent, with assisting the decision makers of academia in making better-informed decisions. Therefore the burden of describing past and present utilization of institutional resources falls upon the office of research. To synthesize the complete picture of personnel, facilities, supplies, and dollars of an institution, research must have access to information about all units of organization.

Before the days of the multiversity, much of the synthesizing needed for relating resource use to allocation decisions was done in the president's or dean's head. As a matter of fact, synthesis is still performed in this manner at many colleges and universities. But the president is likely to find himself forced into a decision (for which he is likely to be called to task) with virtually no empirical information to support a choice. When a decision is concerned with resource allocation, usually in the form of budget building, the dean may feel that he cannot rely completely on data supplied by the requesting academic department, and the president may feel that the data submitted by the dean should not go unchecked. In the same situations, an office of institutional research, through its reputation for thorough, impartial analysis, could help to expedite decision. In rare instances, presentation of analytical information can amount to a de facto decision commanding more objective authority than any of the parties around the negotiating table.

It should be noted that two other offices might conceivably furnish analytical support. Since the business office deals with the dollar values of all resources, theoretically that office is in a position to provide complete descriptions of how the institution is using its means. Traditionally, however, these offices have not organized financial information in a way which best aids the management of educational programs or the planning of future programs. For a number of reasons they have instead concentrated on control and accountability of funds, keeping records largely on the basis of expenditure by object and organizational unit. Formally organized budget offices sometimes produce the integrative analyses needed to support budget decisions. To the extent that such offices perform this task, they are engaged in what is here referred to as institutional research.

Generally, however, it is the institutional research office which is concerned with the need to relate operating characteristics such as class size, faculty salary levels and teaching loads, physical space utilization, and educational objectives to the budget decisions which have to be made. It seems to be the office of institutional research which is increasingly pressing or responding to the need for comprehensive and integrative analysis relating current and prospective use of resources to educational programs and institutional aims.

Total Resources Accounting

Accounting for the use of institutional resources requires at least some notion of what is to be achieved. Economic theory examines at great length the problems of maximizing profits and optimizing the use of production factors. But it always assumes as given whatever is to be maximized or optimized.

In higher education, however, assumptions seem to be everybody's business and therefore nobody's business. Ideally, criteria for evaluation of resource utilization presuppose acceptance of a single, well-conceived set of intended results by all who participate in the allocative process. Then, although we might not be able to measure whether or not higher education actually achieved what we had in mind, at least we would be able to say that so much of our endeavor and dollars were expended toward this or that purpose. As suggested earlier, such conditions rarely prevail. Students and their parents, by and large, expect college to help ensure high occupational and economic status. Public officials expect assistance in the solution of pressing domestic and international problems and in accelerating the rate of economic progress. And substantial numbers of academicians feel that the university should be operated, in large part, for the benfit of the faculty. Though it might be possible, coincidentally, to distribute the available means of an institution in a way which would bring acclamations of praise from all these divergent interests, it is more likely that what would be regarded by one group as the best use of institutional resources would be condemned by the next as diverting the direction of the university from its highest purpose. Indeed, within the constituencies, different values and value weights would undoubtedly be proclaimed.

Reconciliation of differences, even in matters as paramount as institutional objectives, is not the province of institutional research. But one of the most productive roles which institutional research can play, in behalf of more effective use of resources, is that of a gadfly forcing all units of the organization to articulate concise goals and objectives rather than mere banalities. This done, research can work in concert with the organizational units to identify physical and financial expenditures which are dedicated to accomplishment of those objectives.

Neither task is easy. For years one of the common formulas espoused by presidents, deans, and department chairmen for achieving the goal of excellence has been to hire the best faculty who can be found and then let them do what they want. This unwritten policy explains in part why so many colleges and universities are devoid of goals which can be related to their operational activities. As long as the goal of faculty excellence is accepted without defining excellence, no problem arises; but acceptance on faith alone is vanishing. While many agree that the three overriding purposes of a university are instruction, research, and service, in practice these three goals turn out to be merely large rubrics under which individual faculty members carry on a wide variety of activities which they, as individuals, regard as conducive to one or more of these aims. Often the academic department represents only a loose grouping of individual faculty entrepreneurships, each entrepreneur having his own objectives and activities. Under this circumstance, it is not at all clear how the department (and therefore the college and university), as an organization separate from the individuals who make it up, can possess objectives to which its resources can be allocated.

Demands for accountability are indirect demands for identification of specific organizational objectives, and for definition of those objectives in operational terms. Even the largest and wealthiest of multiversities may no longer be able to justify supporting its high-priced expert in celestial semantics on the grounds that he is the world's leading authority in his field. Logically, resources assigned to the support of his work would need to be justified in terms of his contribution to the programs of his department and college. Because academic departments represent important cost centers, or control points, in the allocation and use of resources, competent resource accounting depends upon the departments to spell out just what they mean by the instruction, research, and service to be carried out under their auspices. Granted, these outputs are largely intangible and inextricably interrelated; so description of operational objectives with respect to them is slippery at best.

Consider, for example, the problem of describing instructional objectives in a way which facilitates measurement of the resources devoted to them. The obvious place to begin is with identification of students majoring in the department. If the department is in a graduate institution, presumably the objectives of the department include the production of competent and qualified recipients of bachelor's, master's, and Ph.D. degrees. But what does competent and qualified mean in operational terms? Does it mean that present faculty, curriculum, annual course offerings, class size distributions, admissions standards, attrition, and student examination results are satisfactory, more than satisfactory, or less than satisfactory? What relative values should be placed on large numbers and high attrition? What relative values should be assigned to the Ph.D. program, the master's program, and the undergraduate program in considering an optimal enrollment combination? The list of pertinent considerations for the department's instructional objectives alone is obviously a long one, and the danger of becoming sidetracked into a mire of philosophical platitudes is correspondingly great.

Nevertheless, identification of objectives is essential and for this reason a compromise route to better explanations might well be utilized. Efforts might be applied to both ends of the problem at the same time—that is, to the collection of operational data as well as to definitions of objectives. The problem itself would remain the same—to account for the use of institutiontal resources in a way which would help decision makers make better use of them. But the tactics would force articulation of objectives and programs through confronting operating units with as much information as was available about what they were already doing and then asking them to share in an evaluation of what the data meant.

To some extent a discussion of the need for total resources accounting merely repeats what has already been said in Chapter Eight in the context of management information systems. However three points need to be emphasized. First, all resource expenditures need to be accounted for. The thoroughness of total accounting departs from the methods of traditional accounting. Historically, institutions have accounted primarily for money. Money has been reported in terms of specific budgets, fund sources, or types of expenditures. Educational and general budget expenditures have been emphasized to the neglect of other budgets, departmental expenditures have been analyzed without including the cost of building space used by the department, and so on. Skillful coordination of all resources—faculty, staff, facilities, and equipment—is the key to efficiency, and examination of physical resource expenditures can help decision makers as much or more than dollar accounting. Historically, the extensive data collection and analysis required to account for utilization of all resources provided an excuse to account for dollars only—or for faculty, facilities, or some other partial expenditure only. With the widespread use of automatic data processing, that excuse is losing its credibility.

The second point is the relationship of total resources accounting to an actual system of management information. Total resources accounting necessitates use of the systems approach. Data on faculty and staff must be compatible with data on facilities, and these two units must be compatible with financial information; otherwise complete and integrated analysis cannot take place. If one is to account for all resources utilized by the chemistry department, data on facilities utilization, staff, and dollars should all refer to the same time period. Also the same boundaries should define the organizational entity for all data. If research associates of the biochemical research center are included in chemistry staff data, then the facilities and dollars of the center should also be included; otherwise various statistical descriptions will describe different organizational entities. Obvious as the case for compatible and coordinated data might sound, such coordination has rarely been achieved in large institutions. Persuading the payroll department to alter the format and content of its data system in order to accommodate the staff records office often turns out to be a harrowing experience—perhaps surpassed only by the resistance of the staff records office to modification of its file so that the Registrar can utilize faculty names for the printing of class lists. Specific offices have typically collected information for their own restricted purposes, and they too often take a recalcitrant position when asked to encompass broader horizons.

The third point is the most difficult to apply: total resources need to be accounted for by program in addition to being accounted for by the conventional object and organizational unit classifications. A program is represented by an organized effort which the institution mobilizes to accomplish one of its objectives; it can be defined as a collection of activities (and resources) dedicated to the achievement of a specific purpose. In this definition the offering of a course would constitute an activity, and all the instruction and supporting activities needed to graduate bachelors of science in chemistry would define a program.[2]

If expenditures are to be accounted for in a way which helps educators plan resources needed to carry out programs in the future, then total resources accounting on a program basis is involved. Not

---

[2] Definitions of what constitutes a program, a subprogram, and an activity vary from author to author in planning, programming, and budgeting literature.

only must the analyst furnish data on the utilization of all expenditures, but each type of resource must be costed to the program or programs on behalf of which it was expended. Since faculty members frequently divide their time among several programs, and since other resources are similarly multipurpose, the obstacles to total resources accounting on a program basis are formidable. Nevertheless, the institutional researcher responsible for studies of resource allocation and utilization sooner or later must find feasible methods of measuring the activities of the faculty, the utilization of facilities, and the concomitant dollar costs.

Faculty Measures. Human beings typically constitute the overwhelming preponderance of productive resources available to the institution. (See Brummet, Pyle, and Flamholtz, 1969, for discussion of the developing field of human resources accounting.) Probably the best description of a college or university is a description of what its faculty are doing. Most often such descriptions take the form of a distribution of salary or compensation dollars among the activities performed by faculty members. Though this chapter cannot go into great detail in describing systems of staff accounting, the three basic techniques for distributing faculty expenditures can be explained. One is an ex-ante method which might be called "budgeted faculty assignments." Under this system, each faculty member's assignment is described in terms of his functional duties, and the man's salary is distributed (before the fact) among these assigned duties. The distribution may be determined by the department chairman unilaterally, through discussion and agreement between the chairman and staff member, or according to some departmental load formula based on judgment rather than on empirical measures. An example of formula application is provided by one university which defines a full-time load as one hundred points; instructional activities, administrative duties, and counseling assignments carry standard numbers of points. A full-time faculty member might carry a load totaling less than or more than one hundred points during any single term: his load would be described in relation to that standard, however.

A second basic technique for salary distribution depends on collection of information, ex-post, through some version of the faculty activities report. Typically the professor completes this report himself, recording either average weekly hours or per cent of total effort expended on various endeavors. Again, it is important that the list of endeavors he records bear some relationship to identified departmental objectives. If it does not, as is too often the case, then accounting for the man's salary becomes conceptually ambiguous at best. This method is probably closest to traditional accounting practices because it attempts to aggregate actual costs incurred.

A third basic technique might be called standard costing, under a loose definition of that term. The procedure relies indirectly on ex-post reporting of actual costs, and it bears some relationship to a formula for assigned faculty load. In essence, standard costs are developed through statistical analysis of ex-post faculty activities reports. For example, it might be found that relative effort expended on formal course instruction depends on the discipline, the type of instruction (such as lecture, laboratory, or recitation), the number of course contact hours, and the number of students enrolled. Through the development of standard costs, the salary of an individual could be spread among only those activities which the department defined as contributing toward its objectives, in accordance with the standard cost relationships determined by statistical analysis. Presumably analysis to determine cost relationships is undertaken only periodically, perhaps once every five years. Though this technique holds promise for the forecasting of staff requirements, very little competent quantitative research has been done in the area thus far.

Because all three techniques described above are generally regarded not only by faculties but by many administrators as laborious and irritating, higher education has little reliable information about the differential costs of instruction in various degree programs and various disciplines. It simply has been too troublesome and difficult to analyze carefully the faculty instructional activity patterns which constitute the major source of cost differentials among levels of students taught and among fields of study.

In light of the unpopularity of faculty activity analysis, there exists a great temptation for budget analysts, cost analysts, and institutional researchers to simplify the accounting methods applied to faculty and supporting staff activity distributions. For a number of years the Office of Institutional Research at the University of Michigan has compiled data on the direct teaching costs of credit instruction in two ways: 1) by spreading the instructor's salary evenly over the course credit hours he teaches, and 2) by tabulating his salary according to per cent of his work load assigned to each course he teaches. The first method quite consistently yields a relatively higher direct instructional cost per student credit hour for graduate instruction largely because it fails to adjust faculty effort to the smaller classes at the graduate level. In some institutions the whole man or the entire budgeted position is assigned to instruction or to research or to public service. In other institutions a single budgeted position or person can be distributed among these three major programs only, essentially approximating the first of the three techniques identified above; however, unless budgeted assignments are made in some detail within the area of instruction itself, it becomes difficult to account for differential allocations of personnel resources to levels and disciplines of the students taught.

Accounting for the utilization of personnel according to intended outputs points up a classical problem in economic analysis which pervades not only total resources accounting but the entire resource allocation process. Without digressing to explain that problem here, other issues cannot be clearly presented. The dilemma is portrayed in economics texts as the two-sided phenomenon of joint costs and joint products or benefits. In sum and substance, it is impossible for the farmer to incur the costs of producing beef without also incurring the costs of producing cowhide. It is unlikely that he will reap the benefits of marketing his beef without marketing also the leather. Higher education exhibits the same characteristic in the nature of its instruction and research activity. To a lesser extent institutional service activity is also part of the problem. An example frequently cited is that of a professor of surgery who performs a new type of operation on a patient in the presence of medical residents; the surgeon is engaged simultaneously in instruction of the residents, research into new surgical applications, and service to the patient (assuming he is cured). Questions that can be raised reveal the accounting dilemma: Should the faculty activity portion of his work be charged to the instruction, research, or service program of the medical school? Is the operating room being used as an instruction, research, or service facility? Though surgery is not a particularly common form of graduate instruction and research, cooperative effort involving graduate student and professor in a research project is common. In fact, graduate faculties frequently claim that the primary purpose of their research is to train their students and that discovery of new knowledge represents only a subsidiary purpose.

Accounting for joint outputs becomes particularly crucial in deciding how organized research and graduate instruction can or should be funded. Since graduate assistants are trained in part through their participation in sponsored research projects, and since their services are needed to carry out the research, a case can be made that either output, graduate instuction, or research can legitimately be charged the full cost of the professor's effort; neither could be accomplished without performance of his entire job. As one state budget analyst exclaimed plaintively after spending a day with the dean of an engineering school, "I understand now—instruction means research and research means instruction."

In practice, no satisfactory method has been found to account separately for the contribution of each resource input which, in combination with other inputs, produces joint products. Existing techniques in the field of economic analysis require so many measurements to be taken under such closely controlled production conditions that only crude applications have even been attempted in examining joint-cost, joint-product situations in higher education. Presently, we are simply left with the inseparability of the research and instructional outputs of much faculty activity. And that inseparability renders most difficult the task of explaining resource needs to higher education's quite distinct publics.

Facilities Measures.   Much can be said about the use and misuse of the physical campus and its buildings in progressing toward institutional goals. Accounts of the capital assets of a college or university usually bring a "so what" reaction. Few institutions depreciate the value of their plant or hold reserves for depreciation primarily because they depend on the vicissitudes of capital gift receipts or public appropriations or both for their building needs. Until the Higher Education Facilities Act of 1964, construction of buildings, on private campuses in particular, bore little relationship to the measured space needs of the institution or to the condition and serviceability of its existing physical plant. Acquisition of new facilities depended, instead, primarily on the fortunes and inclinations of private donors and state legislatures. However, as the exploding student population overran the nation's campuses, the crying needs for space to house and teach them became compelling.

Title I of the Higher Education Facilities Act finally focused decisive attention on the status and use of campus physical facilities as well as on the cost of underutilizing what space was available. During the next six years, the Act distributed some 1.7 billion dollars for construction of academic buildings, requiring space utilization data in order to evaluate needs. The passage of Title I probably generated more analysis of space utilization than all that had occurred since the founding of Harvard in 1636. Most of the flurry of activity has been extension and elaboration of methodology first laid out in some detail by Russell and Doi (1957).

Accounting for the use of institutional space has recently evolved into a complex procedure but the purposes are still quite clear. The opportunity costs of wasting physical facilities are high. Not only do maintenance and custodial costs run to a dollar or more per square foot per year, but the alternative uses to which such funds could be put have become real and pressing. Persuasive college officials can occasionally divert potential gifts and public funds from capital to operating purposes through planning for efficient plant utilization. Space analysis can expedite efficient utilization and can make it translatable. Good campus planning remains virtually impossible without reliable and comprehensive knowledge of the present use of facilities. Since the factors which bear on the need for future space are so many and so varied, few existing institutions can plan new facilities without regard to their present life styles and plant utilization patterns.

The straightforward principles of facilities analysis make the actual tasks seem deceptively simple. Building spaces are usually inventoried according to: appropriate use or uses, quantity, physical condition, and built-in equipment or other specialized characteristics. The sheer magnitude of the task in a university of ten thousand students is likely to require several man-years of work, excluding the time required by data-processing staff to put the inventory into a computerized file. But, once the inventory is in hand

and a system of continual updating is in operation, the use of space can subsequently be analyzed more easily.

In the measurement of space allotted to formal instruction, classroom and laboratory scheduling records furnish raw data. If these are not centrally and consistently prepared, the use of instructional space cannot be easily examined. Adequate records of the assignment and use of other types of space often constitute a more troublesome problem. For example some libraries keep data in forms well-suited to utilization analysis; in contrast, the extent to which non-data-keeping departmental libraries, music practice rooms, and other nonscheduled spaces represent relatively good assignment of scarce resources is frequently difficult to determine. A systematic form of spot checking known as ratio delay sampling is sometimes employed to assess the utilization of such facilities, but generally they represent a large fraction of total institutional space relatively neglected in accounting for the use of facilities.

More to the point in a chapter on resource allocation and utilization are the issues posed by physical facilities analysis. The most discussed issue is acceptance of space factors and utilization standards. A second issue is application of measures of relative efficiency or optimization to best possible assignment. A third is relationship of space utilization measures to academic programs. Space factors such as the appropriate numbers of square feet per classroom station, laboratory station, or faculty or secretarial office station have been studied at great length by myriad college planners and architects. While many norms have been calculated and standards have been set by individual institutions and public funding agencies, the most recent and comprehensive effort in space analysis, that published by the Western Interstate Commission on Higher Education (1970a), does not recommend space factors or utilization standards for institutions (though it does suggest, with appropriate caution, some factor ranges for statewide application). Utilization standards are ultimately value judgments best made in the light of immediate circumstances. One science department might prefer office-laboratory combinations while another might elect separation of offices from labs. Whether student advising is carried out in faculty offices or in separate cubicles designated for that purpose might well affect the space factor employed in assigning or planning faculty office space.

As crucial as the factors used in the permanent assignments of space are the standards set for the temporal use of space. One midwestern university grew from an enrollment of 6,600 to an enrollment of over ten thousand with a slight net reduction in the number of classroom stations available. Obviously the rate of classroom and student station utilization climbed dramatically, and maintaining the original norms would have required millions of additional dollars in construction and operation of classroom facilities.

A small western liberal-arts college follows a rather deliberate policy in scheduling as few classes as possible after 2 P.M. to accommodate scheduling of activities involving the greater college community. This college incurs an opportunity cost in potentially higher space utilization for the ability to engage in frequent communitywide activities. In any matter concerned with utilization of space, the point is that standards ultimately depend on judgments which compare the value of optimum use of space with the value of something which might be purchased instead. There are no satisfactory absolutes with respect to space factors or utilization standards.

Most facilities specialists have not yet come to grips with the issue, but there is recognition that currently we do not attempt to measure the efficiency of space use in terms of the appropriateness of the space provided. Present utilization measures assume that all functions are equally well served in the spaces to which they are assigned. In addition, present procedures seldom recognize the degrees of substitutability of one type of space for another. For example, under what circumstances and to what extent can laboratories serve as classrooms? Slack in current facilities capacity due to assumptions about nonsubstitutability of some spaces for others might well be substantial. By the same token, systematic evaluation of possible combinations of spaces and functions according to the qualitative characteristics of each might well improve the qualitative use of space.

The issue of tying the use of space not only to persons and organizational units but also to institutional programs is, of course, central to total resources accounting. Unless the cost of facilities can be assigned to programs, all resources cannot be accounted for in terms of the objectives toward which they were expended. Once the principle of total resources accounting on a program basis is accepted, this is no longer a conceptual issue; however, application of the principle presents difficult if not impossible tasks. Space is not typically occupied on a program basis; it usually houses people— groups of students, individual faculty members, and supporting staff. Most classes include students from more than one degree program; most faculty members contribute to more than one institutional objective, through several programs; and supporting staff members usually assist faculty with their tasks, either directly or indirectly. Thus, we are back to the question of the operating room in the medical school: How shall a resource be accounted for in terms of the instructional, research, and service programs of the university? At this stage, satisfactory techniques for space analysis and program costing are not yet available. If one is a purist, he portends future development of sophisticated and detailed methods for measuring the differential utilization of physical facilities by the program activities carried on, either separately or jointly, in those facilities. If one is a pragmatist, he portends further rule by thumb. In all likelihood, the need for data on how programs use space will bring additional rules of thumb as well as in-depth studies to validate or challenge those rules.

Dollar-Costing Measures. Dollars can be considered resources only in the sense that they represent a fiduciary counterpart of the more tangible resources, men and materials. As long as dollars command the services of these tangible entities, they provide a common denominator which can reflect and measure all resource allocation and utilization; dollars facilitate the process of total resources accounting. Hence the widespread emphasis on cost studies.

As already mentioned, little can be said about the study of capital costs in individual institutions of higher education. Like most of the nonprofit sector of our economy, higher education does not fund its capital facilities in a way which demands close attention to the allocation of monies between operating and capital expenditures. Institutions are not expected to generate revenues to cover capital costs, except in auxiliary enterprises.

The paucity of studies on capital cost seems more than balanced by the abundance of analyses treating operating costs. However, few if any attempts have been made to measure the deployment of all institutional resources to all programs and objectives of the institution. As one observer points out, "costs should, to be useful, be viewed as consequences of decisions, and it is desirable to establish quantitative relationships between decisions, or choices, and the costs which flow from them" (U.S. Department of Health, Education, and Welfare, Social and Rehabilitation Service, 1970, p. xi). We are most concerned, and too often only concerned, about the utilization of resources over which we have some discretionary control. Would a department chairman be deeply concerned about the costs of custodial service and maintenance when both are beyond his responsibility and control? Because of the nature of human concern, most cost studies are specific and partial to the purposes for which they were designed. Studies by state coordinating boards or other state-level agencies deal with data aggregated to a level of generalization not indicative of specific departmental or program resource utilization. Even institutional cost studies often average out, or aggregate out, departmental and program differentials in resource use.

The greatest opportunity for misuse is probably afforded by studies which examine and interpret one input, one output, or one fund source. They are likely to deal only with educational and general budget funds because these are subject to more complete control than are expenditures of restricted funds. Or they are likely to concentrate on the direct salary cost of credit instruction only, which is relatively easy to measure and can be quite closely controlled through manipulation of faculty assignment, course offerings, and class sizes. The shortcomings of such endeavors should be evident. By concentrating on an easily measured, manipulable part of the cost picture, the analyst tempts the administrator to maximize a particular output or the use of a specific resource at the inadvertent expense of another. A favorite faculty example declares that too rigorous an enforcement of large classes and heavy teaching loads brought about by constant attention to reducing instructional costs per student credit hour can conceivably cost more in instructional quality than is gained by reducing direct expenditures. Another possibility can be stated: cramming two or three faculty members into a single office of modest size to make space assignment data look good might well cost more in reduced but unmeasured faculty productivity than would comfortable private offices for each of them.

Since dollars expended can be thought of as proxies for tangible goods and services provided, the complexities and ambiguities inherent in accounting for program allocation of resources hold for program cost-finding studies as well. Most institutions have little experience with cost accounting, and few can boast charts of accounts which make it possible to trace expenditures to institutional programs. These institutions typically employ laborious methods of analyzing the program use of tangible resources first and then spread dollar expenditures to conform. Refined program costing could help them, instead, to pick a discriminating path through multiple fund flows, ignoring organizational and budgetary lines to cumulate all dollars expended in behalf of specific program objectives. Program costing can reveal not only how much it really costs to play the program tune, but also whether the tune is actually called by those who pay the piper. It brings favored-son as well as orphan programs into focus so that needs to reallocate resources, where they exist, can be made unavoidably clear. Mapping of the flow of funds from sources to program uses can also make questions of accountability crystal clear.

Before moving on to a discussion of the analysis and prediction of resource requirements, several final points should be mentioned. The concept of total resources accounting on a program basis is not particularly complicated. It holds substantial promise for institutional administrators who must rationalize their allocation decisions and explain them to the various publics of higher education. However, the generation of data to satisfy the conditions of total resources accounting is a complex and elusive task. In institutions of five thousand students or more, the job demands a computer-based management information system. In fact, if it were not for computer technology, only the most stouthearted and patient could face the prospect of building the elaborate and massive data base needed to track the allocation and utilization of all resources to all institutional programs.

Because sources of quantitative historical information about college operations have been piecemeal, incompatible, and even conflicting, and because institutional researchers often have been given the task of making a comprehensive story out of the pieces, many have become involved in building total resources accounting systems and program-costing systems. To the extent that institutional research is diverted to this task, it cannot perform in-depth analyses in support of better planning and better decision-making. But, without an adequately comprehensive and reliable data base, it cannot make intelligent studies of allocation problems either. During the foreseeable future, institutional researchers will be found pushing, pulling, straining, and probably carrying some of the load in building total resources accounting systems.

Institutional researchers are also obligated to remind decision makers constantly of the dangers of basing courses of action too heavily upon data which tell only part of the story. Limited information about resource inputs or program outputs sometimes encourages administrators to maximize the use of some resource inputs or some program outputs without carefully considering the possible effects on other inputs or outputs. Most institutional cost studies, unfortunately, reflect guilt in this respect. They tend to concentrate on only part of the cost of one output—formal instruction—stated in the form of either student credit hours or student contact hours. Lacking comprehensive data on all resource costs and in-depth study of other institutional outputs, such cost studies are of limited value and are occasionally harmful.

Analysis and Prediction

The complexities and ambiguities of resource allocation seem beyond the capacity of the human intellect to grasp; from most people, they bring forth uncertain responses but, from some sensitive and experienced administrators, they bring forth almost artistic responses. (In Washington a rather apt buzz word used in describing administrative skill is *orchestration*.) Yet even the most experienced and skilled administrators like to reduce to comfortable proportions the range of decisions depending upon pure judgment and intuition. Institutional research has commonly helped narrow the range by providing historical analysis often accompanied by extrapolation of past experience into the future.

Time series or trend analyses comprise perhaps the most useful means of portraying past and probable future directions of individual variables such as enrollments, student credit hours, faculty members, appropriations, instructional space, budgets, and other operating characteristics. Typically included in trend analysis are pertinent ratios bearing on the deployment of resources such as: student-faculty ratios, space utilization statistics, student credit hours or classroom contact hours per full-time-equivalent faculty member or educational and general dollars budgeted per full-time-equivalent student. One of the distinct advantages of trend analysis lies in the fact that it can reveal the direction of activity without ever describing the exact nature of the activity itself. In higher education, where drilling into definitions soon brings up muddy water, this advantage is significant. For example, student credit hours—or rather a continuing increase or decline in the production of student credit hours —can be of great financial significance to some public institutions. Yet the student credit hour as a measure of either work load or output is a rubber yardstick at best. It defies any meaningful definition, but that shortcoming does not seriously jeopardize its use in trend analysis as long as its meaningless definition does not change.

A second common form of resource analysis deals not with self-comparison over time, as does trend analysis, but with comparison of inputs and outputs among similar units. It usually makes more sense to compare chemistry departments, schools of music, or business administration programs with like units across institutions than with one another merely because they are part of the same university. Department chairmen and other resource managers often feel ambivalent about the usefulness of comparisons. They employ them to advantage but deny their validity when faced with an unfavorable comparison. Again, enrollments, budgets, faculty salaries, and student-faculty ratios constitute frequent bases of comparative analysis. However, differences in objectives, programs, nature of the students, and nature of the faculties place severe limitations on the validity and value of comparisons made within and across institutions. Only if the intent and bases of comparison can be spelled out clearly are comparative studies likely to be useful in evaluation of resource utilization.

Probably the purpose served best by comparison is not that

of coming to conclusions about the efficiency or inefficiency of a specific unit, but that of raising questions for further investigation and soul searching. One dean in a professional school, upon finding that his student-faculty ratio was the lowest in the university and only one-third the average for all schools and colleges of the state-wide institution, investigated student-faculty ratios in peer professional schools around the country. He found that his own ratio was above average when compared to those schools but concluded that his whole profession was paying inadequate attention to cost and productivity. He could not justify the lower ratios in his profession on the basis of the nature of subject matter or the prevailing teaching methodologies.

Trend analyses and comparative analyses can be, and often are, combined. Furthermore, comparison of trends in marginal or incremental data sometimes points up, dramatically, subtle shifts in resource allocation. For example, comparisons of annual percentage changes in departmental budgets over a period of years can reveal that what seemed to be quite modest increases in the budgets of several small departments have in fact given them a sizable relative advantage in assigned resources. Analysis of marginal changes, or first differences, can also play a crucial part in enrollment projections and the staffing projections which logically follow.

The traditional analyses referred to above still exhibit the subtle sin of half-truth; they are incapable of telling the whole story. Some means of simplification enabling analysts and decision makers to trace all the major variables of resource flow and resource productivity appears to be indispensable if we are going to improve both the utilization of resources and our capacity to explain what is being accomplished. These problems in simplification constitute an ideal culture for model building so it is not surprising to find both models and model builders increasing and prospering in the world of institutional research.

Allocation and Prediction Models. Good models like good theory add more to understanding through simplification than they detract from understanding through oversimplification. Good models treat all the essentials of a problem adequately but strip away the obfuscating trivia and irrelevancies so the basic structure and operating variables of a complex system can be grasped and hopefully controlled more deliberately and intelligently. Because conceptual simplification and crystallization represent no small part of the answer to questions of efficient resource allocation, there is great temptation to call every simplified way of looking at higher education a model, regardless of whether it refers to a technique for assigning faculty cars to parking spaces or to a comprehensive system for evaluating the economic cost and contribution of higher education.

We hear about predictive models, descriptive models, behavioral models, identity models, stochastic and nonstochastic models, simulation models, micro- and macro-models, and static and dynamic models. Actually several of these adjectives can apply to the same model since a model can be described according to its purpose (for example to predict resource requirements), the sorts of data used as input to the model (for example behavioral data on student curricular choices), or the type of equations used to describe the functional relationships of the model (for example equations taking a stochastic form).

Institutional researchers deal, for the most part, with models depicting resource inputs or service outputs or both at the institutional level (even though the federal government, other agencies, and a number of individual scholars are now setting their sights on state- and national-level models). Most of these efforts treat either all major inputs and outputs of the institution or the input-output relationships of one major sector of the institution—for example the function of formal instruction.

Generally the purposes of modeling exercises employed in institutional research are three: The first is to furnish unambiguous, highly specified, quantitative description of the major elements in an institutional system or subsystem and of the interrelationships which prevail among these major elements. The object is to describe the reality of institutional operations more cohesively and clearly than can be done through qualitative insights into specific elements or processes. This purpose gives rise to what are called descriptive models.

The second purpose that models can serve is to provide more reliable means of predicting the outcomes of actions which change one or more of the major variables in the system. The difference between this purpose and the purpose served by individual forecasts of enrollment, attrition, or some other variable lies in the capacity of the model to describe the combined effects of individual forecasts upon one another as well as upon other events causally related. Not surprisingly, this purpose gives rise to a class of models called predictive models. Predictive models are often extensions of descriptive models; they derive their estimating equations from historical relationships found in descriptive models. Since predictive models often can simulate the outcomes of actions which might be taken, they can directly assist in policy making; hence the terms "simulation model" and "policy model" are applied to some predictive exercises.

The third purpose of models is to make possible the optimum use of resources according to a set of carefully specified output objectives for a sector of the institution or the entire institution. This purpose demands a great deal of model-building sophistication because it assumes the ability to quantify the desired results of institutional activity at all acceptable levels of operation. It also assumes complete knowledge or usefully accurate approximations of the relationships (called production functions) between all resource inputs and all desired outputs at each level. While optimization represents a logical goal of educational model building, few current efforts are this ambitious. Less will be said about optimizing models than about descriptive and predictive models.

Construction of all three types of models demands the same sort of rigorous, often frustrating systems analysis approach to resource allocation. Whether the model entails a comprehensive analysis of resource use in the entire institution or constitutes a subsystem model describing only one segment of institutional activity, the fundamental tasks in model building remain the same. The basic steps are five. First, all major input and output variables of interest must be identified and defined. Second, the organizational structure and processes by which outputs are produced from inputs must be described. Third, significant environmental variables, additional to the input and output variables, must be identified. Fourth, functional relationships (in the form of equations) among all identified variables must be established. Fifth, the model should be tested, preferably with historical data, to see if changes in the values of independent variables produce expected or at reasonable changes in the values of dependent variabes.

The input variables considered as a first step in building resource allocation models conventionally are faculty, staff, facilities, and supplies and equipment. When considered together, they are represented by their common denominator, dollars. Since resource allocation models are most often used to estimate resource requirements, input variables usually constitute the dependent variables in equations.

Definition of the outputs of higher education is largely impossible in any final social or philosophical sense. As already mentioned, there is little agreement on what the final outputs are or should be. Even when there is agreement, we can rarely measure those final results quantitatively. Therefore, in developing analytical models, outputs are typically stated in terms of proxies or surrogates which can be quantified and which are presumed to approximate, at least partially, more meaningful but elusive entities. Student credit hours, student contact hours, courses taught, degrees awarded, and student-years of education have all been used as proxies for output of the instruction function. Even these designations remain too ambiguous to make a model operational. The exacting nature of the exercise usually forces considerations such as: which student credit hours? Registered or graded? Term or academic year? Lower-division students, upper-division students, graduate students, or all three? On the other hand, the specification demanded by some analytic models can force precision beyond our ability to attach meaning to it. We can distinguish between numbers of credit hours completed by two students much more precisely than we can distinguish between their corresponding increments in knowledge. And outputs of the instruction function are, at least superficially, easier to handle than the outputs of research and some service activities.

In performing the second step (description of the structure of the organization and its mode of operation), the organizational structure can be thought of as the maze through which inputs flow and are transformed into outputs. The number and types of outputs depend upon the number and types of exits in the organizational maze. How many academic departments are there, and how many colleges, research institutes, or service bureaus? How are they pyramided to comprise the total institution? There is a second structure which must also be described. It is to a great extent the offspring of the marriage between defined objectives, or intended outputs, and the existing organization. Together, objectives and existing organization determine the program superstructure of the institution. Degree programs, research programs, continuing education, and other service programs all serve as channels for resources and vehicles of institutional accomplishment. They add to the conceptual description of the system as they are properly related to other components of the model. Resources flow into both the organizational structure and the program superstructure. The two are not the same, and therein lies the tale of planning, programming, and budgeting (PPB) systems. The same specification of organizations and programs demanded by PPB systems is also required for resource allocation models which treat inputs and outputs on a program basis.

In the third step, identification of environmental variables significantly affecting the institution as a productive entity entails tagging them with feasible quantitative units. These variables fall into two groups: endogenous variables, which are controllable through policy decision but become parameters in predictive models, and exogenous variables, which are important to the problem but over which policy makers have no control. Major endogenous or policy variables in the usual resource requirements prediction model include student-faculty ratios to be maintained, average class sizes, faculty contact hour teaching loads, salary levels, faculty rank distributions, square-foot space factors and space utilization factors, and faculty-to-supporting-staff ratios. All of these are typically accepted by the model as given parameters in determining resource requirements, but they may be altered if the model is used for simulation purposes.

Much discussion revolves around the best or proper source of the numbers to be used as policy parameters. In descriptive models, no judgmental problem arises because the purpose of the model is to describe the operational reality of the institution. Actual student-faculty ratios, salary levels, or space standards are used. The only problem is that most institutions cannot produce the comprehensive and detailed historical data in the form needed. To the extent that approximations are used, the validity of the results is subject to debate even as a description of the present or past. Policy parameters employed in predicting future resource needs logically come from one of two sources: norms, standards, or policies prevailing in the past; or judgmental decisions of those using the model. If the institution lacks a good historical data base, those using models are forced to set policy guidelines for the future without knowing the past. As long as simulation modeling remains a game which planners play, traumatic perturbations from such policy decisions are not likely to carry beyond the walls of the institutional research and planning offices. But, if predicted resource requirements make their way into budget discussions, each and every policy parameter in the model becomes subject to vigorous scrutiny. Skeptics are most likely to attack the policy assumptions.

Exogenous variables considered here are those materially affecting institutional resource allocation and use. Values placed on higher education, average family income, the academic fields in which students elect to major, the rate of inflation, and amounts of state appropriation are pertinent examples. Some variables might be considered either endogenous policy variables or exogenous variables depending upon the specific institution and its environment. In some public institutions student-faculty ratios are controlled not by the college administration but by the state. Some deans claim they have little control over faculty contact hour teaching loads because these are set within very narrow limits in the academic marketplace. In any event, the use of models generally requires explicit decisions concerning which parameters are to be accepted as fixed and which are subject to control and therefore to adjustment in the model.

In applying the fourth major step, establishment of the functional relationships among the variables, to construction of resource allocation models, one deals with relationships describing the production functions of the institution—relationships between various quantities of educational outputs specified and various quantities of each resource input needed to produce them. Perhaps the simplest illustration is relationship between student credit hours produced and faculty members employed. If all full-time faculty members taught the same number of credit hours, and if faculty members could be employed for any fraction of a full-time appointment, then changes in the number of credit hours taught would be directly proportionate to changes in the number of full-time-equivalent faculty employed. Proportionate changes result in a linear function, commonly employed in predictive models. Linear functions are frequently used because they are relatively easy to handle mathematically and because they can be used to approximate nonlinear relationships, especially over a limited range of values. However, one important class of production functions is curvilinear—incorporating both fixed and variable resource inputs. If the university's physical plant is regarded as fixed for purposes of analyzing operating costs associated with increasing enrollments, then operating costs will climb less and less steeply as enrollment rises because the cost of operating the fixed physical plant will be spread over more and more students. In any event, the functional relationships between each major type of resource applied (personnel, facilities, equipment, and dollars) and the loads or outputs considered (instruction, research, and service) must be defined to operate the model.

In the final step, testing, different values are assigned to the equations of the model. Solving for values of selected unknowns reveals the amounts of the various resources needed for meeting given levels of institutional output.

In estimating resource needs, a model can demonstrate that quantities of students enrolled place work loads on personnel and facilities resources according to predetermined policy parameters and defined production functions. Using specified parameters, production functions, and value(s) of the output variable(s), the model is able to describe the resources required—number of FTE faculty, secretaries, classrooms, offices, teaching laboratories, and—in the more sophisticated models—dollars. Furthermore, simulation exercises permit the user to answer almost any number of "what if" questions too complicated to figure out with brain, pad, and pencil. For example, what if average faculty salaries were increased by 10 per cent but total enrollment and average class size both increased by 7 per cent? What if enrollment in engineering dropped 6 per cent and enrollment in liberal arts expanded by 4 per cent?

Notice that the answers implied above do not suggest that resources will be used optimally. They merely suggest that, given the rules about how resource inputs are to be related to work loads and outputs, the model can juggle all the rules and work loads and come up with summaries of personnel, facilities, or dollars (or all three) needed to do a complex job. To make optimum use of resources for any given combination of outputs, more penetrating analysis and complicated modeling is required. In essence, additional relationships must be established. We need to assess the rate of substitutability of one type of resource for another, and these rates need to be associated with the prices of each type of resource. With such relationships explicit, inexpensive resources can be substituted for expensive resources until the incremental output for each type of resource is proportionate to its unit price.

Good use of resource optimization techniques can be illustrated by some of the curriculum planning carried out in the University of Toronto Medical Center. Through a model known as CIRCUS (Calculation of Indirect Resources and Complete Unit Staff), curriculum planners at the Medical Center were able to simulate trade-offs between higher salaried but smaller numbers of staff members and lower paid but larger numbers of staff members to arrive at an optimum combination which would minimize the sum of direct and indirect costs of both undergraduate and medical specialty training programs. In order to accomplish this, the types of tasks which each level of staff was qualified to undertake had to be identified. For example, interns were regarded as qualified to perform some of the functions usually assigned to medical residents, but not all; residents in turn were regarded as qualified to perform some of the tasks of faculty, but not all. In addition, time profiles were constructed for each staff category to determine the direct salary cost incurred by each staff member performing each defined function. The model accepted the time profiles and salary levels for the various staff levels, along with a number of other inputs, to calculate an optimum staff combination which minimized total operating costs. Only infrequently, however, do we have enough confidence in our production functions and enough knowledge of resource substitutability to give us derivative confidence in the results of optimizing techniques. At this stage of resource allocation analysis in higher education, such modeling usually appears to pile uncertainty upon uncertainty.

A management tool as exciting as the computer-assisted

model inevitably collects its devotees as well as its detractors. Institutional researchers are hard pressed to remain neutral for long. The crucial question is whether the model lends more to analysis through simplification than it takes away through oversimplification. The answer to that question cannot be general; it depends upon time, place, purpose of the analysis, and surrounding circumstances. Certainly few would deny the capacity of computer-assisted analysis to contribute to examination of resource problems many more factors and relationships than would be possible without electronic computation. Few would deny, either, the beneficial work habits which model building forces upon researchers. Disciplined, logical thinking and precise articulation have no better ally unless it is the study of mathematics itself. In this connection, model building can serve as an important educational as well as management tool. It can focus the attention of politically inclined and quality-oriented deans and administrators on the economic responsibilities of their jobs. A model can make the importance of resource allocation decisions devastatingly clear to administrators who tend to think of budgets and numbers as responsibilities best delegated to underlings. In addition, it can educate "underlings" in the dimensions, techniques, and discipline of good staff work. Institutional researchers are afforded an opportunity to furnish administrators with a whole new range of information to support better-informed decision-making. Separation of the wheat from the chaff, however, takes substantial knowledge and much careful thinking about the structure and operation of the institution.

The prime attractiveness of model building is not that it aids understanding of the essentials of complex operating systems, but that it lets the decision maker try out alternative courses of action vicariously, seeing the approximate results before actually committing expensive resources to a course of action. By holding all variables constant except the decision variable, trustees, presidents, or executive councils can assess the resource costs or output results of issues pressing for decision. Conceptually, the decision variables tested in models need not be confined to output variables. Decision makers might want to hold the output of the equation constant (for example number of student credit hours taught by academic staff) and find out what effect a change in the student-faculty ratio would have upon staff, space, and dollar requirements. Used in this way, the model becomes an identity model because the input and output sides of the equation maintain a fixed identity, and only the combinations of input change. In any case, the "what if" questions asked of models present the real payoff in terms of improving allocation and utilization decisions for maximizing given ends.

As with most new developments in any field of endeavor, it is easier to describe the shortcomings of analytic modeling than its advantages. To be fair, one must admit that the problems lie not so much with the techniques as with those who employ them. Some of the halls of ivy, particularly those housing computers, seen populated by a strange breed which would prefer to measure Socrates, Plato, and Aristotle by their physical heights than by their wisdom—because at least the former can be calibrated. Much has already been said about frustration in trying to quantify the output objectives of higher education for purposes of assessing resource allocation. Use of output proxies or surrogates seems appropriate up to a point, but the argument that a proxy is the best measure we have and that some measure is better than none at all does not always hold. The quick use of a monolithic measure can just as easily miscalculate human and inanimate resources as it can bring about improvement. At least at this stage of managerial development, qualitative assessments of both input and output remain absolutely vital to the intelligent use of the billions entrusted to our colleges and universities. Analysts who would rather underestimate the importance of nonquantitative considerations than jeopardize the use of models might paradoxically be impeding rather than expediting the development of models.

Just as debilitating as our lack of knowledge about outputs is our lack of knowledge about the production functions of higher education. Models depend upon these relationships to answer the specific "what if" questions asked of them. Yet knowledge of these input-output relationships depends upon accumulation of vast amounts of empirical data describing actual college operations ideally collected only under laboratory conditions keeping most facets of institutional activity constant. Even if an institution does possess unusually comprehensive and accurate information for self-analysis, it usually gives only a point estimate of relationships, based on one point in time and one set of circumstances. To develop a production function, experiential information about operation at a number of output levels and output combinations is necessary. Until institutional data banks in many colleges and universities include quite elaborate operational data over a period of at least six or seven years, model builders are left with logic, intuition, and a few point estimates in specifying the production functions of their models.

The nature of mathematical equations is likely to impose limitations on the use of models directly proportional to the analytical refinement required. In mathematical equations, all units of a particular variable are generally assumed to be not only identical and interchangeable but infinitely divisible. None of those adjectives apply very well to faculty members, staff, students, or facilities. Buildings are discrete, substantial lumps of steel and concrete. Though faculty, staff, and students are of full-, half-, quarter-, and other fractional time-equivalents, they are obviously not completely interchangeable. In fact most deans probably spend more time dealing with the qualitative nonsubstitutability of human resources than with all other facets of resource allocation put together.

While extremely complex mathematical equations can be written, and while computer programs can include algorithms to treat the indivisibilities and qualitative differences in personnel and facilities, at some point the exceptions and complications are more trouble than they are worth. With respect to modeling applications of allocation problems, that point is probably recognized most readily at the college dean's level. In a reasonably homogeneous college of five thousand students or less, the administrative problems of resource deployment tend to be more qualitative than quantitative. Numerical relationships having to do with budgets, faculty, staff, students, space, and programs can be juggled quite easily with a few computer programs. Usually the results can be grasped conceptually without great difficulty. The dean works closely enough with his faculty and students to understand most of the exceptional and qualitative problems of the college—problems which would be difficult or impossible to incorporate into quantitative models. Most of his managerial decisions cannot be based primarily on quantitative considerations because he cannot deal with his resources statistically. Because the quantities are not large, and because he is close to actual line operations, more detailed and personal understanding is rightfully demanded. Most of his resource allocations choices must be made case-by-case.

As the administrator holds responsibility for larger and larger quantities of dollars, men, and materials, the potential utility of systems analysis and modeling also increases. Not only is he unable to comprehend all the exceptional and qualitative circumstances with which each of his unit heads must grapple, but the resource quantities with which he deals can be treated statistically. The president can allocate three hundred faculty positions and seventy-five classrooms to one of his deans with fair confidence that the numbers are large enough to give the dean the flexibility he needs to handle the unique, internal problems of his programs, students, and staff. What the president needs to know is whether the number three hundred or seventy-five is appropriate, both individually and in combination. That is precisely the sort of decision with which systems analysis and computer models can help. This illustration suggests that allocation models and similar tools will find greatest application at top administrative levels in large universities and at the state and national levels. At these levels, resource decisions usually refer to larger aggregates, and the decision maker cannot hope to comprehend the idiosyncratic natures of all the activities affected by his decision. Models can help define the relationships among aggregate resource inputs and can show their connection to aggregate work loads and outputs—which is the best a decision maker can hope for.

Even at higher levels of decision, prudent researchers frequently concentrate not on comprehensive models incorporating all university activities, but on submodels which describe specific sectors of the total institution. A good deal of work has been done on student flow models to establish the academic behavior of students as they flow through the higher education process (Oliver, 1968). Facilities or space models analyze the facilities loads placed on the campus by predetermined student flows and concomitant staff requirements. Cost models which convert student loads, staff, and facilities requirements into operating budget needs have received a good deal of attention; but, as indicated earlier, when cost models include other than instruction the treatment of the other outputs tends to be simplistic. Nevertheless, submodels designed to describe and predict resource needs in one area of institutional activity gain in credibility what they lose in comprehensiveness; they can treat some of the complexities of reality without becoming unmanageable.

Resource allocation models, in their present childhood, probably serve better as a tool for educating than as one for forecasting future needs. In fact, their educational role might well continue to be their greatest contribution to better management in higher education. Like most quantitative information, descriptive equations and simulation results serve admirably as a basis for asking further questions about the nature and purposes of what we do in higher education.

Planning, Programing, and Budgeting. Little has been said, in the course of this chapter, about cost-benefit analysis, and not much more has been said directly about planning, programing, and budgeting systems. Preceding pages have emphasized the problems of input determination only, paying superficial attention to the benefits of higher education and to the machinations of planning and budgeting that are so firmly welded to problems of resource allocation. Up to the present time, I have seen little in the area of cost-benefit analysis that is of practical use to the institutional researcher. A few applications in other fields, such as public health, have been written up, and the purely economic benefits of higher education have been quite thoroughly investigated by Becker (1964), Bowen (1969), and others. Of course educators and philosophers have expounded eloquently on the benefits of scholarship and the scholarly life, but the institutional researcher is a practitioner who brings analytical methods to the aid of those who need guides for action. So far he has received little help from scholars or from other researchers in the form of findings sufficiently conclusive and specific to be used in measuring benefits of an institution's expenditures. There is a growing body of literature which attempts to measure the impact of the college experience on the student; it holds promise for eventual use by institutional researchers but does not yet lend itself to policy application. We are still settling for proxies which are suspect at best. On the other hand, at least some attention is being focused on the importance of assessing the benefits of higher education in a measurable way. The U.S. Office of Education and such organizations as the Ford Foundation and WICHE are devoting resources to further examination of the problem (Western Interstate Commission on Higher Education, 1970b).

Good planning, programing, and budgeting is the raison d'être of resource allocation analysis. Though large organizations constantly move off in new directions without knowing where they were in the first place, their lack of accountability must surely be a contributing factor to the nervous exhaustion and early retirement of those in charge. A well-developed system for planning the future course of the institution, programing the activities and resources needed to stay on that course, and budgeting the dollars to follow through would be a boon to any executive, helping him to perform three of his most fundamental tasks. It would place him in a better position to explain his college or university to its publics, to lead his colleagues in the achievements envisioned, and to deploy his resources to get the most out of them.

All of the foregoing is put in the conditional tense because few if any colleges or universities can boast a thoroughgoing PPB system. As indicated in Chapter Ten, the obstacles faced in establishing such a system are formidable. Not the least of these is the difficulty of finding out how and to what programs various resources are currently contributing. To reiterate, the professor typically contributes to many programs, but his salary dollars are rarely budgeted or accounted for in program terms. If the future direction of the college is to be charted in terms of objectives and programs, and if management of the organization is to be thought of and explained in those terms and budgets are to be requested in those terms, then current and past resource utilization need to be described in those terms. Requirements for the future must be predicted on a program basis as well as on the traditional basis.

A total resources accounting system, which makes program costing and the construction of descriptive analytic systems possible, acts as one of the cornerstones of successful planning, programming, and budgeting. Though all the tedious systems building demanded by program costing and accompanying resource analysis presents a great temptation to move ahead with a PPB system the easy way (without an adequate program-costing system), the results of doing so would likely have little effect on the way plans are laid and resources are deployed. The grouping of existing accounts on a traditional chart into some program format and the budgeting of funds according to those groupings will rarely have much effect on the planning-management process. There is no reason why they should. For PPB systems to succeed, resources ultimately have to be accounted for according to the purposes and programs in behalf of which they were expended. Only then does the base for planning and budgeting give intelligent consideration to program requirements and implications.

All of this, from total resources accounting to mathematical simulation to program budgeting, places demands upon but offers opportunities for institutional research. The rather desperate need of administrators to find more skillful means of both managing and explaining higher education has fostered the mushroom growth of institutional research. Other offices and departments, in most institutions, have not been inclined, equipped, or designated to fill the void. Assisting institutional policy makers to make better-informed decisions about the deployment of resources is going to require a greater range and depth of analytical skills than it has in the past. By the same token, it will require greater skills in education, coordination, and the politics of persuasion. New ways of doing things are rarely greeted with unrestrained enthusiasm in academia, where the first instinct is to preserve the knowledge and culture of the past.

Bibliography

American Association of University Professors. *Committee Z: The Annual Report on the Economic Status of the Profession.* Washington, D.C., 1961–1970.

American Council on Education. *The Fact Book of Higher Education,* issues 1 and 2. Washington, D.C., 1970.

BECKER, G. S. *Human Capital.* Princeton, N.J.: Princeton University Press, 1964.

BOWEN, W. G. *The Economics of Major Private Universities.* Berkeley: Carnegie Commission on Higher Education, 1968.

BOWEN, W. G. *The Economic Aspects of Higher Education.* Princeton, N.J.: Princeton University Press, 1969.

BRUMMET, R. L., PYLE, W. C., AND FLAMHOLTZ, E. G. "Development and

Implemenation of Human Resource Accounting in the Business Enterprise," *Personnel Administration,* 1969, *32*(4), 34–46.

CAMPBELL, A., AND ECKERMAN, W. C. *Public Concepts of the Values and Costs of Higher Education.* Ann Arbor: Institute for Social Research, 1964.

MILLIKEN, W. G. "Education Must Prove Worth, Politicians Say." *Chronicle of Higher Education,* August 3, 1970, p. 8.

OLIVER, R. M. "Models for Predicting Gross Enrollments at the University of California." In *Ford Foundation Report 68–3.* Berkeley: Office of Vice President Planning and Analysis, 1968.

Regents of the University of California. *Revised Academic Plan 1969–1975 for the University of California at Berkeley.* Berkeley, 1969.

RUSSELL, J. D., AND DOI, J. I. *Manual for Studies of Space Utilization in Colleges and Universities.* Athens, Ohio: Ohio University and American Association of Collegiate Registrars and Admissions Officers, 1957.

U.S. Department of Commerce. *Statistical Abstract of the United States.* Washington, D.C., 1970a.

U.S. Department of Commerce. *Survey of Current Business,* 1970b, *50*(12).

U.S. Department of Commerce, Bureau of the Census. *Current Population Reports.* Washington, D.C., 1970.

U.S. Department of Health, Education, and Welfare, Social and Rehabilitation Service. *Cost and Output of Graduate Social Work Education.* Stamford, Conn.: Cooper, 1970.

Western Interstate Commission on Higher Education. *Higher Education Facilities Planning and Management Manuals.* Boulder, 1970a.

Western Interstate Commission on Higher Education. *The Outputs of Higher Education: Their Identification, Measurement, and Evaluation.* Boulder, 1970b.

CHAPTER **10**

Long-Range Planning

Elwin F. Cammack

❧❧❧❧❧❧❧❧

This chapter considers: factors which have given impetus to long-range planning activities in higher education; various approaches to the planning process, with one possible approach outlined and discussed in some detail, and some problems and cautions in developing and implementing long-term plans. Attention is given to the interface between institutional research and long-range planning.

Incentive

Planning has been carried out in some aspects of higher education for many years. In fact, the Yale Faculty Report of 1828 looked at the goals and objectives of Yale University as they related to the future. However, more recently there has been an increasing expectancy that higher education demonstrate accountability. The demand for accountability has been motivated by increasing costs,

251

by competition for scarce resources, by questioning directed toward the nature and amount of values aided by education, and, especially, by student expressions of discontent with the institutional value system held by higher education. Discontent has been crystallized in demonstrations demanding change in undergraduate programs and in allocation of the resources of colleges and universities.

During the past decade enrollments have increased rapidly in most colleges and universities. Since funds have tended to follow students, new programs started with monies appropriated for additional students often did not necessitate phasing out other programs. However, the increases in numbers of students and programs in combination with the increases in faculty salaries and with decreasing faculty loads have raised dramatically the costs of higher education. And money available from federal sources and private donors has considerably decreased. The combined result has tended to increase the burden of state governments for public higher education and has necessitated fee increments in private colleges and universities. Planning is necessary if accountability is to be demonstrated to those paying the bills.

Another incentive for institutional planning has been the expansion of statewide, regional, and national planning efforts. State boards of higher education, coordinating councils, and other state agencies have looked carefully at duplication of effort in attempting to design coordinated systems of higher education which would meet the educational needs of the state in the most efficient and effective way possible. Along with interest in statewide planning has been an increasing tendency to develop plans designed to serve regional and national needs. A tendency on the part of regional and national planners to relate the educational programs to the manpower needs of the state or nation introduces an entirely new dimension to most college and university planners. Whereas in the past, institutional goals and objectives have been set primarily by departments and their faculties, the emphasis on manpower training casts doubts on the need for many of the programs offered by colleges and universities.

During the next decade an entirely new set of planning parameters will become operative. Many institutions are now faced with leveling enrollment growth, either by self-imposed or externally imposed limitations on the numbers of students served. With reduction in the rate of growth and with continually increasing costs, institutions have much less flexibility than formerly. This means that, if new programs are to be started, old programs must be evaluated carefully and cut back or eliminated to obtain resources for programs more viable in the institutional setting. Since most resources are tied up in salaries, and since faculty members with tenure cannot be immediately transferred or terminated, reallocation often requires that plans be effected over a period of years.

Reasons for Neglect

Planning is such an obvious thing to do that one wonders why it is not done. The reasons are many and not always obvious. Here are a few. Leadership is lethargic or indifferent—not really concerned with anything except present comfort. Loads are heavy, and planning is delayed until time can be found. (Talk about planning is evident but no actual planning is done.) No one has the knowledge or the competency to start an activity although some persons may talk knowingly about it. Dynamic administrators of the wheeler-dealer type prefer to act on the bases of expediency and opportunism. Motivated to enhance their own reputation, they leave to successors the task of picking up the pieces. Plans are seen by such individuals as hampering their freedom. Some administrators despair of writing a plan which will satisfy everyone, and they fear arousal of the antagonism of some segment of the constituency. Public institutions are especially concerned with legislative reactions —optimistic projections may provoke reprisals, and pessimistic ones may be readily accepted as an excuse for inadequate appropriations. Some persons see a plan as a self-fulfilling prophecy which, once made, inexorably forces the institution in that direction. Faculty members often prefer to harbor and promote unrealistic aspirations than to see development of a plan which may explicitly deny them. Concern is often voiced that planning overemphasizes financial considerations and tends to deny creative developments.

There are those who are certain that no plan is needed because the obvious goal is expansion—in size, numbers of programs, amount of research, and amount of service. They think the only problem is finding resources and that that is the responsibility of the administration, the board, or the faculty entrepreneurs. A department voting out its chairman because he had not brought in enough outside money would exemplify this view.

There are some who insist that planning is impossible unless you know what to expect and that, if you do know what to expect, planning is either very simple or unnecessary.

In actuality, planning is needed to cope with rapid change and to provide ways to deal rationally with the unexpected. It provides ways to deal with the unexpected or undesirable because it establishes a basis for rejecting inappropriate proposals and unreasonable demands. Clark Kerr has said, "The more one attempts to deal with short-run problems, particularly next year's budget, the more likely one is to encounter resistance to the analysis of alternatives and political commitments that cannot be changed." As planning horizons move further into the future, people become more objective and more inclined toward rational analysis.

Strategies

The preceding comments on the problems and difficulties of planning indicate the desirability of carefully considered strategy. Although it is quite possible that the final strategy in planning will emerge only as some of the initial steps have been carried through, it may be wise at an early stage in talking with faculty, board members, students, and others who will be involved to point to the fact that planning does not necessarily require a highly stereotyped approach. In particular it does not necessarily require financial considerations to dominate. The following strategies might be developed in combination, or any one of them could be used exclusively. First, it is assumed that the general commitment of the institution is to high standards of academic excellence and that all planning is oriented to obtaining that goal. Planning, then, proceeds largely by deciding upon the steps which the institution needs to take in order to move in the desired direction.

Second, the primary concern may be with relating needs of programs to available resources. In this case, academic standards, admissions policies, and enrollments may be related to provision of operating income. An extreme of this strategy would be to determine the resources which are available from sources acceptable to the institution and to develop the program accordingly.

Third, another strategy is to decide a priori the various programs that the institutions would like to have or would permit, to place these in some order of priority, and then to develop and carry on only those programs for which support can be found.

Fourth, an optimistic strategy takes the point of view that any detailed formal planning is unnecessary because the institution will develop any programs for which resources can be found. This strategy may have been the most commonly used in the past and has gotten many institutions into difficulty.

Fifth, a strategy frequently used in rapidly developing institutions is to do everything possible to attract outstanding faculty members, to provide these persons with as much support as possible from internal sources, and to encourage them to seek outside resources for any programs that they would like to develop. The availability of federal support made this a very attractive strategy in the 1960's.

Discussion of possible strategies brings into the open some of the fears that people have of planning, and open discussion may make it possible to proceed, at least in the early stages of planning, without arousing resistance or antagonism.

Approaches

A good first step in any attempt at planning, and one to which we shall shortly return in discussing the steps in planning, is that of combining an adequate statistical base with description to indicate just where the institution is and how it got to this point. Other steps may readily be deferred until descriptive material has been put together and everybody has acquired familiarity with it as a common background. Background data and the trends suggested by it may markedly affect the assumptions made and the goals stated.

One critical decision must be made in respect to the purposes of the institution, the role of the institution with respect to service to its area, the relationship of the institution to other institutions, and the size of the institution. Agreement must be reached on whether the institution will continue to maintain the character it now has, whether it will redefine and narrow its goals and range of services, or whether it will marketdly expand its goals and services. Unless major new support from a donor or foundation is in the offing, most institutions will find that contraction and redirection rather than expansion are dictated. The prestige accorded to the university pattern—with emphasis on graduate and professional education and on research—affects even the smaller liberal-arts colleges. At some stage of rethinking on programs, there will inevitably be some—faculty members, administrators, and maybe even full departments—who call for inauguration of new degree programs, including possibly master's programs and doctorates, regardless of needs or costs. At this point the advantages of letting everyone have his say and of placing all possibilities on the table must be weighed against the arguments, loss of morale, and delay, should virtually impossible moves have to be carefully discussed and tactfully rejected. To impose severe limitations on or to completely negate the possibility of new programs is to immediately dampen interest and enthusiasm of faculty; but to entertain all possibilities is to encourage unrealistic, pie-in-the-sky proposals. If it is pointed out, however, that every proposal must include some realistic attention to the financial commitments involved and that the ultimate resources and goals must be in balance, aspirations for expensive new programs may be somewhat weakened by realization of the effects on salaries. Segments of the faculty sympathetic to the problems involved may respond by uniting to set a priority on salaries or on improvement of existing programs, thereby effectively sidetracking discussion of expensive new ventures.

A problem perhaps more difficult to deal with is that of an influential person (a board member, a prospective donor, or a political power) who takes advantage of planning to insist that the institution take a certain step, for example adding another graduate program in engineering or introducing a school of law or veterinary medicine. A great deal of pressure can be generated by such an individual, and the possibility of incurring his ill will or of losing out on a major gift may result in ready yielding to a demand which is inappropriate and even deleterious to long-run development. Even without aspirations for new degree programs, planning attempts may elicit proposals for additional courses in specialized areas.

A tendency to equate quality with student-faculty ratio can lead to projections of faculty needs on the basis of constant or even decreasing student-to-faculty ratios. For most small colleges, however, the student-to-faculty ratio could be increased most effectively by the elimination of unnecessary courses and small classes without increasing the faculty credit or contact hour load. In any case, such a simple index should not be accepted as a basis for planning until its implications in reference to the structure of the curriculum and to the specific instructional program have been carefully examined. The faculty should also be forced to examine the implications of new technology in any consideration of new ways to provide significant educational experience with less demand on the faculty.

There is likely to be considerable discussion on the matter of enrollment growth. Some institutions have gone far astray in predicting growth in the student body because they have examined only the intake of new students and have not considered the implications of attrition and transfers. Many private colleges find that the differential costs between publicly supported institutions and private institutions lead parents to insist that students, after one or two years in a private college, transfer to a less costly state college or university. Considerable attrition occurs simply because many students do not find the college program challenging and are not motivated to stay until completion of the degree. Thus it is desirable, in any approach to planning, that the faculty should be forced to rethink the academic program—the courses, the curriculum, the sequence of experiences, the range of experiences provided, the bases for assessing the progress of students, and the competencies that students are expected to acquire by the time of graduation. It is difficult to correlate curriculum review with long-term planning; and yet, unless faculty are forced in planning to consider review, all that may be assured by their efforts is the continued life of the institution. Innovations stimulated by review could offer, in addition, service to the educational needs of the future.

The problem of curricular organization and instruction is closely related to operational costs. Tuitions in all colleges and universities have been going up, and some of the private colleges have practically priced themselves out of the market. This is especially apparent in the New York Area, since open admissions has been declared as the policy in the New York City institutions. Only by restricting program offerings and operating more efficiently will it be possible for many of the private colleges to survive. Only program elements which can be justified by educational quality, institutional mission, and resources should be maintained.

Another planning area to which an institution needs to give serious attention is the matter of minority groups. Almost all colleges and universities have been trying to meet an acknowledged obligation by seeking black, Indian, Asian, and Chicano students who can benefit from higher education. They have modified traditional admissions requirements in order to admit these students, but they have not always faced up to the costs involved, costs such as financial assistance, special educational programs, and counseling services. There is no point in admitting disadvantaged students unless they are given a reasonable chance to succeed. Providing students only with an opportunity for failure is neither equitable nor economical, and it is not likely to promote good will toward higher education.

Planning may be done without regard to the fiscal implications, or it may be focused almost entirely on resource requirements with little regard for the program aspirations of the college or university. Numerous institutions have developed long-range planning documents which speak to goals and program objectives, and which provide overall directions to the university or college without presenting detailed analyses involving revenue requirements. The danger in this kind of planning is that it becomes an academic exercise which does not provide guidelines which will be used by faculty, administration, and governing boards. Plans developed without considering the fiscal implications tend to be unrealistic. On the other hand, if the primary design of a plan is fiscal, it can overlook program implications and thereby provide no means for innovation and future reevaluation. A composite approach can be taken, that is, some attempt can be made to bring together the program delimitation and the fiscal projections. If this is done, a decision must be made as to how projections of fiscal resources are to be determined. Two alternatives are possible here: one is to arrive at program delimitations and carefully project the fiscal resources required to implement these programs; the other brings closure between the fiscal and program projections by projecting resources available over a given period of time and then fitting programs according to assigned priority rankings to these fiscal limitations. This technique is especially useful for short-range planning and for interfacing the budgeting process with the planning process.

As the planning process is initiated, attention must be given to relationships between statewide plans and the roles of other institutions of higher learning in the state. For some fields, such as the health sciences, and for graduate study, both national and regional planning should be considered. There is an increasing tendency to give more attention to manpower-oriented planning at the national level than has been the case in the past. This in part is a reaction to an overproduction of Ph.D.'s in certain fields that have been traditionally supported by federal dollars. Shortages in the health science fields clearly constitute a national problem.

Steps

This section suggests what may generally be an appropriately ordered series of steps in planning. In practice, several of these may be started simultaneously, and there may be movement back and forth between the various steps as the planning proceeds. Thus the goals, assumptions, and programs may have to be reexamined when one finds that the program development outruns the resources anticipated.

The first step of a planning effort requires that a statement of assumptions about the future be developed. There is always difficulty in obtaining agreement on external trends; we can only seek the judgments of those who specialize in predicting social and economic developments. Internal matters, such as size of the institution, faculty salaries, and facilities are much more comprehensible and controllable, tending to be closely related to goals. The process of developing assumptions and specific goals related to these may be one of the more difficult points upon which to obtain accord. Some examples of assumptions which might be considered are: inflation will continue at the rate of five per cent per year over the planning period; there will be an increasing demand for higher education due to an increasing tendency of high school graduates to go on for a college degree; and foundations and federal dollars will follow the major graduate institutions in the nation as a result of an American Council on Education study which suggests a diminishing need for education at the doctoral level.

The second step is to review past operations, trends, and assessments of the current status of the college or university. In the context of a program and budget plan, a systematic information system could help in answering the following questions: How well has the institution performed the task it was created to perform? Have the graduates been successful? Is the institution filling both social and economic needs locally, regionally, and nationally? What have been the relationships between program development and costs? What is the history of students who have entered the institution and completed programs successfully? Have resources been allocated according to stated objectives? Questions concerning the research program must also be asked if the college or university is a graduate institution. Has it been contributing to the advancement of our social and economic welfare? Has the research contributed to the program of graduate education? Questions about the public service function must also be asked. Have faculty resources been wisely utilized in extending the boundaries of the campus to serve its region? Has competition with other institutions caused wasteful duplication of services? Have satisfactory lines of communication and modes of cooperation been developed with other agencies performing functions which are closely allied to that of higher education?

The answers to these questions involve looking at variables such as the student population, the faculty and its characteristics, the educational programs, the physical plant, and the sources of income. To the extent that they are already on record, plans for improvement or addition of programs are a part of the present state of the institution. The utilization of facilities is an important consideration. Data on class size, patterns of instruction, and other characteristics of the instructional and curricular program are useful in understanding the present scene. In addition to sheer statistics, descriptive materials indicating some of the major stages in the development of the institution and some of the major problems faced can be helpful. It is here that the institutional researcher can probably make his greatest contribution to the planning process. Time can be well spent in careful study of this data collection, in analyzing its implications, and in using it to make projections as to where the institution may be going if the observed trends continue.

The third step in planning, which actually may be developed coincidentally with the second, is the clarification of goals. This includes delineation of the role of the institution in society, the constituency which it serves, the particular emphases of the institution, and its relationships with the community and with other institutions. Obviously clarification is more than a matter of reading a statement of goals or purposes in the catalog. It may involve review of many documents including various presidential speeches, board actions, committee statements, and the like. These may reveal crass inconsistencies as well as disparities between intention and actual operations. (At this point we are not talking about those esoteric, very general statements which are really pious expressions characteristic of a ministerial sort of president, quite unrelated to the actual operation of the institution and probably unknown to the faculty and the student body. We are talking about broad institutional purposes which are operationally evident in the functions of instruction, research, and public service.)

When we speak of objectives, we are talking about fairly specific definitions of the types of characteristics or competencies that students are expected to acquire by being in the institution. When we speak of goals, we are talking about ends viewed for graduate or professional programs, for commitment to the liberal arts, for innovation, and, more recently, for programs such as environmental quality.

In defining goals, one of the major considerations—particularly in respect to state supported institutions—is the role definition of an institution in the total of state programs. Here we have a very touchy point. Each state institution desires autonomy to enable it to develop every possibility and especially to enable it to become a large graduate institution. Goals may be derived from mission statements, especially those that appear in statewide master plans for higher education or those that the institution has developed with specificity sufficient for providing real direction in program development and planning. For example, a state with a major public university and several state colleges may have a state master plan that assigns all professional and doctoral work to the state university whereas the state colleges are assigned undergraduate education, master's work in education and other disciplines, and perhaps also emerging specialist degrees (such as Specialist in Education). Each college or university would thereby be obligated to determine goals that are consistent with these broader statements of mission.

Institutional goals may include very broad educational objectives. An example of an objective broadened to the status of a goal applies to the new University of Wisconsin campus at Green Bay. Here the commitment is to develop an interdisciplinary approach to education with a focus on environment that prepares students to solve problems facing society by drawing upon the several disciplines which may contribute to an understanding of and may provide solutions to particular social or economic problems.

A final step in the planning process is the projection of existing and anticipated new programs. Pioneering work on projection techniques is being done in the University of California's Research Program in University Administration, funded by the Ford Foundation. Here, consideration is given to problems such as the outputs of higher education, mathematical analysis of structural control in a graded manpower system, the stability of faculty input coefficients, an economic theory of doctoral education, production bounds for new faculty positions in a budget plan, analytical planning for university libraries, cost accounting analysis for university libraries, models for predicting gross enrollments, an equilibrium model of faculty appointments, and a control theory solution to optimal faculty staffing; these and many other studies are being applied to educational planning and decision-making. Sophisticated models for prediction of resource requirements are being developed and tested. Noteworthy among projects employing models is the work at the University of Toronto and the work being done by the Western Interstate Commission for Higher Education (WICHE). These programs are discussed in greater detail in Chapter Eight.

Projections for long-range planning require application of a multitude of parameters for which sophisticated projections models are only now being developed. Projections of student enrollments according to current program by level of student and by program are a must as are the enrollments anticipated for any new programs that might be planned. It is necessary to analyze the input of new programs not on the basis of that program alone but also in relation to the input or other programs. For example, consideration must be given to the implications that a new program in engineering has for the mathematics department, for the English department, and for all other departments which will service the engineering major. Along with projections of students goes the need to project faculty members, faculty mix, the loads of faculty, induced course enrollments, and the desired complement of faculty competencies that will need to be brought together. Most professional programs and some arts and science majors require a minimal complete staff to provide all courses and educational experiences required; their staff needs would apply even if only one student were enrolled.

One of the greatest shortcomings of long-range planning efforts at most institutions has been the lack of interface between the facilities plan and the academic plan. All too often, campus master plans and specific facilities plans are considered without the benefit of an a priori detailed academic plan. Instead of examining only such variables as total student enrollment and perhaps considering, too, some very gross statements of programs to be developed, those projecting facilities should follow guidelines established in a careful specification of the programs projected; these are the programs for which implementation is desired. If the academic plan is considered, a better fit can be accomplished among classroom sizes, functions, and program requirements, between the office spaces required and those provided, and between research facilities provided and research needs. Models specifying amounts and types of spaces needed for students, faculty, and specific types of programs can provide immeasurable help in bringing program projections into one-to-one correspondence with facilities projections.

The following guidelines are from specifications for planning documents made available to all state agencies in Wisconsin. Program information should include a brief description of the programs and services now provided by the institution or group of related institutions; a description of the way in which these current programs may be expected to expand and modify over the years to 1985; a description of the major new or alternate programs that may be implemented by 1985, such as a new hospital or a major new facility for alcoholics; a description of the way in which the agency's major mission may be shifted in response to changing characteristics in society; a description of the social, economic, and program technology factors which offer potential for changes and evolution in the methods of operating the program by 1985; and a general schedule for the occurrence and accommodation of these conditions.

Information on populations should include projections of the program populations to 1985 categorized by major groups; descriptions of the changing attributes of the program populations; and an estimate of staffing needs to 1985 categorized by major types. Information on facilities should include a description of the existing and authorized facilities available to accommodate program demands describing both the quantity and the quality of the facilities in general terms; a description of the facilities that will be needed by 1985 to meet program requirements, employment projections, and general space guidelines; a description of anticipated changes in existing facilities to 1985, identifying buildings to be razed, major conversions from one space to another, and major rehabilitations; a description of a general schedule of new construction to 1985 showing how facilities changes are to accommodate the program needs on an orderly basis; and a description of land acquisition needed to accommodate program and facilities developed to 1985.[1]

Application of guidelines or steps in planning should answer the questions of where we are and how we got there. Steps or guidelines can also help to answer the question of where we want to go. Interrelationships of goal descriptions and assumptions provide bases for planning how to get to the desired goals. In the process of planning, it may be desirable to consider a number of

[1] Roger Schrantz, State Building Commission, State of Wisconsin, February 1970.

alternatives and it is likely to be necessary to make some modifications in the desired goals in view of reality.

When all the improvement factors and other costs of new programs and facilities are added up, it is highly unlikely that available resources will match these. If institutions could charge students full costs for their education, there would appear to be no problem on this score; yet, even then, institutions might very early in planning find that they have included so many programs to be continued and so many desirable but not absolutely necessary new programs and services that charging full cost would rule the operation out of the competitive market. Always, then, one must face the problem of obtaining closure on a plan by matching the academic program and related services to the resources actually available.

In contending with limited resources, attention must first be given to the possibility of redefining goals and purposes. Redefinition of goals may require changing other goals and purposes of the institution, or it may involve limiting the goals to be obtained over a span of time. One can adjust plans to resources by establishing a set of priorities and indicating that he will go as far through this list as possible in terms of resources available in a given year or period. One can modify groups of goals, eliminating certain ones which are major sources of expenditures or deciding to postpone them until a later time. In the case of education, it may be possible in some cases to employ outside services for taking care of some needs on a less expensive basis or to introduce ways in which costs can be taken care of outside the operating budget. A simple example is a decision that science or art supplies be a special fee item or that arrangements be made for students to buy these directly. Similarly, individual music lessons may be placed on a special fee basis. Food services may be contracted rather than provided under college management. It may also be cheaper to contract special courses with another institution than to provide them within the institution; however an alternative applied in many places around the country is to organize consortia in which collaborative effort will either reduce cost of existing programs or provide programs, at minimal cost, to institutions who do not presently have them.

The manner of bringing closure in balancing resources and programs must not be perfunctory. At various points, estimates of costs have to be made and, at some points, it is likely that income will not match these. If, when this happens, the procedure is simply to go back and lower certain cost estimates, or, on the other hand, to simply increase the tuition or the expectation of gifts, the significance of the plan is undermined. If an institution is strongly committed to everything that is put down in the way of programs, it may well place emphasis on how it can find additional resources. In fact, the existence of a well-thought-out plan and the indication that certain things will have to be discontinued if additional money cannot be found is a very strong entering wedge for obtaining additional resources. This is true whether the source of funds is a legislature, a foundation, or an individual. It is at the point where resources and programs are to be balanced that the most serious thinking must be done about the goals, the programs, the priorities, and the financing of the institution; however, at this point, some of the unrealistic schemes and demands not eliminated earlier can be abandoned. In respect to special funding, it must be kept in mind that the aftermath of categorically given foundation and federal grants may be feelings of overcommitment and desire to escape. Thus planning in itself is beneficial for it results in application of new insights to more realistic goals.

It is probably unwise to attempt to plan too far into the future. To develop an academic and financial plan beyond five or six years may be unrealistic although it may be well to have a ten-year or longer development generally in view. Particularly in connection with the planning of facilities, a ten-year projection including new and renovated academic and auxiliary facilities which assume program plans is desirable because of the lag time between initial planning, raising of funds, and actual construction. In fact, in new and rapidly developing institutions, the overall facilities master plan should be projected beyond ten years—perhaps as much as twenty or twenty-five years—to allow for appropriate land acquisitions and campus master plan development.

If a long-range plan is drawn up in adequate detail, then it is desirable and it should be possible with limited effort to provide a revision each year. For example at the end of the first year of an academic and financial plan, the operating budget for that year should be examined in relation to the goals set. Major modifications should be indicated and the next year should then be visualized in reference to the modified plan; any major departures over additional years will be included similarly so that the plan is always current for at least five years ahead. When new proposals are brought in, they can readily be evaluated in reference to the scope of the plan. If a proposal is highly unrealistic, calling for resources unlikely to be obtained, the existence of the plan provides a handy budgetary referent for denying the request. A proposal with good possibilities for funding that seems well within the general purposes of the institution may seriously be considered, and the plan may be revised to include it. One hazard is that most new programs involve continuing and cumulative liability, and those proposing them are likely to underestimate both the original and the continuing costs.

As has often been pointed out, the commitment of tenure to a faculty member involves a long-run expenditure of hundreds of thousands of dollars. Financial aid is another good example of long-term commitment. If aid is extended to two hundred freshmen each year for four years and the program is successful in keeping all of them in college for four years, aid would be granted to eight hundred students by the end of the fourth year. It is likely, also, that the average amount of aid would have increased.

Planning is an arduous job. It requires a great amount of time on the part of many people, and the task is never finished. It must be continually updated, and this can be done only after at least one individual is given the continuing charge to review the plan, to analyze how well the institution is filling it, to raise major questions about departure from it, and to insist that the necessity of such a deparure means that replanning is necessary. The problem is that no one person can do the entire job. An ad hoc committee on long-range planning recommended establishment of an academic planning council comprised of faculty working with the academic vice-chancellor. As the committee explained:

It is recognized that academic planning takes place at the departmental or interdepartmental level by individual faculty members. A procedure would be established to provide a faculty review of these individual plans from a campuswide point of view and thereby develop academic plans for the University of Wisconsin, Madison Campus. In addition, a planning system would be developed to provide analyses on the consequences of alternative combinations of resource allocation in meeting the objectives in teaching, research, and public service. . . . Initially the Academic Planning Council would establish a provisional academic plan by taking inventory of our present enrollment and resource distributions, accepting the current campus enrollments, and then extending the program and resource targets for each academic unit . . . and each service unit . . . in a straightforward extrapolation. Research extrapolations would include funds, space, and personnel targets for academic research, student service, and community service activities. Enrollment extrapolations would include student and credit loads by level. In setting the extrapolated targets, the recent history of each academic unit would be considered along with any special information available on other factors which might indicate a marked departure from the standard extrapolation.

Each academic unit would be asked to initiate long-range planning based on the extrapolated targets at the departmental or operational level, and information would be collected for a program-by-program review of the provisional academic plan. The enrollment targets would be analyzed to determine if they were realistic in terms of the resources available and the effectiveness of the program. A simultaneous review would also be made by the College of Deans providing college-level coordination of the program unit planning for the council. Each service unit would also be asked to initiate long-range planning so that nonacademic needs of the institution can be evaluated. The provisional plan then would be altered as warranted by the data and planning goals presented by each academic and service unit. At this point the long-range planning already approved and implemented would be built into the academic plans.[2]

[2] Report to Chancellor Edwin Young from the Ad Hoc Committee on Long-Range Planning, The University of Wisconsin, Madison Campus, April 1970.

In employing these plans, the council could establish mechanisms for selecting priorities, allocating resources, and resolving conflicts which may occur between long-term and short-term objectives. Admissions policies, hiring policies, and even promotion and tenure policies would need to be related to the plans for effective application.

As has been mentioned earlier in this section and in previous chapters, planning models now being developed by a number of colleges and universities can aid materially in the planning process. They are especially helpful in achieving closure in establishing relationships between a program and the operating and facilities capital needed to implement it. But no plan can be really effective unless its implementation is assured by acceptance of its obligations and limitations and by development and adherence to policies and practices consistent with it.

Control

Administrators and faculty have at times resisted planning because they feared loss of control. It can be argued, and rightfully so, that long-term planning commitments result in some inflexibility in the annual budgeting process. If commitments have been made over a long period of time, and if faculty expectations are consistent with them, then it is natural to expect that the budgeting process will follow these commitments.

At the same time, there are necessities during long-term commitments to eliminate inequities, to reduce costs, to improve quality, and to phase out programs. It is impossible, for instance, to decide this year that a program should be phased out and to accomplish that in one budget year. To merely phase out a program involves relocating or reassigning faculty who may have tenure, reassignment of facilities which are not readily adaptable to other uses, and disposition of equipment which may be expensive and not at all adaptable to other programs of the institution. Change in institutional direction comes slowly, especially in such things as the improvement of quality; hence any major redirection must be a long-term commitment if it is to be realized. If every action necessary during the life of a plan made it necessary to reopen the plan for debate, the plan would shortly be discarded.

Higher education can be expected to demonstrate a greater degree of accountability to its many publics. By providing a rational basis for decisions, planning will save us all from decisions arrived at through the vagaries of the moment. It will demonstrate to the funding agencies, whether they be legislatures, foundations, or individuals, that the college or university does indeed have a plan of action—one that can be evaluated and one from which the funding agency can obtain a sense of the benefit to accrue as a result of the resources invested.

Past history suggests that planning is most likely to be realistic and successful in an institution when it is done, in part, as a result of externally imposed roles and limitations—limitations which make it evident that faculty and administrative aspirations to make their institution another Harvard, Michigan, Amherst, or Swarthmore are quite impossible to realize. Financial exigency is undoubtedly the greatest spur to serious systematic planning in institutions of higher education.

Bibliography

BARTRAM, J. W. "Long-Range Planning at Utopia U." *College and University Business,* 1958, *24*(6), 25.

BOLIN, J. G. *Institutional Long-Range Planning.* Athens, Ga.: Institute of Higher Education, University of Georgia, 1969.

BOWEN, H. R. "How to Plan Around Things That Can't Be Planned." *College and University Business,* 1963, *35*(1), 31–33.

"Campus Planning," administration study 6. *College and University Business,* 1961, *30*(5), 48–65.

CLOSE, W. A. "Plan for Planning." *College and University Business,* 1966, *40*(6), 41.

D'AMICO, L. A., AND BROOKS, W. D. "The Spatial Campus: A Planning Scheme." *Bulletin of the School of Education, Indiana University,* 1968, *44*(5), 1–116.

DREWRY, G. N. (Ed.), *The Administrative Team and Long-Range Planning.* Athens, Ga.: Institute of Higher Education, University of Georgia, 1967.

EBERLE, A. W., AND MC GUTCHEON, S. C. "A Systems Model for Institutional Planning," *Educational Record,* 1970, *51*(1), 66–71.

ELLIS, E. "Efficient Planning for Growth in Higher Education." *The North Central Association Quarterly,* 1968, *33*(2), 169–173.

EMCH, A. R. *Long Range Planning for Colleges and Universities.* Chicago: Booz, Allen, and Hamilton, 1960.

EURICH, A. C. "Plan or Perish." *College and University Journal,* 1970, *9*(3), 18–22.

EWING, D. W. (Ed.), *Long-Range Planning for Management.* New York: Harper and Row, 1964.

FARMER, J. *Why Planning, Programming, Budgeting Systems for Higher Education?,* monographs for college and university presidents, 1. Boulder: Western Interstate Commission on Higher Education, 1970.

GLENNY, L. A. *Autonomy of Public Colleges, The Challenge of Coordination.* New York: McGraw-Hill, 1959.

HARTLEY, H. J. *Educational Planning-Programming-Budgeting: A Systems Approach.* Englewood Cliffs, N.J.: Prentice-Hall, 1968.

HATHAWAY, D. E. "What Is the Responsibility of the Faculty in Institutional Long-Range Planning?" *Current Issues in Higher Education.* Washington, D.C.: Association for Higher Education, National Education Association, 1960.

HYDE, R. M. "A Small University Charts Its Course." *The Educational Record,* 1962, *43*(1), 62–67.

JOHNSON, E. L. "Planning for Educational Planning." *Liberal Education,* 1964, *50*(4), 489–498.

KETCHUM, D. S. "Implementing the Plan." *College and University Journal,* 1970, *9*(3) 23–27.

KNORR, O. A. (Ed.) *Long-Range Planning in Higher Education.* Boulder: Western Interstate Commission on Higher Education, 1965.

LARKIN, P., AND TEEPLE, J. "Education Must Anticipate Shifts in U.S. Goals." *College and University Management,* 1969, *47*(4), 83–84.

LEWIS, J. P., PINNELL, W. G., AND WELLS, H. B. "Needs, Resources, and Priorities in Higher Educational Planning." *AAUP Bulletin,* 1957, *43*(3), 431–442.

MC GRATH, E. J., AND MEETH, L. R. (Eds.) *Cooperative Long-Range Planning in Liberal Arts Colleges.* New York: Bureau of Publications, Teachers College, Columbia University, 1964.

"Management Methods—Long-Range Planning." *College Management Magazine,* 1969, *4*(3), 58–63.

MAYHEW, L. *Institutional, State, and Regional Long-Range Planning.* Washington, D.C.: Government Printing Office, 1969.

MEETH, L. R. *Selected Issues in Higher Education: An Annotated Bibliography.* New York: Teachers College Press, 1965.

MEETH, L. R. "Functional Long-Range Planning: Purpose and Process." *Liberal Education,* 1967, *53*(3), 375–384.

RUSSELL, J. D. *Manual of Space Utilization of Colleges and Universities.* Athens, Ohio: American Association of Collegiate Registarts and Admission Officers, Ohio University, 1957.

SCARBOROUGH, C. "Management Use of Simulation in Long-Range Planning for Colleges and Universities." In C. FINCHER (Ed.), *Institutional Research and Academic Outcomes.* Athens, Ga.: Association for Institutional Research, 1968.

SPIRO, R. H. "Toward a True Master Plan." *College and University Business,* 1967, *42*(2), 47.

STUHR, R. L. "Developing an Academic Blueprint." *College and University,* 1963, *38*(3), 284–288.

THOMPSON, L. M. "Institutional Research, Planning, and Politics." *The Journal of Experimental Education,* 1962, *31*(2), 89–91.

TICKTON, S. G. *Letter to a College President on the Need for Long-Range Planning.* New York: Fund for the Advancement of Education, 1963a.

TICKTON, S. G. "The Need for Planning at Private Colleges and Universities." *Liberal Education,* 1963b, *49*(1), 13–21.

TICKTON, S. G. *Studies in the Future of Higher Education.* Denver: U.S. Office of Education, National Science Foundation, and Bureau of Health and Manpower, 1966–1969.

WETZLER, W. F. "The Essentials of Planning." *Junior College Journal,* 1962, *33*(3), 156–158.

"What Goes into Academic Planning." *College and University Business,* 1969, *47*(2), 31–39.

WHEATLEY, E. "Putting Management Techniques to Work for Education." *College and University Business,* 1970, *48*(4), 55–59.

WILSEY, H. L. "Institutional Long-Range Planning: A Formulation of Procedures." *Current Issues in Higher Education.* Washington, D.C.: Association for Higher Education, National Education Association, 1959.

WILSEY, H. L. *Long-Range Planning for Colleges and Universities.* Chicago: Booz, Allen, and Hamilton, 1962.

WRIGHT, P. S. (Ed.) *Institutional Research and Communication in Higher Education.* Berkeley: Association for Institutional Research, 1970.

CHAPTER 11

Conducting
Self-Study

Paul L. Dressel, Elwin F. Cammack

⊰⊱ ⊰⊱ ⊰⊱ ⊰⊱ ⊰⊱ ⊰⊱ ⊰⊱

Since this entire handbook examines the use of research by an institution to solve its own problems, the presence of this chapter requires some explanation. Institutional research generally is institutional self-study in the sense that it is done by individuals associated with the institution and used by others in that institution. Since coordinating or control boards are integral to the system which they coordinate or control, studies of institutions conducted by staff members of these boards qualify in an extended sense as institutional research, although the individual institutions may very well feel that the research is done to or for them rather than by them. This, however, is not the self-study of our title. An institution may also contract with individuals or consulting firms to make studies. Unless this contract is part of a larger program of study involving active participation and direction by faculty, students, and administrators within the institution, this too is not self-study.

In this chapter, we direct our attention to the self-study process. The substance or problems to which self-study may be directed have been adequately discussed in other chapters. Successful self-studies do not just happen. Experience indicates that some approaches are likely to be more productive than others.

Self-study is initiated, planned, carried out, and acted upon by persons directly associated with the institution. The strength of this approach lies in the involvement of those affected by the subject under study; gradual molding of receptivity for the changes proposed is a usual result of the study. Not all self-studies realize this ideal. Some collapse because of unresolvable differences, and others fail because the recommendations are rejected. Nevertheless, the development of widespread understanding of problems and the cultivation of a readiness for change are essential elements of a successful self-study.

An extensive self-study may be very expensive, and much of the cost may be hidden or absorbed by unpaid overtime. Recognition of the costs in time and energy can subtly operate to encourage serious consideration, rather than the outright rejection that has too often greeted self-study conclusions and recommendations.

Self-studies are typically conducted by committees, commissions, or task forces made up of elected or appointed representatives of various sectors of an institution. Depending on the nature of the problem to be studied, representatives may be administrative officers, trustees, junior faculty, senior faculty, undergraduate students, graduate students, alumni, and, in some circumstances, even private citizens. (At the University of Wisconsin, self-study is perpetuated through a group of laymen appointed by the Board of Regents. This group, the Board of Visitors, reports to the regents on the state of the university.) In some cases there may be reason for representation from college or departmental units. Sensitivity to the concerns of minority groups almost demands that representation from these groups be consciously sought. More emphasis is also being placed on faculty and student participation, whereas a decade or so ago it was not unusual to find a self-study committee completely dominated by administrators. The selection of personnel and leadership is surely one of the major factors in the success of any self-study. Selection strategy is discussed in detail later in this chapter.

Purposes

The adjective *comprehensive* is sometimes conjoined with self-study to imply all-inclusive examination of the total operations, problems, and goals of an institution. Such an extensive effort may be a prelude to planning or a synonym for it. It may be undertaken as a requirement for accreditation or a major foundation grant. When the goal is the attainment or preservation of accreditation or the attainment of a grant, success in attaining the goal too often is the signal for filing and forgetting the self-study. In both circumstances, the study is done under pressure and may be aimed more at attaining the immediate goal than at studying the institution in any fundamental way. Even so, a successful comprehensive self-study is truly a major effort in data collection, assessment of strengths and weaknesses, reexamination of goals, and detailed analysis of present and needed resources.

Points to be considered in a comprehensive self-study include definition or clarification of purposes and goals; examination of the adequacy of physical and financial resources; study of the effectiveness of the governance and decision-making process including roles of various groups; appraisal of the quality, morale, and activities of the faculty; review of the strengths and weaknesses of current curriculum organization and of instructional methods; consideration of the campus climate or environment, the role of students, and their satisfactions or dissatisfactions with programs, and services; and collection of evidence on the effectiveness of the educational program and processes in fostering student development. Information on these points should reveal numerous issues or problems to which solutions should be sought. Tentative solutions should be put into operation and their effects evaluated. Too frequently, self-study for accreditation barely meets the deadline of the accreditation visit, leaving little chance for institutional action on the weaknesses uncovered. Thus, the self-study becomes a status study, and if an accreditation agency finds the status satisfactory, that success may be used by faculty members or administrators as an argument that no changes should be made. A delay between completion of a self-study and an accreditation visit makes it possible to consider the impact rather than simply the quality of the self-study.

Studies conducted in support of special funding requests (such as the improvement grants made by the Ford Foundation or the Centers of Excellence grants of the National Science Foundation) have tended to place great emphasis on new programs, projections of financial need involving matching funds, and ultimate assumption of financial responsibility by the institutions for a new level of performance. These self-studies, of necessity, have focused on planning as much as or more than on current status and probably have had more impact on the institutions than accreditation self-studies usually have. Accreditation has its greatest impact on the marginal institution which finds accreditation highly desirable for both attracting students and assuring eligibility for federal programs and cooperative fund-raising efforts. In these marginal institutions, the comprehensive self-study report for accreditation may and should be only a step in a process of continuing self-analysis and improvement.

The majority of self-studies are narrowly conceived. They may be aimed at assessing or evaluating a particular program or finding a solution to a specific problem. Topics that may be covered according to the narrow definition of a self-study are general education requirements, ROTC or physical education requirements, grading practices, faculty organization and governance, desirability of adding a new program, honors and independent study, administrative reorganization, admissions, personnel policies (such as work load, salaries, and promotion), and fringe benefits.

Self-studies may be limited to a particular unit (a department or college) or may apply to the entire institution. They may be devised to look at particular policy issues such as grading practices, student discipline, or undergraduate instruction. Typically groups charged with the study of specific issues find that the issues are much more complicated and far-reaching than anticipated. A change in general education requirements may affect the load and staff of several departments. The development of new general education courses calls for immediate extra expenditures and may involve long-term budget commitments. Admissions policies go far to determine the character of an institution, and changes may create ripples far beyond the campus. Discussions of honors or independent study are inevitably seen by some faculty members as an attack on the vitality of their courses, as a diversion of resources from existing programs, or as a step in the direction of abolishing faculty control and scholastic standards.

Evaluation of any existing program is always a threat to those involved in it and may even be perceived as a threat to academic freedom and professional integrity by others who rally to the support of the threatened unit. An attempt to solve a specific problem such as too many small classes or too little space may raise other issues. On one campus the lack of adequate classroom space led to a study committee which quickly focused on the fact that almost no classes were scheduled after 3 P.M. because a strong program of student activities required that all students be free from classes after 4 P.M. The problem was one of institutional priorities.

Some of the difficulties of self-study committees can be avoided by recognizing in advance some of the pitfalls and then organizing the study so as to either avoid them or eliminate them by identification and open discussion. There are ways to facilitate self-study; the right strategy, operational patterns, and support are as essential in self-study as identification of the problem and scope of the study.

Facilitation

Since a self-study is likely to require much time, effort, and some funds, a number of questions should be answered before deciding to launch a self-study and especially before designating the personnel involved and phrasing the charge to them. The following are key questions. First, is the problem one which requires restudy of goals or of basic operating policies? Some problems are primarily the result of a failure in leadership. An ineffective administration may create low morale, wasteful use of resources, and lack of direction. Because self-study usually avoids pinpointing individual weaknesses, it, therefore, is not likely to correct problems created by poor leadership. An outside consultant or group of consultants, with no vested interests in the operation and no fear of repercussions or personal threats, can easily submit proper recommendations. A self-study is no substitute for lack of administrative willingness to deal forthrightly with a well-defined issue.

Other examples of situations not requiring self-study are an undue number of small classes when policies already call for elimination of small classes or of courses which regularly produce them; redefinition of instructional load, especially when the flight from teaching to research is involved; and determination of budgetary priorities in development of various disciplines. In solving such problems, administrators may gain assistance from existing faculty committees or from invitational advisory committees, proceeding by presenting the problem along with some proposed courses of action. In these circumstances, individuals or committees can give tacit support to an obviously needed action without having to originate it or to actively support it.

Second, is the problem one which should be considered and resolved through existing committees or through other agencies of governance? Committees are of several different types. Some are ad hoc, set up for a particular purpose and terminating when that purpose has been met or when the committee is found to be ineffective. Standing committees are assigned areas of continuing responsibility such as curriculum, retirement and fringe benefits, or promotion and tenure. Standing committees by their delineation of responsibilities or by virtue of the personalities of those involved take on any of several roles. They may attempt to administer an activity. An example is an admissions committee which insists on meeting to review every application and to decide by vote whether to accept or reject it. This, regardless of actual designation, may be called an executive committee pattern.

A second type of standing committee attempts to write general policies; the application (and perhaps even interpretation) is left to an administrator who may officially be the chairman or secretary of the committee. Such a policy committee may meet to consider doubtful cases, clarify ambiguous points in policies, or serve as an appeal board for rejected applications. A third type of standing committee is advisory. It provides a sounding board for discussion of ideas and policies and perhaps for collection and reporting of reactions to them. It is, however, advisory to some administrator, who may accept, reject, or simply ignore the committee. The latter is likely to happen if the committee attempts to move from advisory to policy or executive status.

Executive and policy committees are seldom effective in self-study roles. They become involved in current operations and, in some sense, become a part of the establishment. Because of individual and committee roles, they have neither the time nor the disposition to study a situation or a set of problems in a way which may alter or eliminate these roles. Such committees, in fact, may be a significant part of the problem.

Advisory committees can and often do play a continuing self-study role. As proposals or problems are identified, they may be referred (by faculty committee or by an administrator) to an advisory committee for study and recommendation—but not for final disposition. The recommendations must still be processed through normal channels.

Standing advisory committees suffer from the fact that, unlike ad hoc self-study committees, they seldom have any release time for their efforts or any assigned staff. To substitute any other standing committee for one of their activities would also set an expensive precedent. But advisory committees can handle many items which may otherwise justify a formalized committee for self-study. The danger is that advisory committees may be misused. They may be asked to meet regularly and, to justify their meetings, may be asked to consider trivia or ideas an administrator wants to dispose of because he regards them irrelevant, impolitic, impractical, or simply asinine. (Self-study committees have been misused in the same way.)

Standing committees are appropriately used for discussion and resolution of issues closely related to their responsibilities. They are not usually appropriate vehicles for self-study, although no item that appropriately can be referred to a standing committee should be made the basis for setting up a special self-study committee. The criteria for making distinctions between issues for standing committees and issues for special self-study committees involve distinctions between minor changes in current practices or policies and possible major changes or innovations which call for alteration in priorities or structure or for redirection of the institution. The time factor and the intensity of the effort required are also criteria, for ad hoc self-study groups can be given time release, special assistance, and freedom from day-to-day decisions.

Third, is the problem sufficiently significant to justify allocation of resources for support of in-depth study over a period of weeks or months? Will the faculty generally recognize the importance of the task so that some will be willing to carry part of the ordinary work load of those assigned to the self-study task? Can staff support be provided to assist in collecting materials and data and making special studies? Can funds be allotted to bring consultants to the campus or to send committee members to other campuses? Unless the answers to several if not all of these questions are positive, the problem is not of sufficient importance to justify a self-study. Seldom can a self-study of any significance be pursued unless adequate resources can be assigned to permit concentration in depth over a period of time.

Fourth, are the incentives or pressures which appear to require the self-study of sufficient gravity to cause general acceptance of the need for the study, willingness to contribute to it, and readiness to attend to the results? A self-study required for accreditation or for a grant almost automatically satisfies these conditions, although accreditation reviews for large universities seldom create much pressure. Unless there is widespread recognition of the existence of a problem, a self-study is usually seen as being generated by administrative officers with the intent to achieve certain changes which they desire but which they could not attain through ordinary channels.

Prelude to self-study may be afforded by a series of studies which point up certain problems, by a number of special cases presented by students or faculty in which there is contention that present rules or policies have caused an injustice, or by visits of one or more consultants who have highlighted a problem and the consequent need for careful consideration of change in practices, policies, or goals.

Fifth, are administrative officers willing to make available to a self-study group all the information required to fully understand the problem and the implications of various solutions? Are they willing to entertain exploration of all possible ramifications and to consider any well-reasoned and well-documented analysis or recommendations? In some institutions, presidents regard certain types of information, such as budget, salaries, and reasons for certain policies, as highly confidential and refuse to permit access to such information even when it is clearly relevant to the charge given to a committee. Reasonable questions raised in a self-study have been dismissed with the statement that these are matters of policy determined by the trustees. A group of individuals should not be asked to undertake study of a problem unless full cooperation is assured and given in providing any information needed.

However, some requests from members of a self-study committee can legitimately be rejected as irrelevant. A study of faculty education requirements hardly provides a member of the committee with a justification for requesting access to the salary of every member of the faculty, although a study generated out of concern about promotion and salary policies may require exactly that information. Usually not every member of a committee requires details and many needs for confidential information can be satisfied by summaries which take into account factors such as years of service, rank, and specialization. The general principle remains clear; individuals or committees should not be asked to resolve problems unless they are provided access to all relevant information and are permitted to ask what under other circumstances may be regarded as impertinent questions.

Operational Strategy

The first strategy in setting up a self-study group involves the selection of the committee members. Some comments have already been made about the possible criteria for the breadth of representation of various groups. Obviously representation, in part, depends upon the scope of the study. A study initiated within a department of mathematics and concerned with departmental curriculum problems is not likely to call for representation from the board of trustees or the college of fine arts, but it could and probably should include some contacts with or representation from other units, such as engineering and physics, which utilize mathematics. It may also use one or more outside consultants. A study of a department initiated from outside the department should certainly involve representation from outside the department and utilize one or more off-campus consultants. The desirability of representation from outside a unit under study when the unit itself initiates the study should be obvious. Departments, especially, frequently are so concerned with their own problems and status that they lose sight of their obligations to the institution and the impact of their decisions on others in the institution.

Self-studies of all-institutional problems require that especially careful consideration be given to the selection of the study group. Two questions which are regularly raised and some largely personal answers follow. First, how should study group members be selected? The alternatives are numerous and include election by academic units (usually colleges in a university since departments are too numerous); selection by deans and advisory committees of colleges; appointment by the president after nomination by a committee on committees; appointment by the president; and some combination of election and appointment.

Although many faculty members and students argue for an elective method, problems are posed by this approach. The individuals elected are too often highly visible and popular, largely by virtue of views they hold; yet they are not likely to be persons with any special competency in the problem to be studied. Election by units involves, additionally, expectation and acceptance of responsibility for representing the interests of the unit represented; this can directly conflict with responsibility for attempting to find a solution in the best interests of the institution. (Conflict of interest is also a commonly noted weakness of standing committees.)

A completely appointed committee, acceptable in some institutions, runs risks of nonacceptance in many others, and appointment by no means ensures an able group. A combination of elective and administrative appointees seems to be the most reasonable alternative. The nomination-with-administrative-selection method can also be successful.

In some cases administrators such as a director of institutional research or registrar serve committees as consultants, study directors, or ex officio members. Regardless of faculty attitudes to-

ward administrators and regardless of administrators' own defer-
ence to faculty views, administrators' views tend, through intimida-
tion, to prejudice the report. Any administrator who participates
in a self-study committee is in a delicate position when the report
is ultimately delivered to him; faculty members who dissent from
the recommendations readily suspect that they were dictated by
administrative preferences.

Second, what personal criteria should be considered in
establishing the membership of a self-study committee? Individuals
who already have strong and announced convictions on the issues
to be studied are seldom good committee members. Individuals
respected by their associates are essential, but overattention to this
criterion can result in a group with little knowledge and perhaps
even no great interest in the problems.

Individuals who may advance themselves through committee recommendations are questionable choices, but this possibility is
not easily foreseen. The chairman, in particular, should be a person
of recognized stature with an already well-established career, especially when some new unit or administrative office is a likely recommendation of the committee. More than one self-study chairman
(or committee member) has been disillusioned when a committee
recommendation which he espoused did not lead to his own advancement. Committee members should be those who will be
pleased to have been of service and happy to return to their earlier
assignment.

Self-Study Charge. Typically each member of a self-study
committee receives a letter appointing him to the committee and
briefly stating the task. The committee may meet first with the
president or a vice-president to have the charge repeated or enlarged upon with some opportunity for questions and discussion. If
the committee elects its own chairman (generally very unsatisfactory), the election may be held at this time. The interpretation of
the charge is likely to consume many hours. What seemed crystal
clear becomes clouded by questions: Does our charge include looking at X as well as Y? (It does not clearly say so.) To whom should
our recommendations be addressed—the president or the faculty?
Is our job over when we have prepared recommendations, or are
we expected to shepherd the recommendations through the normal

channels? Are we expected to continue as a committee to monitor and evaluate the results of the recommendations? Should our sessions be regarded as confidential, or are we free to discuss our deliberations with others? Are we to submit progress reports to the president and the faculty, or is a final report sufficient? What does the president really want? (Should we meet with him again and ask him to be explicit with regard to his expectations?) Must we agree on a single report, or can there be minority reports? Should we seek for the best possible solution or for one which is likely to be acceptable? (to whom?) What is the deadline for our report? Who writes the reports? Should we prepare a questionnaire to ascertain student or faculty views? How frequently are we going to meet? Can we get funds to visit some other institutions and see what they are doing? How much secretarial and research assistance can we have?

Argument with regard to the charge will recur periodically and likely will be the subject of a lengthy section in the final report. Many of the other questions asked at first meetings are premature and can be decided only as study progresses. Some issues such as the deadline, the assistance and funds available, the disposition of the report, and the future role of the committee do need to be clarified as part of or addenda to the charge. The answers to some questions asked are reasonably obvious, but the the committee should be privileged to look at anything and have any data relevant to its charge. If appointed by the president, the commitee should report to him unless otherwise directed. If elected or appointed by the faculty, it should report to the faculty. The task is over when the report is prepared, though the chairman and individual members can be influential in interpreting the report and in gaining support. In fact, committee deliberations probably should include consideration of the steps and the strategy for placing its recommendations in operation.

Strategy within the Study. In the process of defining the task and simultaneously getting acquainted, each individual should have adequate opportunity to state his concerns, raise questions, suggest relevant data, indicate sources of help for the committee, and suggest procedures. At this stage, the chairman should caution individuals against arguing for a particular view or solution. Following each presentation of a personal view, a few questions of clarification may be permitted, but general discussion should be postponed until all have had their say.

If some requested data are already available, they should be prepared for distribution and explained by those responsible for collection. Usually a number of identified resource persons should be invited to make presentations to the entire committee. If relevant studies are suggested, the office of institutional research, other appropriate agencies or individuals, or committee staff should be asked to initiate them. It is rarely profitable to record all statements and discussions in detail, but a member of the committee or a study director (possibly the chairman) with stenographic assistance should be asked to keep minutes and to process these for distribution at or before the next meeting. Invited statements by resource persons or by consultants and research reports should also be reproduced and distributed for later use and to ensure that absent members have the benefit of this information.

For comprehensive self-studies, separate committees or subcommittees may be designated at the outset. If so, an overall coordinating committee or council is essential, and the suggestions presented thus far would apply to combined sessions when all committees meet. If subcommittees have not been identified previously, early discussions usually define reasonably discrete aspects of the task and subcommittees can then be identified on the basis of interest in these topics. In forming subcommittees, it is usually wise to add some individuals to each subcommittee who do not serve on the main committee. If resources permit, each subcommittee benefits by having available a staff person to follow up on its requests and to assist the subcommittee chairman in maintaining records of its deliberations.

In large institutions it is sometimes helpful to identify in each college a liaison person or subcommittee to consider the particular issues and problems of that unit. However this procedure can become very cumbersome, and the same ends can usually be achieved by scheduled hearings at which individuals or groups can, by prior appointment, present their concerns to the subcommittees or to the total committee.

It is desirable that the entire campus be kept apprised of

progress, but early reports should avoid any implication that final recommendations have already been reached. Emphasis should be on the analysis of the issues, the range of factors considered, and alternative solutions which have been suggested. As individuals or groups (committee or subcommittee members or people outside the study) develop strong views and begin to argue persuasively for them, they should be asked to put these into position papers with their names attached. These can be circulated and discussed at an appropriate time as alternatives. Emphasis should be placed on inclusion of relevant data as opposed to mere expression of opinion. As position papers accumulate and as subcommittees come up with tentative recommendations, the information can be circulated widely. Open hearings may be scheduled at which individuals may express their reactions to certain of the views expressed and rebut if they wish. As studies are completed, the evidence may effectively invalidate certain courses of action which have been suggested.

Individuals and committees must take into account the financial implications of their recommendations. These may completely rule out some suggestions, such as giving all advisers a percentage reduction in teaching load. In other cases, when cost estimates are related to available resources, the necessity of establishing priorities or of tailoring recommendations to reality emerges.

Subcommittee reports are likely to be overlapping and contradictory. Joint sessions may resolve some contradictions; others may have to be argued out in total committee and resolved by compromise or by majority vote. At this point the issue of minority reports arises again and must be resolved. Though minority reports ease the conscience of those who dissent from the majority, they do cast a shadow over the report. Nevertheless, if the integrity of the committee is to be maintained, minority reports must be allowed. They will hopefully be presented within the perspective of the final decision.

A good committee report is not written by a committee. Rather it is written by one or more individuals who are sensitive to the feelings and insights of the individuals who make up the total committee and to the rationale and the data supporting the recommendations. The chairman, secretary, study director, and no more than one other individual selected by the committee constitute a maximum writing group. After committee deliberations have been completed, an interval of several weeks should be allowed while a draft of a final report is prepared and circulated to the entire committee. It is probably not wise to distribute this report widely, for it may arouse from some individuals such intense reactions as to influence individuals or the committee to reopen old and resolved issues. The entire committee should be brought back together for a page-by-page review of the report. Purely editorial suggestions should be deferred, but the committee should be permitted to question phraseology which is ambiguous or which appears to violate earlier agreements.

If the self-study was commissioned by an administrator, the report should go to him, and with him rests the decision of wider distribution. He would be very unwise if he failed to distribute the report to all the faculty and to the board. Students should have access to it, but it may be overly expensive to distribute it to all students, most of whom are likely to be indifferent. If the report is voluminous, a digest of recommendations or a briefer version may be prepared; it is far more likely to be read than the unabridged version. Background data, studies, and major position papers can usually be assigned to appendices or to a supplemental volume available in limited quantity.

The order in which recommendations are presented may seem to be a minor matter but actually may be a major factor in their acceptance. Recommendations are usually interrelated, and some may be corollaries of others. If interrelated or independent recommendations can be juxtaposed, this kind of organization may forestall reactions based upon judgments that certain factors have been ignored or depreciated. When this course is not possible, parenthetical notes appended to recommendations should specifically indicate significant relationships and should perhaps provide comments on the implications.

Since neither the order nor the content of recommendations necessarily indicates to whom recommendations are addressed, consideration should be given to the inclusion of a section in which recommendations are grouped according to the administrative officer or unit which must authorize or approve the change. By this device, many changes can be effected without formal processing

288 Institutional Research in the University

through the committee structure and the hierarchy of administrative officers. Recommendations regarding changes in certain courses, for example, if addressed to the departments involved, may be immediately made. (If the departments refuse recommendations directed to them, the recommendations may then be processed through other channels.) A recommendation regarding a new central administrative office is naturally addressed to the president, who can act at once if funds are available and if it is apparent that the recommendation is widely accepted. A recommendation regarding procedures in searching for a new president should be addressed directly to the board. Thus, action on a self-study report can be expedited directly through the many persons and offices involved rather than through ordinary channels, which would also have to refer parts to the same committees and individuals.

Seldom can an administrative officer put a set of self-study recommendations into effect by fiat. And the impact of a study will be lost, along with most of the recommendations, if the whole report must be fed from the self-study group through the slow, nit-picking process of standing committees. If, however, the conduct of the study has created an attitude of receptivity and if each of the recommendations is strongly supported by a majority of the self-study group, many of the recommendations will have been accepted and effected by large numbers of those most directly concerned before the final report is ready for distribution.

Maximizing Impact

No self-study can be regarded as effective if it does not produce change; improvement is the justification of self-study. On occasion, change has been reflected only in a strengthened conviction that everything is well with the institution—although it is difficult to believe that institutions exist which are so good that they cannot be improved. The extent to which a study has impact depends upon the state of readiness for the study, the clarity of the charge given to the committee, the membership of the committee and committees, the tact and leadership of the chairman, the availability and quality of the staff assistance available, the cooperation extended throughout the institution in providing relevant information, the effective use of consultants and other resource persons, and the quality of reportage.

In addition, continuing communication among committee members, administrators, faculty, and students throughout the study is critical. There is no such thing as secrecy on a campus; partial, confused, and erroneous revelation and rumor are the result of any attempt to maintain it. If a committee takes the posture (as some individuals will) that it has been asked to resolve the future of the institution and that in due course all will be revealed, the study is well along toward failure. If the committee views its job partly as educational, it must regularly communicate its concerns, studies, and developing points to the entire institution. If the committee also views its job as a unifying agent and a synthesizer of ideas, it solicits opinions, proposals, and reactions so that everyone may feel that his view has been heard and understood, even though it did not finally prevail. In the resulting communication, opinions are changed, and the emerging views of those on the committee and those in other areas of the institution may coincide. When this consensus occurs, the self-study has been eminently successful.

Achieving implementation of the recommendations is relatively simple if the educative functions of the self-study have been effectively performed and if opinions which have been crystallized are congruent with the recommendations. The duration of the self-study can be adjusted to accommodate dissemination of information and expression of opinion. If it is apparent that on some issues there are widely diverse opinions, extension of the study period to provide for further analysis, collection of data, and full exploration of contrasting views may be desirable. Anyone who observes legislative operations is made aware of the fact that some very good pieces of legislation are the results of months and even years of embryonic attempts to solve serious problems. There are meritorious ideas for which the time has not yet come. Individuals have to be introduced to them and meet them several times before they agree to live with them.

Thus any appraisal of the effectiveness of a self-study based upon how many of its recommendations are immediately adopted is unfair. A sensitive evaluation seeks to determine, two or three years later, whether practices have been gradually modified in accord with recommendations even though the recommendations were never formally accepted; recommendations, perhaps somewhat modified, have been adopted at a later date with or without reference to the self-study report; or changes in policy and in practice have been made which differ from the self-study recommendations but which have emerged as a result of the continuing ferment induced by the study.

In all of the foregoing circumstances, it is interesting to trace the role of the self-study group. As individuals, they frequently continue to promote ideas which are not at first accepted. Not infrequently, some of them become administrators and, in this role, accomplish what the self-study did not immediately accomplish. A self-study may solve immediate problems or may redirect an institution but, in either case, it is also an investment in the education of people who, in the long run, influence the course of the institution.

Role of Institutional Research

In the preceding discussion of self-study activity, incidental reference is made to the roles of institutional researchers. An institutional self-study is unlikely to be effective unless adequate groundwork for it has been laid. Institutional research reports can provide much of the necessary background. Analysis of such diverse problems as student difficulties in fulfilling general education requirements, high numbers of waivers of requirements, and patterns in changes of majors may enable researchers to document, too, the existence of larger issues affecting problems presented to them—issues such as the necessity of changing not only curriculum requirements but the courses used to fulfill them.

Institutional researchers can assist self-study by collecting or grouping available local, regional, or national data; by making surveys of opinion; or by conducting requested studies. Research may be carried out even when an office of institutional research does not exist; those who do it are at that time engaged in institutional research.

Although the term self-study as ordinarily used implies a committee, task force, or research group with membership on some representative basis, it is possible for an office of institutional research to define a needed study, select a committee, and give direction to the deliberations of the committee. However the nature of the problem must be considered before study is undertaken by an office of research. Study of a problem which faculty members or students consider to be in their domain of responsibility probably cannot be so initiated even if institutional research investigations have pointed out the problem. An effort to improve statistics available on departmental operations and budgeting procedure may be so developed because of general recognition that the office of institutional research has special concerns and competencies appropriate to the task. The acceptability of recommendations in this case comes out of the cooperative efforts of the office of institutional research in working directly with departmental representatives to develop data systems which they consider valid and useful.

The distinctions between institutional research and self-study are essentially these: an office of institutional research is a continuing operation with permanent personnel, whereas a self-study is limited in time and carried out on an ad hoc basis; an office of institutional research is typically charged with continuing study of a wide range of problems, whereas a self-study is focused on a particular set of problems; and an office of institutional research is concerned primarily with pointing up and analyzing problems through data collections and studies whereas a self-study is initiated to resolve these problems through proposing new policies or structures.

Thus an office of institutional research and a self-study task force can be viewed as interacting and supporting groups. Each becomes effective through the presence and judicious activity of the other. However, many of the problems pointed up by the office of institutional research can be resolved through existing channels. Self-study activities should be occasional in nature, initiated only when the complications of the task require that study be conducted outside normal activities, that widespread representation be involved for educational purposes, and that a synthesis of views be attained to assure the feasibility and acceptability of the recommendations.

CHAPTER 12

Wider Research

Paul L. Dressel, Sally B. Pratt

෴෴෴෴෴෴෴෴

In a number of the other chap-
ters, there have been references to the impact or the interrelationship of local institutional research with respect to research done by
state coordinating boards, regional agencies, federal agencies, and
national associations. A significant part of the activities of an institutional office of research are instigated by the demands made by
various state, regional, and national groups for statistics and summary reports; state, regional, and federal agencies also engage in
reporting summary statistics in studies which must be described as
institutional research because of their interest to or impact upon
institutions. This chapter discusses the subjects studied by external
agencies and also attempts to differentiate a study in the area of
institutional research from the broadly conceived study of higher
education. Attention is focused upon studies of either nature having
immediate implications throughout the field.

State Coordinating Systems

State coordination of higher education appears in various forms. It may involve a single board as a governing agency over a number of institutions. This set-up implies centralization of power and may result in the elimination of all individual institutional boards or reduce them to an advisory role. There are also boards with limited powers. These coordinate or control limited aspects of the activities of institutions but do not have general governing or administrative powers. In some cases coordination proceeds on an entirely voluntary basis, with representatives of individual institutions meeting to coordinate activities of common concern.

Much of the concern for coordination, at least in the public institutions, has arisen out of the hope that it may increase efficiency, prevent excessive duplication of offerings, curb institutional aspirations to offer new graduate programs, and, through these accomplishments, save money. There is, in fact, some reason to believe that coordination has resulted in good presentation of the needs of higher education, has thereby acquired a higher support level than it may otherwise have achieved, and has therefore justified itself by providing a program of higher education designed to effectively meet the needs of the entire population.

Coordination immediately creates a need for hard data and for studies of its implications. For example, in all but three or four states, coordinating boards have the responsibility of approving new degree programs. Such responsibility is not adequately met by a quick yes or no based upon reading a proposal submitted by an individual institution. The desire of the institution to introduce the new program introduces a bias in the data selected for inclusion or omission in the request and in the way in which the data included are exhibited and interpreted. An institution desiring a new doctoral program is likely to be motivated partly by prestige and partly by pressures from its departmental faculty and is likely to have little concern for whether the program is justified by the need for manpower in the particular field concerned. Enrollment projections in new programs are likely to be optimistic, and the costs are likely to be underestimated. Thus the responsibility of approving or disapproving new programs, if conscientiously carried out, forces a coordinating board to specify in detail just what kind of data must be presented to support a request and to develop means whereby data on manpower needs, potentials already existing in institutional programs, and, probably, resources available can be brought together in making a judgment.

In most cases the coordinating role involves consideration of needs—for new institutions, new facilities, or money. To deal with these matters intelligently, a coordinating board must develop an adequate data system and regularly collect data on existing facilities, space utilization, academic programs, enrollments, income, and expenditures for each of the institutions coordinated. If the responsibilities of the board include planning for the expansion of existing institutions and for the development of new ones, then extensive surveys are required, and these must be brought together to provide what has generally been called a master plan for the state. Any master plan requires review and revision every five years, and a completely new plan may be needed at intervals of ten years.

The development of a master plan is a major task. The California Master Plan of 1960 addressed itself to the following topics: the structure of higher education, functions, coordination, selection and retention of students, scholarships and fellowships, institutional capacities and needs, physical plant utilization levels, faculty supply and demand, adult education, estimated costs, and student fees. In addition to these items, all of which deal specifically with the institutions, projections of enrollments must be developed; policies must be stated with regard to the types of programs available and the qualifications of the students admitted; and some indices must be developed to suggest, for at least the professional, technical, and vocational fields, what the manpower needs are likely to be.

In the early days of state coordination, operating budgets were limited and staffs were small. The natural aversion of individual institutions to development of a professional research staff in a coordinating board led easily to the dependence of boards upon voluntary or part-time researchers from the staffs of the institutions coordinated. Aside from having the usual problems—finding competent people and deciding whether the chores should be designated as overload, budgeted institutionally, or reimbursed individually as part-time assignment—this approach was found to be undesirable in other ways. Most studies conducted from the vantage point of the coordinating board have implications for each institution, and hence an individual from any one of those institutions immediately has a divided loyalty. Even assuming that he resolves this dilemma satisfactorily, his data, his interpretation, and his recommendations are likely to be reviewed with suspicion by those who are disadvantaged by the study. Frequently the most competent persons could not be co-opted into such activity, seeing no future in it and preferring to pursue their own interests. Recruitment difficulties meant that the individuals finally procured for projects were often not completely competent. Lack of continuity in staff and lack of time to concentrate on particular studies were other causes for coordinating boards' finally moving to the employment of their own research staffs. It is still possible to use individuals from individual institutions for particular studies, and it is a widespread practice to set up advisory committees made up of persons from the institutions involved to review staff plans and to discuss and react to findings and recommendations.

Perhaps the greatest pressure exerted on institutions by coordinating boards has been in the direction of improving their basic data systems, which are used in justifying budgetary requests and allocations. Most of the western state coordinating boards have encouraged, if not pressured, institutions to join in the WICHE sponsored development of management information systems and to apply information systems to planning and budgeting. In many states (Texas and Florida serve as examples), the move toward formula bases for appropriations has led to extensive study of staffing needs and university operations in order to determine ways in which research, service, and various support activities can be incorporated in the budget on some uniform basis. Such studies typically require extensive data on the history of expenditures in various categories, and they may lead to the development of rather sophisticated mathematical models for determining budgetary needs and final allocations. Typically, however, unless such formula-based appropriations are formalized as line item budgets (such as the budgets of the California state colleges), the internal budgeting operations of individual institutions proceed with little relationship to the formula, illustrating the fact that institutional research activity carried on at a distance from an institution (geographical or otherwise) may have little impact upon it. Institutions develop great facility in masquerading their aspirations as patterns imposed by a coordinating board, and, thus acquiring financial resources, they display facility in employing them, too, in a manner departing from the rationale on which they were acquired.

Another difficulty with institutional research activities in state coordinating systems is that they tend to require a large amount of detailed data while lacking the facilities or the personnel to deal effectively with those data. And people who find themselves dealing with data collected for determining the resources allocated to the institution become suspicious of their accuracy. They tend to seek new definitions or new types of data with greater accuracy and validity. Institutions, too, are suspicious of each other's data and are quite prone to point out, as they are often completely justified in doing, that certain existent data patterns do not account for a particular institutional idiosyncrasy which justifies a different or special treatment. Thus data needs and requests grow from year to year, and the ability to utilize the data lags far behind. Despite all the data gathered, it is possible for limited items, combined in some oversimplified way never publicly revealed, to become the basis for decision-making.

Requests by coordinating boards for data on individual students or faculty members are infrequent, but still a matter of occasional concern. Whatever may be the justification in reference to a particular study, there remain some questions about the wisdom of permitting personal records to be collected in an office remote from a campus and largely devoid of the kinds of controls and security precautions that usually surround them. And, once the records are available and not surrounded by such precautions, there can be no control over some further and unstated use which may be unjustifiable or possibly a clear violation of confidentiality.

Perhaps the most serious problem in connection with state-level institutional research is violation of autonomy. As long as individual institutions operate independently with regard to programs, faculty loads, credit and degree structures, and the like, all data collected from a group of institutions involve some translations from local patterns. Summaries of state patterns give a superficial appearance of equivalence or uniformity which, in the hands of individuals insensitive to institutional differences, may be misinterpreted and misused. To attempt to overcome the problem by demanding conformity not only in data reporting but also in program would be a next step in curbing the autonomy of the institution and destroying some of its originality, creativity, and adaptiveness to the local scene.

Regional Agencies

The Southern Regional Education Board (SREB) is composed of representatives of fifteen southern states. It carries on a multifaceted program, conducting cooperative efforts in areas such as institutional research, adult education, and computer science. It sponsors annual legislative work conferences to study current developments in higher education. It has sponsored a student contract program for all regional students, permitting the annual enrollment of over a thousand students in health sciences, social work, and special education programs. Perhaps its major responsibility is to provide for the coordinated growth of higher education in the several cooperating states. In meeting this responsibility, the SREB provides governors and legislators with reliable information and recommendations which take into account the needs and the developments of the fifteen-state area. Thus its research program stresses the importance of planning. The following are from the wide range of research publications which express the concerns of the Board: *Curriculum Change; Tax Support and Costs of Education; Equalizing of Educational Opportunity; Federal-State Relations; Effective Use of Resources; The College Campus in 1969: Faculty; New Directions in Higher Education Coordination and Planning; Recruitment to Graduate Study, 1965; Statistical Supplement to State and Local Revenue Potential, 1969; State Support for Private Higher Education;* and *On Time and the Doctorate—An Inquiry into the Length of Doctoral Programs, 1965.* Since the purpose here is only to document the involvement of SREB in institutional research, complete titles and references for these studies have not been given. Many of these items are described in Dressel and Pratt

(1971), which was developed in connection with this volume. This bibliography is useful in relation to all topics discussed here as well as those discussed in other chapters.

The Western Interstate Commission on Higher Education (WICHE) carries on a great variety of programs. In general its role in the group of thirteen western states is similar to that of SREB. There are a number of regional programs concerned with subjects such as medicine, nursing, continuing psychiatric education and mental health, continuing education for library personnel, mineral science education, and state personnel. Many of these programs have called for surveys of activity, accumulation of data on needs and deficiencies, and development of recommendations to improve education through interinstitutional cooperation, state cooperation, or the development of new programs. WICHE also carries on a legislative work conference designed to foster communication among legislators, public officials, and educators of the thirteen western states.

Two items in the WICHE program of great interest to institutional researchers are the college and university self-study institutes, which are held annually, and the management information systems program. The former consists of presentations of research on and discussion of current issues in higher education, covering a new and timely topic each year. The latter was started as a program largely limited to the WICHE states and was expanded to a national effort in designing, developing, and implementing management information systems with a common set of uniform data elements. It has resulted in development of space analyses manuals and resource allocation models. Specific projects have resulted in a data element dictionary, a program classification structure, and resource requirements prediction models. Other projects have dealt with student flow models, input-output indicators, cost-finding principles, information exchange procedures, and faculty activity analysis. A personnel classification manual has also been developed. A number of publications have already emanated from this project; numerous others are being developed.

The range of WICHE involvement has had a major impact on institutional research developments in the western states. The activities of the management information project extend far beyond the WICHE states, and they are certain to have a significant impact nationally. At the least, the reporting for the Higher Education General Information Survey conducted by the U.S. Office of Education will be modified by the definitions developed in the management information systems project, and the potential for affecting the basic data systems of institutions and the procedures and emphases of offices of institutional research is almost limitless. The inclusion of the planning element along with activities traditionally associated with institutional research may markedly change the conception of what institutional research encompasses.

The New England Board of Higher Education (NEBHE) is composed of delegates from the six New England states. The primary purpose of the Board is to develop areas of cooperation and mutual interest among the New England colleges and universities. Its programs include the following: the New England Regional Student Program (to maximize availability of post-high school education for the youth of the New England area), the New England Library Information Network (to coordinate acquisition and use of various kinds of research materials, use of teletypewriter and other communications facilities for interlibrary services, and production of joint holdings and want lists), and the New England Council on Higher Education for Nursing (an approach to the improvement of nursing care through higher education in nursing). NEBHE conferences have dealt with matters of interest to institutional researchers. The 1962 conference theme was on institutional research and the following years' focused successively on academic effectiveness, time and space in educational planning, and academic decision-making. Since then NEBHE has had limited involvement in institutional research activity but continues to have interest in this area.

There are six regional accrediting associations. Each of these conducts accreditation activity for all colleges and universities in its area. In connection with this activity, the accrediting associations encourage institutions to engage in self-study and prepare written reports which are used as the basis for initial accreditation or for review. At various times accrediting associations develop handbooks outlining institutional self-study procedures and defining the basic data required for accreditation or successful review. Occasionally an accrediting association may sponsor or encourage some contribution to study of the accreditation operation which turns out to be relevant to institutional research. For example, because the review of literature in higher education related to the consulting and examining process sponsored by the North Central Association of Colleges and Secondary Schools encompasses a broad selection of relevant literature, it includes items of interest to institutional researchers (North Central Association, 1967).

Special professional agencies confer accreditation in fields such as architecture, art, business, chemistry, dentistry, engineering, forestry, law, and medicine. Occasionally these accrediting agencies carry on studies of practices and requirements which provide useful background for certain types of institutional research activity.

The Federation of Regional Accrediting Commissions of Higher Education has undertaken to establish a national consensus on accrediting in higher education for regional application. In so doing, the Federation has prepared statements of policy which serve as guidelines for the constituent commissions in carrying on their accrediting activities. Among the policy statements adopted by the Federation are the following: eligibility for consideration for accreditation; relations between the Federation of Regional Accrediting Commissions and the National Commission on Accrediting; relations between general and professional or specialized accrediting agencies; accreditation of educational institutions conducted by religious communities for their own members; evaluation and accreditation of college work; code of good practice in accrediting in higher education; collegiate programs on military bases; external budget control; general education requirements in technical, specialized, and professional programs; innovation; institutional integrity; accreditation of off-campus programs; undergraduate study abroad programs; substantive change; and accreditation of United States institutions outside the United States. These policy statements are available from the Office of the Executive Director, Federation of Regional Accrediting Commissions of Higher Education, 5454 South Shore Drive, Chicago, Illinois 60615. Some of them have possible relevance to certain phases of institutional research activity.

One widely prevalent concern of all accrediting agencies is the lack of adequate evidence upon which to base accreditation decisions. Institutional research and evaluation which have yielded data adequate for assessing the operation of an institution and for determining its quality are rare. If the accreditation process is to do more than look at the day-to-day operations, actually appraising the quality of the product, emphasis has to be placed upon comprehensive institutional research and self-study.

Federal Agencies

The U. S. Office of Education was originally established to collect statistics and facts related to the condition and progress of education. It was also charged with diffusing such information as would help in the establishment of efficient school systems and would generally promote the cause of education. Various legislative acts and executive orders have added numerous related functions, including responsibility for federal assistance to education and for special studies programs. The many statistical reports of the Office of Education are well known to institutional researchers and generally familiar to higher education administrators. Perhaps the major complaint about them has been long delay between collection and presentation of data. Within the Office of Education a National Center for Educational Statistics is responsible for developing the statistical program, coordinating information-gathering activities for all programs, and performing special analyses and dissemination of the data gathered. It is divided into three divisions: Survey Operations, Statistical Information and Studies, and Survey Planning Analysis. This office is responsible for the Higher Education General Information Survey, which is sent out each year. Among the many reports which emanate from this center are those on fall enrollment, financial statistics, physical facilities, inventory, degrees conferred, and students enrolled for advanced degrees.

The National Center for Educational Research and Development is also an arm of the Office of Education. It is responsible for the administration of programs to improve education through support of research and related activities conducted outside the office. It includes several research divisions; the higher education division can be contacted for information about funds available or support of a particular type of research project.

The Office of Planning and Evaluation has primary responsibility for planning and evaluation of overall Office of Education programs. It also provides guidance and coordination of bureaus and staff offices in establishing their objectives for program planning and evaluation.

The National Science Foundation has the basic purpose of supporting research and the education of scientists. It is presently moving in two other directions: attention to research problems affecting society and examination of the problems of science education for nonscientists. One of its programs provides grants for interdisciplinary research relevant to the problems of society. The activities of the Foundation include development and dissemination of information relating to scientific resources (including manpower), aimed at facilitating national decisions and strengthening the scientific effort of the nation; awarding grants and contracts primarily to universities and other nonprofit institutions in support of scientific research; maintenance of a current register of scientific and technical personnel; provision of a central clearinghouse for data on the supply of and need for various scientific and technical resources; awarding of graduate fellowships; development and support of programs aimed at improving scientific education in special institutes through improving the competence of teachers of science, mathematics, and engineering; support of projects to modernize materials of instruction and courses of study and projects to afford opportunities for high ability secondary school and college students to secure added scientific experiences; and support of programs encouraging development and use of the computer and other scientific methods and technologies.

Although much of the foregoing suggests programs and possible support for institutional research, the changing emphasis in the Foundation makes it risky to predict the future. In reorganizing to focus on problem solving and providing increased support for the social sciences, the Foundation may put heavy emphasis on social indicators; economic and econometric studies; social, legal, and political science research; urban anthropology and the effects of urbanization; and crime. To the extent that such emphases require extensive collection and manipulation of data, it is possible that there will be unforeseen developments quite relevant to the concerns of institutional researchers. Studies such as the following ones conducted in the past have certainly been relevant to institutional research: *Toward a Public Policy for Graduate Education in the Sciences* (National Science Board, 1969b); *Graduate Education: Parameters for Public Policy* (National Science Board, 1969a); *Impact of Federal Support of Science on Publicly Supported Universities and Four-Year Colleges in Michigan* (Dressel and Come, 1968); and *Federal Support to Universities and Colleges, Fiscal Year 1967* (National Science Foundation, 1968).

The Association for Institutional Research (AIR) is composed of individuals interested in various aspects of institutional research. Each year AIR has an annual conference on pertinent topics; the 1969 and 1970 conference themes, for example, were Challenge and Response of Institutional Research and Institutional Research and Communication in Higher Education. Earlier conference emphases and proceedings focused on the instructional process, academic input, design and methodology of institutional research, and conceptual framework of institutional research. From time to time, too, the Association issues studies, the most recent being a self-study on members of the Association. Another publication is an annual annotated bibliography of institutional research.

The American Association for Higher Education (AAHE) is an individual membership group open to administrators, faculty, students, and others interested in higher education. It is concerned with the entire spectrum of issues and developments in the field. Its annual convention in Chicago provides extensive coverage of current issues in higher education through speeches, discussion groups, forums, and the like. The proceedings of the conference are published as *Current Issues in Higher Education*. In addition the Association cooperates with Ohio State University in the publication of *The Journal of Higher Education*. It has as its own publication the *College and University Bulletin* and has, in the past, published the *Literature of Higher Education*, edited by Lewis B. Mayhew, and the *Bibliography of Higher Education*, prepared by Roger Kelsey. The improvement of college instruction and the study of governance in higher education have been other themes of concern to the Association.

The American Council on Education conducts a number of programs of interest to institutional researchers. Its Office of Institutional Research has turned out reports dealing with topics such as campus disruption, institutional characteristics, national norms for entering college freshmen, planning techniques for university management, college and university faculty, and quality of graduate education. The Council also publishes numerous books and brochures not directly sponsored by it which have relevance to higher education problems. The major project of the Office of Institutional Research has been the development of a research data bank for higher education. It has been developed for a large-scale program of longitudinal research on student development based on the assumption that the principal concern of an institution of higher education is to produce changes in student behavior. A major objective of the program is to determine how the college environment affects student performance. The initial goal, to develop and maintain a comprehensive longitudinal file of information about the personal development of students attending many different types of colleges and universities, provides a basis for assessing change. In addition, the file will contain comprehensive data concerning the characteristics of the college environment.

The data bank, developed for longitudinal research, also has potential uses for cooperative and collaborative research. The information included in the file is not only extensive but carefully planned in respect to a research design. One of the problems discussed elsewhere in this handbook, however, applies to it—the difficulty of effecting change in higher education through elaborate data collections and studies. Institutional researchers are typically too busy with their local concerns to do much with the extensive information available from the reports of annual surveys. On most campuses the best that can be expected in reaction to an extensive survey report is appearance of a brief summary of some of the interesting highlights of student responses in the student paper. It may also be the subject of a brief laudatory or critical comment by one or two administrative officers. But nothing happens.

In the course of time one may expect that a good many social scientists will become interested in data collections and make a number of interesting studies, but an old-time institutional researcher may predict with some confidence that if these studies have any impact, it will be in developing gradually some national consciousness which will affect the allocation of funds to higher education rather than in bringing about change on individual campuses. The reason is simply that such studies, unlike those of institutional research, do not speak to the specific problems and decisions with which administrators, faculty members, boards, and legislators must deal. Nevertheless, the studies should be encouraged, and, as the assessment of the impact of higher learning becomes more sophisticated, they may ultimately deserve and receive more than passing interest.

The National Association of State Universities and Land-Grant Colleges serves as a liaison between member institutions and the federal government, with its primary concern being the organizational development of member institutions. This association performs a significant service to its members through the information disseminated in its newsletter, and through its occasional data summaries on research reports. One report deals with the impact of private investment on public colleges and universities (National Association of State Universities and Land-Grant Colleges, 1969). The Association also issues a report on appropriations of state tax funds for operating expenses of higher education.

The American Educational Research Association, through its annual conference and publications, touches on all fields of educational research and is not limited to higher education. Nevertheless, its publications, which include *Review of Educational Research, Encyclopedia of Educational Research, American Educational Research Journal,* and a monograph series, are very useful to the institutional researcher.

The American Association of University Professors (AAUP) has had far-reaching impact on the universities through its powerful faculty organization. AAUP is concerned with all phases of faculty life, including standards, policies, salaries, and academic freedom. Through its committee structure all aspects of the academic community are discussed and individual institutions are sometimes censured. The AAUP publication, the *AAUP Bulletin,* contains extensive salary information of use to the institutional researcher. In addition, the various committees have turned out reports on academic freedom and tenure, professional ethics, and other topics of interest when the institutional researcher finds himself carrying on studies that suddenly impinge on them.

The National Education Association includes many organizations, a number of which are primarily concerned with higher education. Recurrent publications of NEA of particular interest to the institutional researcher are *Salaries in Higher Education* and NEA research bulletins. Other periodic research reports may also be of interest.

Local Implications

Accumulations and reports of data by the various organizations and associations discussed in this chapter constitute useful resources for the institutional researcher. One of the major difficulties with much of the data is that they do not become available early enough to meet the current needs of local researchers, who are, therefore, often forced into collecting data needed for a current study by questionnaire or phone call. In addition, the collection and study activities of many of these groups frequently impinge on local offices as questionnaires arrive in the mail. Diversity in definitions and in methods of questioning can sometimes be a source of grief and irritation. The institutional researcher whose own report on salaries does not accord with his report as issued by the AAUP is not in a good position to explain exactly why; the problem may be complicated by the fact that the local AAUP chapter insists on collecting these data for itself rather than accepting those available from the institutional research office. When state coordinating agencies collect and organize their data in ways somewhat distinctive from those most useful on the local campus, the institutional researcher again gets caught in a time-consuming task of explanation and usually ends up with a feeling that no one is completely satisfied.

Yet, on the whole, the impact of the demands by external agencies for data and of the feedback from them is useful for institutional research. If the time comes when there is uniformity in data and the computerization of data yields fast processing and quick feedback, many of the current problems can be resolved. The institutional researcher may then find that much of his routine work—reshaping data for various purposes and explaining the differences and discrepancies—can be eliminated in favor of time spent examining the implications of data for improving the operations of the institution.

Bibliography

Academy for Educational Development. *State Planning for Higher Education.* Washington, D.C., 1969.

BLAUCH, L. E. *Accreditation in Higher Education.* Washington, D.C.: U.S. Office of Education, 1959.

BRUMBAUGH, A. J. *State-Wide Planning and Coordination.* Atlanta, Ga.: Southern Regional Education Board, 1963.

California State Department of Education. *A Master Plan for Higher Education in California, 1960–75.* Los Angeles: California State Department of Education, 1960.

COX, L., AND HARRELL, L. E. *The Impact of Federal Programs on State Planning and Coordination of Higher Education.* Atlanta, Ga.: Southern Regional Education Board, 1969.

DRESSEL, P. L., AND COME, D. R. *Impact of Federal Support of Science on the Publicly Supported Universities and Four-Year Colleges in Michigan.* Washington, D.C.: National Science Foundation, 1968.

DRESSEL, P. L., AND PRATT, S. B. *The World of Higher Education: An Annotated Guide to the Major Literature.* San Francisco: Jossey-Bass, 1971.

GLENNY, L. A. "State-Wide Coordination of Higher Education: Plans, Survey, and Progress to Date." In G. K. SMITH (Ed.), *Current Issues in Higher Education.* Washington, D.C.: Association for Higher Education, 1962.

JAMRICH, J. X. "Research Techniques in State Surveys of Higher Education." *College and University,* 1960, *35*(2), 195–203.

MOOS, M., AND ROURKE, F. *The Campus and the State.* Baltimore: Johns Hopkins Press, 1959.

National Association of State Universities and Land-Grant Colleges. *Margin for Excellence and Opportunity: The Impact of Private Investment on Public Colleges and Universities.* Washington, D.C.: Office of Institutional Research, National Association of State Universities and Land-Grant Colleges, 1969.

National Education Association. *Salaries in Higher Education 1969–70,* higher education series research report 1970–R6. Washington, D.C.: Research Division, National Education Association, 1970.

National Science Board. *Graduate Education: Parameters for Public Policy.* Washington, D.C.: National Science Foundation, 1969a.

National Science Board. *Toward a Public Policy for Graduate Educa-*

tion in the Sciences. Washington, D.C.: National Science Foundation, 1969b.

National Science Foundation. *Federal Support to Universities and Colleges, Fiscal Year 1967.* Washington, D.C., 1968.

North Central Association. *Review of Literature in Higher Education Relevant to the Consulting and Examining Process. June 1966– May 1967.* Chicago, 1967.

PLINER, E. (Ed.) *Coordination and Planning.* Baton Rouge: Public Affairs Research Council, 1966.

USDAN, M., MINAR, D., AND HURWITZ, E. J. *Education and State Politics.* New York: Teachers College Press, 1969.

CHAPTER 13

Toward the Future

Paul L. Dressel

❦❦❦❦❦❦❦❦

Although various attempts to define institutional research are both explicit and implicit in the preceding chapters, the careful reader will have noted that there is not complete unanimity among the contributors to this handbook. This discrepancy may reflect differences only in the points of view or dispositions of individuals. In some part this is surely the case. In addition, in some respects, it represents differences in the ways institutional research has come into being in individual institutions and in the ways it is regarded there. Rarely can an individual define a subject and then engage in it according to his own likes; but it is likely to be a sad situation if an individual engages himself only with the demands made upon him, accepting without question the limitations implicit in these demands.

Differing views of institutional research result from some of the major differences in definition. If one emphasizes research and views institutional research as a form of applied research, he may search for truth, understanding, predictability, and control, but avoid involvement in current operations. If one views institutional research as almost entirely a means of expediting the day-to-day operations, another kind of emphasis arises.

With the first view, an individual is likely to be conscious of the many shortcomings in operations in higher education but profoundly concerned with the lack of definite goals and the lack of clear-cut values in decision-making. Hence he is generally concerned with studies that force administrators and faculty members to reexamine their goals as well as their practices. A researcher who has this view should not be involved in day-to-day operations. He should not try to effect change directly, but rather should concentrate on identifying problems, producing data which force attention to them, and suggesting alternatives. Faculty committees, administrative officers, and others can, through distribution of his studies, be enabled to look at problems in a new way in order to come to resolutions. With this view and consequent method of operation, the institutional researcher should not have much concern with whether he or his office is directly credited with the accomplishment.

With the second view, an institutional researcher is likely to emphasize efficiency more than effectiveness. He is in danger of becoming so involved in operations and so identified with adminstration that he unconsciously accepts the limitations of the present scene. He does not have time to probe deeply into the internal workings of the various aspects of the operation, although he probably has little interest in doing so. In particular, with this view of institutional research, one is likely to become totally involved in formulation of budgetary requests and collection and manipulation of financial data; his energy is spent in meeting the demands of the budget procedures, and his focus is on the internal operations primarily oriented to allocating resources.

In the first view—the sanitized version of institutional research—institutional research becomes the conscience of the university in raising questions if not in proposing solutions. This view has probably never been widely accepted if one is to judge by the practices in offices of institutional research. It may be that the increasing emphasis on management, as evidenced through the development of management information systems, program budgeting, and the like, will force institutional research into this purely operational role. If the office were so staffed as to carry on both research activity and operational activities, this might be no problem. But those who have become involved in the operational aspect of the university—especially in respect to budgets—have generally found that this aspect becomes all-absorbing in terms of time, energy, and resources available to institutional research.

A third view of institutional research perhaps will be increasingly found. The institutional research office, in this case, serves not so much for carrying out research as for providing knowledgeable staff and resources to coordinate institutional research activities of other offices and to advise other researchers who need help. A faculty committee desiring assistance may contact the office of institutional research not with the expectation of getting data or research done by that office but with the assurance that knowledgeable persons are there to help them define what they need and to point out the offices, data banks, or individuals which will be able to supply it. An office operating in this manner coordinates certain data files.

This third view of research is consistent with the idea that institutional research itself should not be engaged in long-term specific activities. Rather, it should be an innovator and an inspirer of action, readily willing to withdraw when a point has been made or a new procedure has been institutionalized and to turn its attention to other matters. Viewed in this way, the director of institutional research can be a catalytic agent in the university as he encourages and aids institutional research activity on a widespread basis without incurring the detail of specific projects for the office itself.

Organizational Placement

The appropriate placement of an office of institutional research depends on which of the several views just discussed holds in a particular institution. If the office is going to be engrossed primarily in studies of operation—especially the academic program—it probably belongs in the office of the provost or vice-president for academic affairs. It should be placed there with a charge that clearly designates it as an all-university office having access to data accumulations anywhere in the university and having service responsibility to all units and individuals on the campus making legitimate studies on university problems. In short, the office should serve the faculty, the administration, student groups, and individual gradute students engaged in dissertation studies involving university operations.

If the office is primarily identified with management and the budget, it probably should be placed in the president's office. In this position it still may be able to have some influence on the academic program. If placed in the office of the vice-president for business, the office of research becomes effectively removed from the academic area, is very definitely limited to financial and budgetary activities, and may not be able to study academic budget problems. Of course much depends upon the roles assigned the various vice-presidents. In the occasional institution where the vice-president for business has the responsibility for making the academic budget, the placement of institutional research in his office may be justified.

If the third view of institutional research discussed in the preceding section obtains, the head institutional research officer can well be designated as a vice-president concerned with planning and institutional studies with clear indication that, in this role, he is to be assisted by all units of the university as required by his activities. The combination of planning and research responsibilities, however, suggests that such a vice-president should not have assigned to him a large number of operating offices to coordinate and that he should not be involved in too much routine day-to-day activity. The planning function as well as the institutional research function suffers greatly when individuals do not have time to sit back and think about long-range problems on a universitywide scale.

Problems

One concern exhibited in several chapters of this handbook is that institutional research inadvertently prolongs the deliberations of faculty and of faculty committees as well as the time required for making adminstrative decisions. As faculty become more and more involved in study of problems and in the development of policies, they experience a number of frustrations. One is the sheer amount of time required of them. Another is the general lack of secretarial and stenographic assistance; as a result of this latter problem, additional duties often fall upon already overloaded secretaries in departmental offices or possibly in the dean's office.

Furthermore, any committee that wishes to do more than discuss a problem faces the difficulty of getting together data, analyzing it for its significance, and developing some possible recommendations consistent with the evidence. Even should a committee contain individuals with all the necessary competencies, the task of data collection remains very time consuming. And if the data required must be collated from the files of a number of different offices, the task may be completely hopeless.

Whatever the pattern of institutional research in a given institution, it is desirable for several people of academic stature to be associated with the office and to be available for consultation and assistance as requested by the faculty. In the long run, this requirement is likely to have a desirable impact on the whole decision-making process of the institution because those respecting their judgment will turn to relevant information before considering general surveys of opinion and practices.

One of the continuing problems faced by institutional research and by planning offices is that the constant pressure for short-term decision-making not only interferes with long-term planning but forecloses some options before they have been identified. Short-term decisions call for quick accumulations of data, sometimes in new patterns which require a great deal of organization. One may hope that the development of management information systems will bring a day when, with a minimal amount of programing, most any pattern of data can be brought readily to an administrator or committee in a form appropriate to their task. As indicated in previous chapters, complications in developing information systems are many, costs are great, and it is probably overoptimistic to expect to see widespread development soon. Furthermore, despite all attempts to simplify organizational structures and improve management, universities seem to become more complicated as time goes by. It can be anticipated that new types of questions and new patterns of data will always be demanded to deal with the questions. The problem of the institutional research is to find some way to responding expeditiously to these needs and requests while reserving time for longer-range studies.

The increase in interinstitutional cooperation in programs and studies places another burden upon institutional research personnel. And seldom does an interinstitutional enterprise define a project in quite the same way as a single institution would. This different definition may be beneficial, but in the short run it poses problems for those who must make institutional data files accommodate interinstitutional definitions. Similarly, demands for data from state, regional, and national sources are time consuming on the one hand and troublesome on the other because of yet another set of definitions. WICHE, in some of its work on definitions, has indicated that many definitions can be made at a local level. This certainly could alleviate many problems eventually, but it by no means solves the problem of contributing data on a uniform basis as now requested for studies in which results will be compared among a group of institutions.

Whenever uniformity must be achieved interinstitutionally, it is almost certain that the office of institutional research will have difficulties. Neither external demands nor internal patterns are permanent. One can reasonably predict that, no matter how extensive the work done on a national or regional level, individuals taking over an activity later will decide to alter it in one way or another. And no matter how well an institution may be functioning at some point in time, it will be only a year or two before some reorganization will complicate compilation of comparable data and perhaps even require a complete reprograming.

The role of the computer and the problem of coordinating analytic data systems have increasing implications for the efficiency of institutional research activity. In the long run, there may be no conflict between the needs of day-to-day operation in various offices and the needs of institutional research and planning offices. Short-term problems include the disinterest of individuals in revising an existing system; the heavy burden already carried by data-processing offices on most campuses; the inability of administrators to identify the data they need; and the lack of personnel and dollars to integrate computer-based data systems, planning activities, and institutional research. Thus it may be that the third view of institutional research suggested earlier, which would place the office at a vice-presidential level incorporating planning activities and institutional research, constitutes a model for an adequate system. Institutional researchers could be placed strategically in various offices in the institution (such as the registrar's office, business office, and provost's office), and the vice-president for planning and institutional study could coordinate their activities, drawing from various places the data needed for long-term studies and planning and thereby helping administrators and faculty committees to define their requests and to channel their data needs to the appropriate person or file.

Training of Researchers

The lack of unanimity on a definition of institutional research raises difficulties for planning any training program for institutional researchers. Some regard higher education programs as effective training. An unpublished survey found that, of 160 graduate schools in education, fifty-seven offered programs in higher education. Eight reported a specific concentration, sixteen offered courses, and twenty-two included it as a topic. Others regard preparation for educational research as essentially synonymous with preparation for institutional research.

Yet there have been effective institutional researchers whose training was in economics, business, political science, mathematics, statistics, and law; any one of these disciplines has elements in it which are quite germane to the work of institutional research. An individual well grounded in economics, accounting, statistics, computer science, social survey techniques, tests and measurements, and educational research is (assuming the appropriate pattern of interests and personality characteristics) a real gem for institutional research. In fact, a number of institutional researchers have come close to attaining this array of accomplishments by necessity as they have worked at their jobs.

It would actually be unfortunate if institutional research became narrowly defined as a profession with a specific doctoral program in any one department or college of a university. It would be equally undesirable if, because of the array of knowledge and skills needed, someone developed a program requiring one or two courses in each of these various fields. Any individual with a strong quantitative background can readily assimilate much of the knowledge and skills required for successful work in institutional research. An individual obtaining his research training in any of the several fields mentioned above should be able to fit quickly into the job.

It may be helpful to consider personnel who have served in one institutional research office, that of Michigan State University. One individual with a background in the field of business is a CPA and has earned a Ph.D. in higher education as well. Another has a Ph.D. in counseling and guidance. A third taught literature in college with a master's degree plus work beyond but ultimately obtained a Ph.D. in higher education. Another has a background in business and economics with a Ph.D. in higher education. Another has a background in engineering and business, and the formal study of one person was entirely in the field of mathematics. An office formed with such a diverse group of individuals gains added strengths and also presents credibility to faculty members who distrust doctorates in education and can be mollified by the presence of individuals trained in a number of different disciplines (perhaps their own) in administrative and quasi-administrative operations.

Though in theory one can always go to particular departments and disciplines and request assistance, the pressures in higher education are such that it has become very difficult to enlist any extensive cooperation from faculty members. So there is a definite need for the development of a team approach bringing together a number of different competencies. That team approach may well extend to individuals occupying positions in a number of different offices in a university rather than grouped together.

In any professional activity, there is always the problem of professional ethics. Earlier in this volume the point is made that the institutional researcher is in a role different from that of the researcher in a university department or an institute. The institutional researcher is, by virtue of his job, given access to much data which must be regarded as confidential. In addition, he obtains insights into operations through his examination of data, his contacts with people, and the general necessity of developing familiarity with the total structure and activity of the university. He is often in the position of working with an individual or group which desires to maintain confidentiality of their data and results of them. At the same time he may be involved in other studies which deal with the same problems. If the institutional researcher, at this point, begins to see himself as the individual who should solve all the difficulties, he will almost certainly try to use his knowledge from all sources to justify and push for his point of view. If he views his role, instead, as that of helping each group gain insight into their problems and the data relevant to them, then he may be able to successfully avoid divulging information on either side or making statements which compromise his role.

The institutional researcher also must recognize that much as he may want to have his studies and his data disseminated widely, this course is not always wise. A contrary situation, which he must resist as strongly, is the attempt of an administrator to completely squelch a study, which perhaps denies distribution even to those persons who may take some responsibility for change in the situation. One can live with limited distribution of confidential data as long as the data are used in such a way as to have some significant impact. But if studies which bring critical issues to view are regularly being buried, institutional research is serving no function, and the researcher will do better to resign in protest with a public statement of explanation than to wait and be fired.

Criticism of the ineffectiveness of institutional research obligates individuals in the field to point out that the ineffectiveness often rests elsewhere than in the office of institutional research. In many cases, it rests elsewhere because the administrator, in selecting institutional research personnel, picked very inadequate persons. The attitudes, values, strategy, and ethics embraced in institutional research are not directly teachable, but the prospective institutional researcher must be able to assimiliate them—perhaps by observation and experience.

Possible Model

Many individuals are searching for new models for governance and operation of institutions of higher education. The demands by faculty for increased involvement in educational policy have slowed down the decision-making progress, have made administrative innovation difficult and have even made it difficult to move toward increased productivity and efficiency. The student demand for involvement has made the usual pattern of committees, councils, summits, and the like even more cumbersome. In addition insistence on formal representation comes from various minority groups. In some cases representation involves such a complex selection procedure with so much competition among subgroups trying to obtain control that at times it looks as though the institution may simply become ungovernable and destroy itself by its own excesses.

The deep-seated suspicion with which many faculty members regard administrators tends to undermine the expertise which administrators can bring to problems and to place administrators under great pressure to refer all decisions to committees—thereby avoiding decisions rather than risking confrontations. Administration has become such a difficult chore that assignments are accepted only by those who ardently wish to become professional administrators— a characteristic which makes them immediately suspect to many faculty members. The suspicions held by some faculty members and even some students are carried to such extremes that a faculty member with expertise in an area is regarded as an inappropriate person to serve on a committee studying or developing policies for that area. Thus, some faculty members would prefer to see a professor of English or history rather than a professor of economics, business management, or accounting on an academic budget committee.

There is no good way to bring to bear upon the problems of the university the expertise of many faculty members who are consultants to other institutions or to business and industry yet are seldom called upon by their own campus to make an enlightened analysis or to offer advice. At the same time, we have developed on many campuses programs in higher education which purport to train administrators; personnel specialists; and various others such as registrars, directors of learning services, evaluators, and institutional researchers. Such programs often offer a Ph.D. in higher education. Here Ph.D.s are trained for a career in higher education in spite of the fact that most administrators in the better universities come from the faculty ranks. Could anyone regard his doctorate as sufficient training to immediately become a dean or a president, merely because his specialization is higher education? Unless courses in administration are taught by persons with extensive administrative experience, they can have little relevance to the problems of higher education administration. And research on higher education done by professors of higher education is likely to be limited in scope unless those involved possess competencies from many other fields. The question, then, is how to tap the total resources and provide a wide variety of training programs for persons going into various roles in the university.

A single department or college should probably be avoided. Whether one talks of training researchers or administrators or coordinators of service in higher education, one should not overlook the many units in the university that can make some contribution. Numerous centers for the study of higher education have been established, but most of these have been related to a college of education, and those which have not have tended to be primarily research units apart from the day-to-day operations of the university. Though the research units have conducted good studies, they have had limited impact on higher education because the studies were not immediately relevant to true-to-life operational decisions which could be reported on.

One possible approach would be to set up, in some major university, a total center for the study of higher education, involving the teaching of research and administrative services in the context of the operations and problems of the institution. In this center could be placed personnel with ongoing responsibilities for institutional research and additional responsibility and funds for attracting members of the faculty into the center for concentration on particular studies. Research personnel who were particularly interested in improvement of instruction, curriculum, and evaluation could be available to the faculties not only of the immediate university but of other universities to provide help in the study and improvement of these fields. At the same time the center could be budgeted so that faculty members wishing to spend a period of time on the study of instruction or the improvement of curriculum could be brought into these programs.

The center could include space for individuals working on an advanced degree with particular interest in some higher education problem. Their doctoral programs might be in any of several fields (mathematics, engineering, business, the social sciences, or education). By an internship or a research experience in the center, they would not only add to their insights into the problems of higher education but would gain, by their experiences in working with colleagues representing various disciplines and sharing a general concern about the improvement of higher education, attitudes and values which would lead them to be useful members of the higher education enterprise. The program itself would not award a Ph.D. in higher education. It would, instead, serve to unite many persons working toward Ph.D.s who have identified a particular interest in higher education or have had a significant experience with it. The university itself (perhaps through a service role of the center, in conjunction with a number of other colleges and smaller universities) would provide the laboratory in which this experience was made available.

The model suggested above would simultaneously assure the relevance of graduate preparation to higher education, the significance of the study of higher education, and application of the competencies of faculty in diverse disciplines to the problems of the university. Such a model, at least in theory, could resolve many of the problems which have been raised with regard to the definition of institutional research and the training of institutional research workers. It would also seem to facilitate widespread involvement in study of the university, thereby avoiding the possibility that a new breed of institutional researchers may ultimately be identified and then, like others who have names, tend to wall themselves off from other groups in the university.

Unfinished Business

In the initial stages of planning this handbook, a number of us felt that it should go far toward defining the field of institutional research. No doubt in some senses it has, and yet, in developing this last chapter, we have been forced to acknowledge that there is not unanimity even among the contributors to this handbook as to what institutional research is or as to what it should be. The sanitized version of institutional research discussed as the first view at the beginning of this chapter is not likely to be popular because of its cost, because of its propensity for making critical examinations of the institution, and because those who have not experienced it do not readily see how it can contribute to simultaneous improvement of the quality and the efficiency of operation of the university. The dirty, workaday version of institutional research (the second view presented earlier) incorporates a group of activities which are increasingly essential, but it would be unfortunate if, in emphasizing this aspect, we lost the broad research concept. And it involves the further problem of relating research and planning functions in a meaningful way.

The combination of institutional research and planning which seemed rather inappropriate to some of us at the beginning stage of thinking about this handbook now holds considerable promise for future exploration. Because both institutional research and planning are far-reaching and because they are interrelated, they need to be spread throughout the institution with some coordinating office tying together the whole operation. This, in substance, constitutes the third view of institutional research presented at the beginning of this chapter.

The interrelationship of decision-making and institutional research is another unresolved item. Those who insist on seeing institutional research through to policy and action seem ultimately to become so co-opted into the action that they do no research. At the same time, it is entirely natural for individuals who have concentrated on research to become impatient or dissatisfied if they do not perceive incorporation of their work in campus decisions. Researchers are likely, also, to want some recognition for themselves.

Reflection on the problem of recognition suggests that this problem lies not only in the natural desire of the individual for attention but also in an absence of any clear sequence of career development for an individual who becomes involved in institutional research. A department chairman may look forward to the day when he can return to his professorship, his graduate seminar, and his research, or he may develop a desire for advancement and aspire to a job as dean. Relatively few department chairmen would see that chairmanship in itself as a career but this, too, presents alternatives. A dean of five years' standing is already beyond return to scholarship, but deans can and do accept the deanship as permanent assignments. And the dean who is under fifty may aspire to a vice-presidency or a presidency. Anyone in a vice-president's role in an institution can accept this as a sufficiently dignified title and role to remain in it until retirement, or he can look forward to a presidency. Assistant deans, assistant provosts, and assistant vice-presidents can anticipate the possibility of moving to another institution with the removal of the qualifying adjective even if they can seldom achieve promotion at home.

But where does the director of institutional research look for advancement? Some move into line administrative positions, but there is no established pattern for doing so. The faculty in a large university expects academic administrative positions to be filled with persons from an academic background, and the mere possession of an academic Ph.D. in a discipline hardly satisfies such persons. Furthermore, institutional researchers, if they have done their job, have raised enough questions about both administrative and faculty behavior and irresponsibility that they are not likely to be popular candidates for an administrative position. The Association for Institutional Research (AIR) is neither large enough nor prestigious enough to give the institutional researcher any great professional stature by his activity in it. The usual research journals are not suitable for publication of institutional research reports.

A congenial possibility seems to be presented in tying institutional research activity with broad study and education in higher education. The problem of doing this within the context of a single department or program of higher education in a college of education is the lack of interaction with other university faculties. Furthermore the limitations of a professional school may deny the particular interests and background of the person considering institutional research. So we return to the universitywide center suggested earlier in this chapter; it presents a possible pattern in which the institutional researcher, by continuing interaction with faculty members from all segments of the university, by work with doctoral candidates in many fields, and by conduct of studies of higher education broadly conceived enough to justify national distribution, would find an integrative identity for himself—an identity somewhat approximating that of persons who have worked in or developed interdisciplinary centers and institutes. He may at the same time, through his pattern of associations, achieve sufficient recognition to be accepted as a valuable resource and as a prospect for promotion into line administrative positions in his own institution.

At the moment it is unclear as to whether an institutional research position can be a satisfying career for a large number of people. It would be very unfortunate if a pattern developed revealing that such jobs were held for a limited period of years by individuals moving through them to something else; it actually requires several years in such a position in most universities to arrive at sufficient understanding of the institution, its resources, and its data to begin to make significant contributions to its problems. Nevertheless, if institutional research can be related to some phase in the administrative hierarchy, the upward movement of individuals with institutional research background into vice-presidencies and presidencies would undoubtedly enhance the impact which this office has on higher education.

Realization of one other possibility may give some individuals satisfaction with their careers in institutional research. On many campuses the institutional research coordinator or director is shrouded by ambiguity. His title (usually director) is one which has relatively little meaning in terms of the administrative hierarchy. Many other people, too, are designated as directors of programs within departments, within colleges, and at the all-university level. Some of these are designated directors by formal board action and, like a director of continuing education, are tacitly understood to be the equivalent of a dean in rank; other directors have only informal designation by department chairmen or deans, no budget, and no authority. In such cases, the institutional research director's importance in the administrative structure may be unknown. If granted an additional title such as assistant provost or assistant vice-president, he risks being regarded more as an administrator than as an institutional researcher. Possibly a clarification of the placement of the office in the administrative hierarchy would resolve some problems. The possibility of designation as a dean of institutional research would make some individuals happy; but even the title of dean has some ambiguities surrounding it. The dean of a college is a figure with reasonably assured status, but deans of admission, deans of men, and deans of records are often regarded as curiosities resulting from some president's ill-advised desire to build up an administrative superstructure.

Finally, there is the relationship of institutional research to research on higher education. The latter is often so far removed from the realities of operation that such research is not read by people on the line and would not readily be applied by them if they did read it. Social psychologists, for example, may write on some of the affective impacts of college. Yet, even the deans of experimental colleges and particularly faculty members of such colleges have only passing interest in such studies and focus their attention on it only insofar as it seems to have something commendatory to say about their programs.

A center such as has been described in this chapter, by bringing together persons doing both practical study and theoretical research, may ultimately bridge the gap between institutional research and the well-conceived study of higher education. Faculty would be exposed to a broad conception of research on the higher education enterprise; at the same time, administrators would be shown clearly that some research going well beyond the day-to-day operations may have far more significance for planning the future of the university than do those studies which seem at the moment to speak loudly.

Other Resources

Lou Anna Kimsey

❦❦❦❦❦❦❦❦

This appendix provides the reader with a selected list of resources (services) available to the institutional researcher from sources outside the institution. The section on instruments includes some of the important standardized tests which the researcher can use for measuring variables associated with such concepts as collegiate environment, attitudes, and personality. Since organizations associated with higher education can be a source of information as well as direct assistance for the institutional researcher, a section on organizations has been included. Though the list is not exhaustive, knowledge of the services provided by the selected organizations can help the researcher save valuable time in the pursuit of answers to a vast array of questions. The information in this section corresponds very closely to that of Chapter Eleven.

A. INSTRUMENTS

Biographical Inventory for Students

This instrument, developed by Laurence Siegel, describes students by using ten scores—action, social activities, heterosexual activities, religious activities, literature-art-music, political activities, sociometric status, economic independence, dependence on home, and social conformity. This inventory is designed for research on students in grades twelve and thirteen. It is not for clinical use. (Available through Educational Testing Service.)

College and University Environment Scales

CUES, developed by C. Robert Pace, provide measures of such variables as practicality, community, awareness, propriety, scholarship, morality, quality of teaching, and student-faculty relationships, which help institutions define cultural, social, and intellectual climates of the campus. This instrument summarizes student consensus with regard to the existence or nonexistence of measured characteristics on a campus. (Available through Educational Testing Service.)

College Characteristics Inventory

The CCI, developed by George Stern and C. Robert Pace, is an environmental index designed to measure the press of the college environment on students. The thirty variables of the Activity Index are represented as a press and thus became the scales of the CCI. The result is thirty press scores and eleven factor scores, some of which are aspiration level, intellectual climate, student dignity, academic climate, group life, and social form. The instrument can be used to determine interinstitutional differences as well as intrainstitutional student variations. (Available through National Computer Systems, 1015 South Sixth Street, Minneapolis, Minnesota 55415.)

College Student Questionnaire

The College Student Questionnaire, a technical manual developed by Richard Peterson, provides biographical and attitudinal information about college student bodies. Part I, which is basically for entering freshmen, covers the student's background, attitudes, and plans. Part II, which can be used at the end of a student's first or second year, assesses the student's educational and vocational plans, college activities, and attitudes. The package also includes a control test for academic aptitudes which differentiates various groups along this dimension. (Available through Educational Testing Service.)

Evening College Characteristics Index

The ECCI, developed by George Stern, Clifford L. Winters, Jr., N. Sidney Archer, and Donald Meyer, is an outgrowth of the College Characteristics Index and is designed for nonresident colleges. With the deletion of the CCI resident-oriented questions, the ECCI becomes an effective index for assessing environmental presses in community colleges, two-year junior colleges, or evening colleges. (Available through National Computer Systems.)

Group Dimensions Descriptive Questionnaire

This instrument, developed by John K. Hemphill and Charles M. Westie, provides thirteen group dimension scores: autonomy, control, flexibility, hedonic tone, homogeneity, intimacy, participation, permeability, polarization, potency, stability, stratification, and vicidity. It has application for research into campus organizations at a particular institution and the same organization at many institutions. (Distributed by Educational Testing Service.)

Institutional Functioning Inventory

The Institutional Functioning Inventory, developed by the Educational Testing Service in conjunction with the Institute for Higher Education, Teachers College, Columbia University, is designed to assess institutional characteristics which, in conjunction with the aims of the institution, help determine validity. The IFI has eleven scales which measure such things as freedom, concern for undergraduate learning, concern for innovation, and institutional esprit. The instrument can be used in self-study to view the overall institutional picture of interdepartmental differences as seen by faculty, administrators, or students. The results of periodic administration of the IFI can serve as indices for gauging institutional change. It also has application in determining interinstitutional differences. (Available through Educational Testing Service.)

Omnibus Personality Inventory

The OPI, developed by the OPI Research Team at the Center for Research and Development in Higher Education at Berkeley, assesses

personality characteristics of groups of college students. Scales (sixteen on Form C and twelve on Form D) include such dimensions as
thinking introversion, theoretical orientations, estheticism, autonomy,
developmental status (Form C only), impulse expression, social
maturity (Form C only), lack of anxiety, and response bias (Form
D only). This instrument can readily be used for describing and
comparing college student groups because of the availability of
norms based on definable groups. This instrument is solely for research, and it is not appropriate for clinical use. (Available through
The Psychological Corporation, 304 East 45th Street, New York,
New York 10017.)

Stern Activity Index

The AI, developed by George Stern, assesses personal needs along
with twelve factor scores based on combinations of need scores.
Among the needs are friendliness, sensuousness, closeness, permissiveness, and orderliness. With college norms available, research may be
done on student body needs or on the needs of various subgroups of
the student population. (Available through National Computer Systems.)

Survey of College Achievement

The Survey of College Achievement, developed through the Institutional Research Program for Higher Education of the Educational
Testing Service, provides a measure of group achievement in the
first two years of college. Subject areas include English, humanities,
math, natural science, and social science. The instrument can be
used as a basis for comparisons of freshman class by subgroup or by
normative group as well as for comparisons of growth and change in
achievement of student groups along dimensions such as sex, aptitude,
attitudes, major field, or GPA. It could also be used to delineate
needs for curriculum reform especially with respect to remedial programs. (Available through Educational Testing Service.)

The following is a list of some of the "secure" testing programs which generate data that can be useful to the institutional
researcher.

Program Administrator	*Program*
American College Testing P. O. Box 168 Iowa City, Iowa 52240	ACT Program Examination (for college admissions)
College Entrance Examination Board Box 592 Princeton, New Jersey 08540 (Program administered by Educational Testing Service)	Scholastic Aptitude Test (for college admissions) Placement Tests Advanced Placement Tests
Educational Testing Service Princeton, New Jersey 08540	Graduate Record Examination Teacher Education Examination Program (for program evaluation) National Teacher Examination (for teaching candidate evaluation)
National Merit Scholarship Corp. 990 Grove Street Evanston, Illinois 60201 (Program administered by Science Research Associates)	National Merit Scholarship Qualifying Test

B. ORGANIZATIONS

1. TESTING AGENCIES

A. *American College Testing* conducts secure testing programs related to admissions and advanced placement as well as conducting research on the effectiveness of these programs. The following services of ACT are of particular interest to the institutional researcher.

a. *Class Profile Service* provides a description of the entering freshman class of an institution as a whole or by subgroups. It is also possible to obtain a description of students who did not enroll but who requested that their ACT scores be sent to the institution.

b. *Institutional Self-Study Service* is a program designed to study the opinions and the development of various student populations on a campus as well as the institutional evaluations of nonstudents '(adminstrators, faculty, and alumni). The results of this specially designed questionnaire can, for example, delineate trends in student opinion and development; determine student evaluation of facilities, instruction, policies, practices, and services; assess student academic and nonacademic development; and determine reactions to the institution by the nonstudent groups. The information gleaned from the questionnaire provides campus officials with a data base for evaluating concerns such as institutional goals, quality of instruction, effectiveness of student services, needs and characteristics of the institution, and nonstudent views of the institution.

c. *Basic Research Service* analyzes the relationship among ACT scores, high school grades, and first-term overall GPA.

d. *Standard Research Service* helps the institution develop prediction equations as well as providing a description of potential and achievement of the freshman class.

e. *Profile of Financial Aids Applicants* provides a summary of students who apply for financial aid on the basis of the ACT Comprehensive Financial Aids Report.

f. *Management Reporting and Analysis Service* assists in evaluating financial aids programs and award-making policies as well as providing information necessary for the completion of the Federal Fiscal Operations Report.

B. *College Entrance Examination Board* is best known for its work in admissions and advanced placement testing. CEEB's prime research thrust has been in investigating the transition from high school to college. However, wider interests are reflected in its publications (for example, *Patterns of Admission for Transfer Students, Professional Development of Financial Aids Officers*).

C. *Educational Testing Service* conducts secure testing programs such as the Graduate Record Examination as well as constructing and publishing tests such as the Group Diminsions Descriptive Questionnaire. Research programs pertaining to measurement problems in education constitute an important part of the program. However, the following services are probably of most interest to the institutional researcher.

a. *Institutional Research Program for Higher Education* is designed to provide information about the environment of the institution by using the following instruments: College Student Questionnaire, Institutional Functioning Inventory, Survey of College Achievement, and the College and University Environment Scales.

b. *College Board Validity Service* (in conjunction with CEEB) provides a method through which individual institutions can determine the effectiveness of College Board scores, high school records, and other information in predicting both overall collegiate success and curriculum success.

c. *College-Level Examinations* (in conjunction with CEEB) are designed to measure college achievement in order to evaluate students whose educational patterns are atypical, establish criteria for awarding credits in classes not taught by traditional methods, provide criteria for selection of students for upper division study, and help institutions evaluate the effectiveness of their curriculum.

d. *College Placement Tests* assist institutions in the placement and sectioning of enrolled students.

e. *Comparative Guidance and Placement Program's* twofold purpose is to assist two-year institutions in curricular guidance and course placement of entering students and to provide self-study information.

f. *Teacher Education Examination Program* is designed to help institutions evaluate their teacher education programs.

g. *Undergraduate Program for Counseling and Evaluation* provides measures of achievement and ability which are important in assessing individual student achievement in liberal arts or within curriculum areas, furnishing information for academic counseling, evaluating competence for further study, and providing data for self-study of curriculum and departments.

D. *National Merit Scholarship Corporation,* in conjunction with its National Merit Scholar Program, has conducted continuous research on vocational, intellective, and nonintellective predictors of achievement and related topics. A financial need analysis is also inherent in the National Merit Scholar Program. NMSC publications reflect other interests (*Analysis of College Effects, Career Programs of Merit Scholars*).

2. COUNCILS

A. *American Council on Education* conducts large-scale programs involving environmental effects on student development in addition to having as members organizations such as the American Association of Junior Colleges, the Association of American Universities, and the

American Association of Colleges of Pharmacy. Through annual conferences and a variety of publications (*Educational Record, Fact Book on Higher Education,* directories of higher education institutions, "Higher Education and National Affairs"), ACE makes a meaningful contribution to higher education. Of further interest to the institutional researcher is the fact that the ACE data files, primarily a result of its annual survey of entering college freshmen, are available for use by qualified researchers.

B. *National Education Association* has many member organizations (for example, the American Association of Colleges for Teacher Education, the National Association of Women Deans and Counselors). Though primarily a teacher-oriented organization, NEA has shown an increasing interest in development as manifested through the sponsorship of National Training Laboratories. Of the numerous publications of NEA, one that is of particular interest to the institutional researcher is *Salaries in Higher Education 1969–70.*

3. Government

A. *ERIC* (*Educational Research Information Center*) is sponsored by the U.S. Office of Education as a nationwide information service whose primary function is to publicize educational documents and literature (for example, *ERIC Research in Education,* a monthly listing of current research). Regional clearinghouses publish bibliographies and usually sell copies of material (for example, microfiche) at low cost. Some of the clearinghouses pertinent to higher education are listed below.

ERIC Clearinghouse on Counseling and Personnel Service
The University of Michigan
Ann Arbor, Michigan 48104

ERIC Clearinghouse on Educational Administration
University of Oregon
Eugene, Oregon 97403

ERIC Clearinghouse on Higher Education
George Washington University
Washington, D.C. 20006

ERIC Clearinghouse on Junior Colleges
University of California at Los Angeles
Los Angeles, California 90024

ERIC Clearinghouse on Library and Informational Services
University of Minnesota
Minneapolis, Minnesota 55404

B. *U. S. Office of Education* disseminates a tremendous amount
of information which is vital to the institutional researcher through
annual publication of statistics (enrollments, degrees conferred, financial) as well as occasional publications such as bibliographies and
special studies.

4. REGIONAL BOARDS

A. *Educational Commission of the States.* ECS, which has forty-
two states and territories as members, is primarily concerned with
political influence on education. However, it is in the process of developing centers for the dissemination of information about govern-
mental-educational relationships (state-federal, state-state, institution-
state, institution-federal). These centers will also conduct research in
these areas. Two publications which are of interest to the institutional
researcher are the *ECS Bulletin* and *Higher Education in the United
States.*

B. *New England Board of Higher Education.* NEBHE is composed
of delegates from the six New England states. Its primary purpose is to
develop areas of cooperation and mutual interest among New England
colleges and universities. Examples of some of the programs that flow
from this purpose are the New England Regional Student Program,
the New England Library Information Network, and the New England
Council on Higher Education for Nursing. Among the useful publications for institutional researchers are the proceedings of NEBHE
annual conferences (1962—A College Colloquium on Institutional Research, 1963—Academic Effectiveness, 1964—Time and Space in Educational Planning, and 1965—Academic Decision-Making).

C. *Southern Regional Education Board.* SREB, composed of
representatives of fifteen southern states, conducts cooperative programs in such areas as institutional research, adult education, and
computer science. In addition, it sponsors annual Legislative Work Conferences to study current developments in higher education. SREB concern for students is manifested in its work to provide educational
opportunities for black students as well as in its Student Contract
Program, which permits the annual enrollment of over one thousand
students in health sciences, social work, and special education pro-

grams. Publications of SREB include *Introductory Papers on Institutional Research*, *Datelines* (quarterly), *Issues in Higher Education* (periodically), and *Statistical Supplements to State and Local Revenue Potential, 1969*.

D. *Western Interstate Commission on Higher Education*. WICHE's breadth of concerns is indicated by the variety of programs which it sponsors. The College and University Self-Study Institutes (annual) consist of presentations of research and discussion of current issues in higher education. The Legislative Work Conference is a forum designed to foster communication among legislators, public officials, and educators of the thirteen western states. In addition, WICHE is concerned with medical profession preparation (improvement of the nursing curriculum, continuing psychiatric education for physicians) and mental health through programs such as the Mental Health Council and the Mental Health Manpower Office. WICHE's current major project is its Management Information System, which is designed to facilitate effective allocation of institutional resources in addition to providing cost data on instructional programs.

5. RESEARCH-ORIENTED PROFESSIONAL ORGANIZATIONS

A. *American Educational Research Association*. AERA through its annual conference and publications touches on all fields of educational research, of which institutional research is a small part. The following publications may be useful to the institutional researcher: monograph series (for example, curriculum evaluation), *Review of Educational Research*, *Encyclopedia of Educational Research*, as well as *American Educational Research Journal*.

B. *Association for Institutional Research*. AIR is composed of individuals interested in the various aspects of institutional research. The high point of the AIR program is its annual conference on pertinent topics (Institutional Research and Communication in Higher Education—1970, Challenge and Response on Institutional Research—1969). Publications include an annual annotated bibliography of institutional research as well as periodic studies (*A Study of Members of the Association of Institutional Research*).

6. SIGNIFICANT OTHER PROFESSIONAL ORGANIZATIONS

A. *American Association for Higher Education*. AAHE is an organization for both administrators and faculty. It is concerned with the entire spectrum of issues and developments in higher education. Through its annual convention in Chicago as well as publications—

Journal of Higher Education (in cooperation with Ohio State University), "College and University Bulletin," *Current Issues in Higher Education, The Literature in Higher Education* (edited by Lewis B. Mayhew), and *AAHE Bibliography on Higher Education* (by Roger Kelsey), AAHE provides valuable information for the institutional researcher.

B. *American Association of Junior Colleges.* AAJC's chief purpose is to represent junior colleges at the national level. It strives to clarify to all parts of government as well as to the American people the role of the junior college in American higher education. It has established commissions on such things as administration, legislation, instruction, and curriculum.

C. *American Association of University Professors.* AAUP has far-reaching impact on the university through its powerful faculty organization. AAUP is concerned with all phases of faculty life (standards, policies, salaries, and academic freedom). Through its committee structure all aspects of the academic community are discussed and, at times, censured. The AAUP publications include *AAUP Bulletin,* which contains extensive faculty salary information of use to the institutional researcher.

D. *Association of American Colleges.* AAC has approximately 900 member institutions of which approximately 50 per cent are small, independent, or church related colleges. AAC fosters the interest of these member institutions through its own efforts as well as through cooperation with ACE. AAC publications include *Liberal Education,* a quarterly journal.

E. *National Association of State Universities and Land-Grant Colleges.* NASULGC consists of a senate and an executive committee complemented by five councils and seven commissions representing the administrative structure (presidents, academic officers, graduate education). The association serves as a liaison between member institutions and the federal government, with its primary concern being to influence legislation as well as to publicize the need for more support of higher education from both public and private sectors. Information is disseminated through its Office of Institutional Research to member schools.

F. *National Society for the Study of Education.* NSSE is concerned with all levels of education. It holds conferences and publishes yearbooks on a wide range of topics. Some of interest to the institutional researcher in higher education are *Programmed Learning* and *Educational Evaluation, New Roles, New Means.*

7. ADMINISTRATIVE ORGANIZATIONS

The following organizations are some of the important professional associations (not previously listed) which represent the administrative concerns of the institution. Most of these associations hold conferences and publish journals and monographs as well as issue statements about their area of interest.

American Association of Colleges and Universities Business Officers

American Association of Collegiate Registrars and Admissions Officers

American Association of University Administrators

American College Personnel Association

Association of College Admissions Counselors

Association of College and University Housing Officers

Council of Student Personnel Administrators

National Association of College Deans and Registrars

National Association of Student Personnel Administrators

National Association of Women Deans and Counselors

8. UNIVERSITY CENTERS

The following is a list of some of the prominent university centers. Each has on-going as well as special research projects, and each disseminates information through publications. However, the intensity of activity varies from center to center.

Center for Academic and Administrative Research
The University of Washington

Center for Research and Development in Higher Education
The University of California, Berkeley

Center for the Study of Higher Education
The University of Michigan

Higher Education Center
Temple University

Institute for Higher Education
The University of Florida

Institute of Higher Education
Columbia University

Institute of Higher Education
The University of Georgia

9. REGIONAL ACCREDITING AGENCIES

Middle States Association of Colleges and Secondary Schools
(MSA)
225 Broadway
New York, New York 10007

New England Association of Colleges and Secondary Schools
50 Beacon Street
Boston, Massachusetts 02108

North Central Association of Colleges and Secondary Schools
(NCA)
5454 South Shore Drive
Chicago, Illinois 60615

Northwest Association of Secondary and Higher Schools
(NW)
Miller Hall
University of Washington
Seattle, Washington 98105

Southern Association of Colleges and Schools
(SA)
795 Peachtree Street, N.E.
Atlanta, Georgia 30308

Western Association of Schools and Colleges
(WA)
1499 Bayshore Highway
Burlingame, California 94010

APPENDIX B

Collapsed Table of Contents, *Brown Book*

Michigan State University

❧❧❧❧❧❧❧❧

7.0 .... General fund expenditures by college
7.01 .... Regular general fund expenditures plus summer
term expenditures by college
7.1-7.15 ..... General fund expenditures by department
8.0 .... General fund expenditures per student credit hour
produced by college
8.0A Graph .. General fund expenditures per student credit hour
produced by all colleges
8.01 .... Regular general fund expenditures plus summer
term expenditures per student credit hour produced by college
8.1-8.15 ..... General fund expenditures per student credit hour
produced by departments
9.0 .... Number of majors (bachelors, masters, doctors)
by college
9.1-9.15 ..... Number of majors (bachelors, masters, doctors)
by department
10.0 .... Number of degrees (bachelors, masters, doctors)
by college
10.0A Graph .. Total number of degrees by all colleges
10.1-10.15 .... Number of degrees (bachelors, masters, doctors)
by department
11.0 .... Library budget, staff, volumes, periodicals, dollars
and volumes per student, and students per staff
12.0 .... Gifts, grants, and contracts
13.0 .... General fund research budget
14.0 .... Operating revenues by source
15.0 .... Revenues for new plant construction
16.0 .... Average faculty salaries by rank
17.0 .... Student loans by sources, number, and amount
18.0 .... On-campus student housing in residence halls and
married housing

Index

341